EXPLORING BRITAIN'S
Disused Railways

EXPLORING BRITAIN'S
Disused Railways
North-West England

Mark Jones

crecy.co.uk

First published 2022

© Mark Jones 2022

ISBN 9781800352575

All rights reserved. Apart from any fair dealing for the purpose of private study, research, criticism or review, as permitted under the Copyright, Design and Patents Act 1988, no part of this publication may be reproduced, stored in a retrieval system, or transmitted in any form or by any means, electronic, electrical, chemical, mechanical, optical, photocopying, recording or otherwise, without prior written permission. All enquiries should be directed to the publisher.

Printed in Malta by Melita Press

Crécy Publishing Ltd
1a Ringway Trading Estate, Shadowmoss Rd,
Manchester M22 5LH
www.crecy.co.uk

Front cover top:
A 1950s view of James Street station on the Liverpool Overhead Railway. *Gordon Suggitt collection*
Front cover bottom:
Rochdale–Bacup line, footbridge north of Shawforth, 2003. *Gordon Suggitt*

Rear cover main:
An apparently much-needed weedkiller train, led by a Class 20 locomotive, heads up the Buckhill branch from Calva Junction to RNAD Broughton Moor in July 1990. *Author's collection*
Rear cover inset from top:
GC St Helens branch siding to Kelbit works circa 2000. *Author*
Sign at Manchester Mayfield station. *Author*

Picture credits
Every effort has been made to identify and correctly attribute photographic credits. Should any error have occurred this is entirely unintentional.

Contents

Introduction 6
1 Setting the Scene 8
2 The Earliest Railways 14
3 The Wirral and Chester 18
4 Mid and East Cheshire 26
5 Warrington & Altrincham 33
6 Liverpool 41
7 Wigan and St Helens 50
8 Bolton and Bury 62
9 Stockport & Tameside 73
10 Manchester 79
11 Oldham and Rochdale 89
12 East Lancashire and Blackburn 96
13 Preston, Blackpool and Southport 106
14 Fleetwood, Lancaster and Morecambe 114
15 Barrow and the South Lakes 123
16 Whitehaven and Workington 131
17 Carlisle and North Cumbria 140
18 Pennine Cumbria 146
19 Exploring Tramroads 154
Acknowledgements 162
Bibliography 162
Index 164

Maps Key

——————— **Operational lines**
·················· **Closed lines**
——————— **Coast and/or lake outlines**

Introduction

An interest in railways, it is pleasing to say, has become fashionable again in recent years and an interest in the lines that no longer see trains is very much part of that trend. Disused railways, it seems these days, have a remarkable fascination for increasingly large numbers of people. Part of that fascination comes from them meaning different things to different people. Nature lovers relish the flora and fauna of the old embankments and cuttings, industrial archaeologists delight in discovering viaducts, tunnels and old artifacts, social historians delight in uncovering the lives of those who lived or worked on the railways and others hark back to bygone days when the now-slumbering line hosted proud, noisy, almost lifelike steam locomotives. There is something for almost everyone.

This book is the first in what will hopefully become a series with national coverage. The aim is to take a contemporary look at the 'lost' railways of the north-west of England, in particular to consider how they have fared since closure and to detail what is still around to visit and explore. To carry out this task effectively, it is of clear value to first consider the original purpose of a line: what was it built for, what did it carry, what made it lose its 'raison d'être' and when and why did it close. It is also sometimes of value to make comparisons with the lines that have survived and those that have thrived and adapted to meet the demands of the modern passenger.

Where this book differs from those that have gone before is its focus on what I will term the post-closure history of our railways. By post-closure history I mean everything from track lifting, demolition of buildings and structures, changes of ownership and access right up to the current condition of the railway in question. Some pre-closure history often adds context; the traffic it carried, notable events and so on, but generally I have not gone into any great detail of, for instance, the types of motive power used on a particular line. Earlier regional (and, indeed, national) books on disused railways tended to shy away from giving too much detail around precisely what remained, on the basis that many closed lines were still evolving in terms of their future use and that any guide would quickly become out of date. This remains true to an extent, but in the third decade of the twenty-first century rather less so; in places there are still such potential and ongoing developments to consider, both positive and negative, and these are discussed on an individual basis in the relevant chapters.

Many histories of the railways of the north-west start with the 1830 opening of the Liverpool & Manchester Railway – but as will be seen shortly, much of interest in our region happened many years before the introduction of locomotive haulage. The histories of such 'early railways', can be fascinating and searching for signs of their existence, perhaps largely undocumented, of considerable value and interest. This in turn leads to the final chapter of this book, when an explorer who has found as much as s/he can of our former passenger lines might wish to turn their attention to these, generally lesser known, tramroads.

Tunnel at Moore, Cheshire, on the original (pre-diversion) route of the West Coast Main Line, closed in 1893. *Author's collection*

Although all passenger and other major lines in the area have been covered, no claim can be made to cover every single minor line, particularly in areas packed with short industrial branches such as the district of Wigan and Leigh. Any book such as this, which seeks to cover a particular area, also has to set boundaries; in this case the north-west is defined as the current counties or administrative districts of Cheshire, Lancashire, Greater Manchester, Merseyside and Cumbria. It will be noted that some lines, when open, were in different counties to these prior to boundary changes that took place in the 1970s or earlier and this is discussed where relevant. Where a line lies partly within 'our' counties and partly outside, I have taken a 'majority' approach so that a line is included if more than half of it lies in the area of the book. This means, to give a couple of examples, that the Chester to Whitchurch line, lying more in Cheshire than Shropshire, is included but the Haltwhistle to Alston branch, lying predominantly in Northumberland, does not qualify. It should, of course, also be noted that railways, by their nature running from place to place, do not always fit neatly into the smaller areas used to define the chapters, but the index can be consulted if there is any doubt as to where to find a particular line.

Perhaps it also worth noting what this book does not have the time or space to include. There is no room to include closed stations on existing lines, though many fine such station buildings survive; I have, however, made an exception with the briefly open Workington North station (see picture), whose story is little told. Generally, the best places to look for these are on non-electrified lines; quite substantial stations such as Shap or Coppull on the West Coast Main Line were pretty much eradicated, though a few surprising remnants such as the former goods shed at Bay Horse, south of Lancaster, survive even here. Disused formation's close to existing lines, but still in rail property ownership, can also not be included, though some fascinating and little-known structures exist here. One example is Acton Grange Tunnel at Moore, south of Warrington (see picture), on the pre-1892 West Coast Mainline before an adjacent formation was built to lift the route over the Manchester Ship Canal at Acton Grange Viaduct. Miniature railways, unless on the site of former standard-gauge lines, are also excluded, though recording their demise is not without interest; a recent example is the lifting of the miniature railway at the now-closed Botany Bay centre in Chorley.

Two further points: to avoid debates around exact opening and opening dates, details of which are carefully recorded elsewhere, I have generally reported just the months and years of these events. Secondly, although outline maps are provided at the start of each chapter, the locations of sites are described within the text and are better located, particularly in urban locations, by cross-referencing to Ordnance Survey (OS) or Google Maps. Grid references have not been provided.

Finally, as will be seen, the majority of the photographs featured in the book are of structures or trackbed of lines after closure. A number of photographs of stations, bridges and even trains from their time of use are included, but good unpublished photographs from fifty or more years ago are becoming more and more difficult to source. I am, however, very pleased with the collection presented in this volume and am most grateful to all those who have contributed. A few images may be from photographers, who despite my best efforts, I have been unable to trace; here I offer my apologies and will be delighted to acknowledge their contribution in any future edition.

Disclaimer: Although every effort has been made to ensure the accuracy of the material presented in the book, the author will accept no responsibility for any errors or of changes that have taken place since the book went to press. Mention of private land in this book does not in any way imply a right of access to such land and it should also be stated that trespassing on open railway lines is a criminal offence, with a maximum fine of £1,000.

Workington North station was a temporary station, built to provide access to that part of town cut off when a bridge was destroyed by floods. It was only open from October 2009 to November 2010. *Derek Fry*

A classic 'disused railway' view. Rusty track with a derelict lineman's hut to one side on the Eden Valley Railway between Appleby and Warcop. *Chris McFarlane*

1
Setting the Scene

So let us consider where we are, nearly a quarter way through the twenty-first century. It has been over fifty years since the last passenger line closure in our area with no intention of replacement by trams, nor are there any immediate prospects of reopenings, save possibly a MerseyRail curve to Skelmersdale and less possibly a reopening of the west–north Burscough Curve to allow a Preston to Southport service. At the time of writing (early 2022) the only vulnerable line in our area would seem to be that from Warrington to Widnes, which served the now decommissioned Fiddlers Ferry power station but is currently kept in operation as a diversionary route for freight. Given current views on coal power there is no likelihood of the power station reopening – indeed proposals exist for a residential estate, together with warehouse facilities, on the site, but it is doubtful that the numbers involved, around 1,600 houses, would justify the provision of new passenger services. Having worked in Warrington for many years around the turn of the century, I feel a degree of sadness as I know that twenty or so years ago, I could go down to Sankey Bridges for an hour at lunchtime and expect to see at least two or three coal trains heading up to or back from Fiddlers Ferry to Warrington's Arpley sidings. So, what might become of this, possibly soon to be closed, railway. Sadly, the route doesn't have a great deal going for it; flat and straight with the fenced-off power station to the north and the lengthy curtain of reed beds bordering the disused, parallel, Sankey Canal to the south blocking any kind of view. The popular and well-used Trans Pennine Trail runs along the towpath on the other side of the canal so there is little prospect of conversion to a cycleway either. Time will tell if my somewhat pessimistic predictions for this line are realised – of course I hope for better.

The last passenger line to close in the north-west was the Oldham loop line in 2009 and its subsequent fate is worth documenting and discussing. Around ten days after the line closed, I paid a visit and took a number of photographs, some of which are included here. I also believe that I was the last person to stand on Oldham Mumps station as I got there literally minutes before the site was fenced off ready for demolition but, thanks to a sympathetic site manager, I was waved through onto the platform. Unlike the first railway-to-tram conversions in Greater Manchester, the routes to Bury and Altrincham, which kept entirely to the former railway formations, those in charge of conversion of the Oldham loop felt under no obligation to keep to what was already there. With trams perfectly capable of ascending or descending quite significant gradients, embankments and bridges were removed; notably the large bridge just to the north of Oldham Mumps station. Stations have been moved, buildings demolished, and sites reconfigured; an example being at Shaw & Crompton, where the tram stop lies south of the

A 2004 view of the south side of Oldham Mumps station. *Phillip Earnshaw*

From almost the same angle as the previous photo, Oldham Mumps in 2009, one week after closure. *Author*

level crossing; the original railway station having been to the north. After a brief period from June 2012 to January 2014 where trams used the former alignment through Mumps and Werneth stations, a new route was configured through Oldham's town centre and the old formation was abandoned. At Mumps, the old route line has just been left overgrown and fenced off, but at Werneth the station site and the tunnel just to the north are now in commercial use.

Let us now go back a little further. During the 1960s there was a quite vocal campaign to convert railways into roads; this was never a straightforward task as dual carriageways and motorways needed a space a good deal wider than that taken up by a double-track railway. However, there are several conversions into roads in the north-west worthy of note; a few of these will be mentioned here rather than in the area chapters as their suitability for exploration is somewhat dubious. One line lost, pretty much in its entirety, is the Seacombe branch on the Wirral, closed in 1963 and replaced by a road giving access to the second Mersey Tunnel. A motorist using the road might notice the impressive, curved sandstone cutting at Poulton but all traces of a once-substantial station at Seacombe have long gone.

A 2003 view of a Manchester-bound DMU leaving Werneth Tunnel, Oldham. *Gordon Suggitt*

Exploring Britain's Disused Railways

Removing the waiting shelter on the Manchester-bound platform at Oldham Werneth, one week after closure, 2009. *Author*

New Hey station, between Oldham and Rochdale, one week after closure, 2009. *Author*

Another example can be found in Blackpool, where much of the former direct route into the town's Central station is buried under the western section of the M55 motorway and its continuation, Yeadon Way. The most recent conversion, and one that may well be extended in future years, is the building of a road along part of the Pemberton loop line, Wigan's east–west avoiding railway. The new road, known as Westwood Way, takes the course of the old line between the A49 road at Goose Green to the south-west of Wigan and crosses the Leeds & Liverpool Canal on a new bridge using the old bridge abutments before the road heads north off the trackbed. Unlike the previous two, this road sits in a suburban area and has wide pavements and links to nearby paths, so a walk along the former line here is safe if not overly exciting.

Let us now turn to finding our former railways; here we have two distinct but complementary tasks, finding where a line went and identifying what remains. We will start with the former. Back in the 1980s and '90s, tracing the course of former railways that were not marked on modern maps was not a straightforward task. In recent times, however, easy access to old maps via the National Library of Scotland and also the 'rail map online' website has made this a much easier exercise; in particular, being able to 'overlay' an old map onto or alongside the current version is a great help. For assessing the situation on the ground, observational skills are needed that are gained with experience, but a few pointers can be given here. A row of modern housing in among streets of older structures might indicate a built-over route and similarly a small group of modern houses on level ground next to a station might have been constructed on a former goods shed area. Bridges that remain in railway ownership are marked as much by their current custodian, the Department for Transport; three examples are included here. Sometimes a knowledge of the relevant chronology is helpful – the short branch from Whitefield to Heaton Park in north Manchester for construction of the reservoir there closed in the 1920s and much of the area was built over soon afterwards with streets of typical 1930s semi-detached houses; but tracing an almost totally vanished line such as this one is an activity perhaps best left to the hard-core devotee.

Much of what is written about disused railways involves discussing official paths, but before doing so I thought it would be useful to take some time to consider the unofficial ones; not obviously private land behind gates or fences that are only accessible with permission, but the paths that are created 'naturally' and are used without restriction to reach one place from another. Sometimes termed 'desire paths', such a path can form without conscious intent where a convenient route does not coincide with an officially set out road or track. In some parts of our area, many sections of former railway lines achieve this status, and it is worth considering in general terms the process involved. Firstly, the landowner(s) must have no objection – any 'keep out' signs, obstructions or other blockages will obviously deter the casual walker. Sometimes, however, a farmer is only too pleased for people to prefer to cross his land via a 'separate' old railway rather than on a public footpath through fields full of crops or animals. Secondly it must be useful – to be both the shortest route between two places people might wish to travel and to be accessible reasonably easily from at least two locations. Thirdly it must 'naturally' remain in sufficiently good condition for people to be able to use it on a reasonably regular basis as no one is taking responsibility for upkeep of such a path – any excess water must have somewhere to drain away and it must not be entirely blocked by nettles, brambles, or other such foliage. Finally, it must have some regular use – the passage of feet, whether human or canine, serves to solidify the route and keep at least a narrow gap free from encroachment by vegetation. It does happen that long-term unofficial paths can become inaccessible; one example is the, now almost permanently flooded, former Great Central Railway's Wigan branch, east of Culcheth station (North Cheshire) passing south of the village of that name towards the former Newchurch Halt.

Shaw & Crompton station, between Oldham and Rochdale one week after closure, 2009. *Author*

Department for Transport markings indicating bridges that remain in public ownership: *Left:* near Market Drayton. *Dave Coogan; Centre:* south of Brinscall on the Blackburn to Chorley line. *Author; Right:* north of Colne on the line to Skipton. *Author*

Turning, now, to official paths or cycleways, these can be created in two ways. The first way is to take over an unofficial path, as described above. Unofficial use demonstrates demand and has established continuity of the route. However, the main long-distance paths such as the Trans Pennine Trail tend to be constructed on formations taken over directly from railway property agencies or possibly bought intact by local authorities. An official path is no guarantee of an easy walk though; in some places, particularly the Trans Pennine Trail east of Lymm, the path has been allowed to deteriorate to the level that access after heavy rain, without waterproof footwear, is not at all straightforward.

A cutting at Hurst Green, Lancashire, on a line that was never built, between Longridge and Whalley. *Author*

Site of former stone cutting on the Seacombe branch, Merseyside, now used as an access road for the Mersey Tunnel, 2003. *Gordon Suggitt*

What if no path is built? Where cuttings and embankments formerly existed, the latter often survive in a more intact form than the former. If a turf cutting has been filled in (stone cuttings are generally steeper), the space taken up by the infilling is considerably wider than that taken up by a single- or double-track railway and is generally not built upon. A quite lengthy example can be seen on the Padiham loop line in east Lancashire to the west of Great Harwood. The removal of a large embankment is an equally major task but with less obvious reward unless it takes up space urgently needed for housing or other uses. The large embankments leading up to the Latchford Viaduct south of Warrington are good examples of earthworks that have survived intact for almost forty years without subsequent use. A contrary example, though, is a completely eradicated embankment on the Barnoldswick branch west of its crossing of the Leeds & Liverpool Canal, its site now lying bare on an empty and unused field.

In low-lying rural areas, sometimes former railway formations are simply removed and returned to nature, with little on the ground to indicate their former presence. Good examples of this can be found on the Chester to Whitchurch line and the Knott End branch in Lancashire.

One point that may help a potential explorer is that lines in such locations were often built straight – there was no need to twist and turn to follow the contours of the land. Another guide can be the sites of road crossings with their keeper's houses or alternatively a line of gates or gaps in walls (or perhaps old walls with the former gaps filled in with different brickwork) indicating the former route.

Another situation that arises every now and then is where you see some remains of a former railway where you didn't expect one to be; I remember once stumbling across the remains of the Ellerbeck Colliery branch, south of Chorley and not previously known to me, quite by accident one day. In previous times this could become something of a mystery, but with access to older mapping the problem can generally be solved, though perhaps you have stumbled across a tramroad, in which case move on to Chapter 19 for further discussion. At Hurst Green in Lancashire (see Chapter 13) or south of Ulverston in Cumbria (see Chapter 15) you might even come across formation that never had a track laid. One last consideration is that lines that served military or ordnance premises are also sometimes missing from maps, but in these cases deliberately so for reasons of security.

2
The Earliest Railways

Railways have existed in the north-west of England for much longer than many imagine, certainly a good bit earlier than 1830 when the Liverpool & Manchester Railway, Britain's first 'inter-city' line, was opened. But before we start documenting and exploring early railways, we perhaps need a definition of what exactly 'is' a railway. There are potentially both general and specific options here: the latter being to refer to such vehicles being carried on some form of rail, but perhaps a broader definition is to simply consider a railway to be a prepared track that guides vehicles in such a way that they cannot easily leave it.

Although there is clear evidence that wheeled trucks with various forms of guidance had been used by miners underground in mainland Europe for centuries before 1600, it is shortly before that time that the use of wagons running on wooden rails developed in England. Our story takes us right back to the 1500s: England was desperately short of copper. As an essential raw material for making cannons, this was a major concern, so the discovery of a vein of copper in the Lake District, close to Keswick, was most welcome. However, sixteenth-century England lacked the technology to effectively mine this copper and Daniel Hechstetter, a mining engineer from Augsburg, was appointed to take charge of this undertaking, bringing 200 German miners with him. The expertise of these miners was far more advanced than the English, both in the underground work of tunnelling, pumping, and hauling to retrieve the ore but, more importantly, in the art of separating and smelting the copper. However, as might be imagined, the arrival of all these 'visitors' did not go down well locally, with at least one German miner beaten to death by an angry mob, but eventually things settled down and a number of German miners married local girls, indeed a number of Germanic surnames still feature among the population of the area. Archaeological explorations of the mines in question have confirmed that the continental 'hund' system was used in these mines, notably at Caldbeck near Keswick, but was only used below ground. This was an early form of underground mine tub with roller wheels on flat boards being steered by a guide pin, similar to that used on a Scalextric track. It was known as a 'hund' from the German word for dog, as the wheels made a sound that reminded some people of a dog barking. While it is entirely possible that such 'railways' might in places have led out of mines to some sort of land- or river-based collection or distribution point, documentary evidence of this is sadly lacking.

The next significant development was the use of actual rails; significantly reducing friction and thus allowing horses to pull much greater loads than hitherto. These were initially made of wood, but with heavy traffic and exposure to water or ice, had the disadvantage of needing frequent replacement. They were mounted on stone sleeper blocks, which survived much more readily and, together with their bolt holes, became a familiar point of recognition for tramway explorers. Use of blocks also allowed the space between sleepers to be cobbled or an alternative hard surface provided for the horses that pulled the wagons.

It is fair to say that very little is known of what is thought to be Lancashire's very first railway line – a primitive, wooden-railed, horse-drawn tramroad at Prescot between St Helens and Liverpool. This line, owned by one Philip Layton, carried coal from a pit near Prescot Hall for about half a mile to Fall Lane, where one presumes a suitable road was available to take the material to where it was needed. It had certainly opened by the early 1600s but was possibly being worked as early as 1594; this would make it England's earliest documented overground railway.

So why did tramroads, and later railways, become necessary? Many sources detail the inadequacy of seventeenth- and eighteenth-century roads, narrow, muddy, deeply rutted and with the ever-present danger of robbery by musket-wielding highwaymen. These tracks could only be negotiated by horses hauling wagons or by trains of packhorses. The first alternative was to use rivers. During the late seventeenth century, Thomas Patten, a Lancashire businessman and merchant, was trading along the River Mersey between Liverpool and Warrington, and,

A bridge at Gathurst station, north of Wigan, carrying the Wigan to Southport line over a minor road (larger arch) and the eighteenth-century Hustlers Railway (smaller arch). *Author*

in order to improve access for his barges to a quay just below Warrington, he cleared some obstructions in the river. In a letter written in January 1677, Patten remarked that it would be advantageous to make the rivers Mersey and Irwell both navigable through to Manchester. Further north, in the early to mid-1700s, a quay was available on the River Lune at Lancaster but due to silting and other difficulties, the Lancaster Port Commission decided to build a dock at Glasson in 1779, later to be linked to Lancaster and Preston by canal (see Chapter 14).

Embankment on the early nineteenth-century Congleton Railway. *Author*

As the industrial revolution gathered pace; involving the development of bigger and bigger workplaces, the demands on the transport infrastructure serving them started to become difficult to manage. For example, by 1786, the huge Ravenhead plate glass and smelting works in St Helens were consuming well over 700 tons of coal per week between them. With these demands, the limitations of the canals as a reliable mode of transport were gradually becoming clear. Delays in traffic were frequent, with canals frozen up and impassable for long periods in the winter months when supplies were most needed. Conversely, water shortages during prolonged periods of dry weather could also shut down stretches of canal. There was also much dissatisfaction with the standard of canal maintenance, with water leaking away at locks and landslips on embankments and cuttings not being promptly made good.

Other options were beginning to make headway. By the early 1740s, wooden tramways were being constructed in west Cumbria linking coal pits to harbours, where boats could take them onwards; much Cumbrian coal was sold and shipped to Ireland, where local sources were limited. These early lines included the Seaton Banks Tramway east of Workington and the shorter Parker Waggonway at Whitehaven, followed not long afterwards by a somewhat longer line heading to the harbour at Maryport; ownership and responsibility for their use seemed to rest with one Sir James Lowther, clearly a pioneer if a somewhat little-known one. Such tramways helped the Cumbrian coalfield to produce an annual output of 500,000 tons by the late 1700s, a fivefold increase on a similar period a century before.

Around this time a further significant development took place, with the first production of iron rails. At first these were no better than wooden rails, being brittle and unable to withstand heavy loads, and an alternative system gained popularity in the mid-1700s; this involved the use of an 'L'-shaped iron rail together with plain, non-flanged, cart wheels and became known as a plateway. The lines around Whitehaven referred to above were early converts to this system and these were needed, as cast-iron wheels on carts and wagons were being introduced at the same time, significantly increasing the weight of load that a single wagon could carry. Plateways eventually fell out of use by around 1820 when a wrought-iron rail became universal, the first of these being known as fish-belly rails from their cross-sectional shape. This pattern of iron rails together with flanged wheels remain to this day the basic format for almost all railways.

It is fair to say, though, that around the mid to late 1700s canals remained the best option and many tramroads were built to connect with them. A few are mentioned here, with others discussed in Chapter 19. One of the first was a line from collieries at Parr in St Helens to the Sankey canal to the north and where a later dock can still be viewed. This tramroad opened in 1757, just two years after the canal, and was also notable for being promoted by a woman. But Sarah Clayton had gained experience of tramways in places as far removed as Bath, Shropshire and North Wales and was undoubtedly a shrewd businesswoman and sound recruiter of staff. Another example can be found just east of Gathurst station on the still open Wigan–Southport route, where a bridge was constructed to carry the line over the originally wooden-tracked, eighteenth-century Hustler's Railway, built to carry coal from pits near Orrell to the River Douglas with a later short diversion to the parallel Leeds & Liverpool Canal. A less common use of wooden railways was in construction; it is recorded that a 'rail road' was put into use in 1773 to facilitate the building of the Chester Canal. On a similar theme, a tramway linked two sections of the Peak Forest canal at Marple from 1800 to 1807, when a flight of locks was completed and opened.

An original stone sleeper from the Congleton Railway. *Author*

The best place in our region to visit, if you want to find significant remains of a really old railway, is in the area to the south of Congleton in Cheshire. Here you can explore the remains of the Congleton Railway, built to bring to the town coal from Stonetrough Colliery, situated in the Biddulph Valley north of the small town of that name. Opened in around 1805, the rails were described in a contemporary account as 'oval or egg shaped', indicating that it was an edge railway rather than a plateway. It brought coal to a land wharf or landsale yard on Moss Road, a mile or so to the south-east of Congleton. However, its opening unfortunately coincided with the bankruptcy of the colliery owners; it is believed that Stonetrough Colliery closed in 1807 and did not reopen until 1810, as did the railway. Fieldwork, published in academic form by Patel in 2018, established a gauge of around 4ft and a somewhat later closure date than was originally assumed; Baxter had the line closing for good in 1807 but a closure date around the 1840s appears more accurate from the evidence gathered.

The similarly located Mow Cop Tramway was a slightly later venture; opening in 1842 and at a 4–5ft gauge, it ran west and slightly north from the newly opened Tower Hill Colliery, adjacent to the older one at Stonetrough, on an almost straight run to reach a wharf on the Macclesfield Canal at Mow Cop. It included two inclines and a now inaccessible tunnel (though a small group apparently entered and explored it in January 2002) of around 370 yards under a ridge of the Cop. It is thought to have closed in 1887 when the collieries were bought by a rival owner and immediately shut down.

Although little has been done locally to provide information about the old lines, a surprising amount can be followed. Starting at the Congleton end, the formation can be picked up from a footpath off Tower Hill Road. It passes through woods, via a short cutting and a fine long embankment close to Hillside Farm. Just north of the site of Stonetrough Colliery, now part of a farm, the two lines crossed, though at slightly different levels as the Congleton line had shut before the Mow Cop route opened. The Mow Cop line, outside of the tunnel area, is quite recognisable; first the incline can be seen crossing fields before the line becomes a rough track on its more level middle section. A further incline of around 1 in 8 then lowered the tramway to reach the canal wharf at Mow Cop.

In the nineteenth century most of the early routes, certainly those that survived and remained busy, were converted to locomotive haulage and many other industrial railways also became referred to as tramroads. A lot of these, often in more remote, hilly, areas, have survived better than many former passenger lines in built-up areas and a number of these make superb walks. In the final chapter of this book, we will explore what remains of a good selection of them.

Stone sleepers on the Mow Cop tramway incline. *Author*

3

The Wirral and Chester

West Kirby–Hooton

This line was opened in piecemeal form by the Birkenhead Joint Railway (BJR). The southern part of the route was opened between Parkgate and Hooton in October 1866 but it took almost another twenty years before West Kirby was reached in April 1886, the first station in Parkgate being replaced at the same time. After a period of prosperity, traffic declined quickly, as almost every place it served was better connected by other lines, and the line was closed to passenger traffic in September 1956, though goods traffic hung on until May 1962. Being in a well-populated area, the railway quickly deteriorated, with photographs of that time showing derelict, vandalised stations, flooded cuttings and much evidence of fly-tipping of rubbish.

However, quite unusually for the time, by the mid-1960s Cheshire County Council had taken an interest in the line and saw potential for a linear park. They were almost too late, as the stations at Heswall and Neston South had already been sold privately, requiring, to this day, short diversions around these locations. But after that time things moved quickly; a report detailing the scheme was published in April 1968 and the line converted to the Wirral Way in stages from 1969 to 1973, a role that it still performs to this day.

Starting at West Kirby's Merseyrail station, the adjacent BJR station, situated west of Orrysdale Road, is long gone but the trail is easily picked up and runs through gentle suburbs to Caldy. There is little left of the next two stations at Kirby Park or Caldy, although the access for the former from road level can still be made out. Thurstaston station, being more rurally situated, has fared better; its two platforms are still extant, as are the former goods facilities, though the station buildings are long gone.

En route to Heswall, a gradient post survives, or at least did until recently, half hidden in the undergrowth, but within Heswall itself the railway formation has been lost under housing development. The station site has gone the same way, although a retaining wall still remains, which helps to identify the site. The stationmaster's house is also a survivor. Where the formation is picked up again, picnic tables offer a comfortable spot for refreshments. Access continues through to Parkgate, once a small maritime town with the tidal River Dee running right up to the sea wall, but now separated from the river by a mile or so of mudflats and tufty grass. At this location there are remains of the second station (the first was on the opposite side of the Neston to Parkgate Road) and its approach path, together with the privately occupied station house. The formation turns due east after Parkgate and passes under the still busy Bidston to Wrexham Central line. East of here, housing engulfs the trackbed again past the site of Neston station, land sold off before the country park was built, but the short diversion required is clearly signposted.

After Neston station comes Neston Rock Cutting and this today provides the best section of formation on the whole journey. The cutting was carved out of sandstone by pickaxe and evidence of the navvies' efforts remain visible today. In botanical terms, the cutting is of particular interest as the north wall of the cutting, slightly higher, drains and stays dry while the south wall is almost permanently damp; as a result, they each support quite different flora. The last station on the route is by far the best; the beautifully preserved and maintained Hadlow Road station retains its station house, booking hall and opposite waiting shelter, although at one time it did face an uncertain future due to council cuts. Along with the two platforms, level crossing gate, trackwork, signal box and signal, this is a gem of the disused railway network. It is a fitting place to stop for a while before concluding the journey to Hooton. At the latter location the derelict land on the left was part of ROF (No. 10), which was built in 1942. It acquired the name Roften and had a siding from the West Kirby line. The walk concludes on the former western platform at Hooton station, which also retains a building, though this is closed and locked. Hooton station itself is still busy and very much a key location on the Merseyrail network to Liverpool, Chester and Ellesmere Port.

Hadlow Road station on the Wirral Way, 2003.
Gordon Suggitt

Birkenhead and its Dock Railway

From one of the country's oldest official paths to what will hopefully soon become one of our newest. The Chester & Birkenhead Railway opened in September 1840 with a temporary terminus in Birkenhead at Grange Lane. The Morpeth & Egerton Docks then opened in April 1847, with the first docks branch opening at the same time from Grange Lane to a goods depot at Cathcart Street. As the docks expanded and trade increased, further lines were built, gradually serving an increasing range of premises on the south side of the dock area. From the south junction of Rock Ferry to the site of the former Bidston Dock, a line approximately 4½ miles long became established. It kept away from the town centre, with a section of the line running through Haymarket Tunnel and a low-level cutting through the centre of Birkenhead that is just about visible from the road flyovers. For much of the twentieth century, the line was busy with freight, primarily for hauling offloaded iron ore from Bidston Dock to the John Summers Steelworks in Shotton. This traffic ceased in March 1980 when the steelworks closed. Goods workings continued on the line to the Spillers Mill on Dock Road until the late 1980s with grain wagon traffic coming in from Whitemoor Yard in Cambridgeshire. Afterwards, a thrice-weekly coal train operated on the line until 1992. A few railtours also visited the line in the 1980s.

Although the former Canning Street North signal box has now been demolished following fire damage, and the rails across the level crossing there have been removed due to the provision of cycle lanes on the roadway, plenty of evidence of the original railway still remains – from the level crossings located at Duke Street and Wallasey Bridge Road to the Monks Ferry and Woodside tunnel portals, which have now been filled in. In 2013, landowners Peel Holdings announced plans to run 'streetcars', smaller and lighter versions of trams, along the line, linking with the Merseyrail network but nothing ever came of these proposals.

Recent proposals for the line seem somewhat complex, but it appears National Museums Liverpool have announced plans for a new transport museum in Birkenhead, with funding coming from the government's Town Deal Fund. A total of £25 million has been awarded to Wirral Council for a range of regeneration projects in Birkenhead that includes work on an 800m stretch of the Docks branch, enabling trams and potentially other motive power to run along it. The rest of the line is earmarked for a community path, bringing access to 'open spaces and landscapes' in the area. Following public consultation in August 2020, an original plan to fill the cutting and bring it up to street level has been reconsidered. The current plans for 'Dock Branch Park'

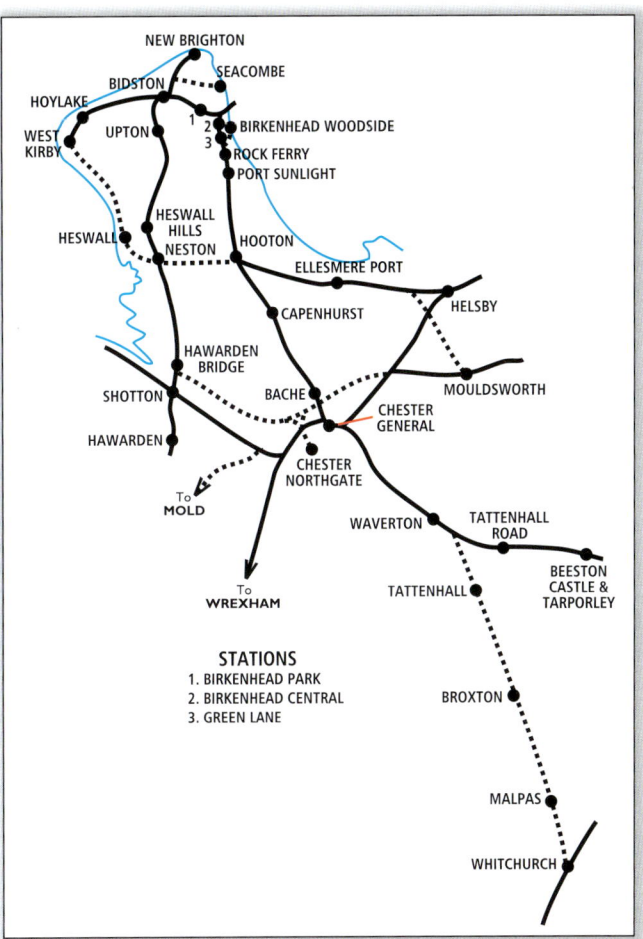

Map showing lines in the Wirral and Chester area.

Wirral Way, the Neston rock cutting. *Author*

Above: Birkenhead Docks (Canning Street) Rail and road bridge crossing water between Egerton and Morpeth Docks. *Howard Harrison*

Left: A view from close to Canning Street North signal box with the line heading right towards Rock Ferry. *Howard Harrison*

Below: Birkenhead Docks; a classic 1980s railtour scene, junction of Patten Street & Beaufort Road. *Howard Harrison*

Canning Street North signal box – the line to the right to Rock Ferry, the line going left to cross Egerton Bridge, the line crossing on the level towards Birkenhead North. *Howard Harrison*

Looking from the signal box at Canning Street towards Birkenhead North from the now demolished footbridge by the level crossing. *Howard Harrison*

The former CLC Warehouse at Birkenhead, 2003. *Gordon Suggitt*

will now see the line be given to the community of Birkenhead for the first time. The ambition is to preserve as much of the heritage of the line as possible while bringing it into positive community use. The park will become, it is proposed, 'a place of natural connection, protecting and diversifying habitats and biodiversity, connecting and creating new communities and a cultural and visitor experience second to none'.

Also worth a view in this area is the site of Birkenhead Woodside station, a distant outpost of the Great Western Railway lying right next to the River Mersey and accessed via a tunnel north of Birkenhead Town station. This tunnel is filled in, with entrances bricked up and secure, but the top part of the north portal's arch can still be viewed. Closed in 1967 and demolished little more than a year later, the Woodside station site, marked by a large wall to one side, remains identifiable with part of it in use as a bus depot. Birkenhead Town station, situated south of Grange Road and more convenient for the town centre than Woodside, had closed as early as May 1945; just one wall from the original booking office remains at this site.

Ellesmere Port

The lines reaching the western end of the Manchester Ship Canal (MSC) can be arguably considered part of the MSC Railway but given their dates of operation (considerably later than the lines discussed in Chapter 5) and the degree of geographical separation, it is felt better to give them brief consideration here. This (now virtually unused) system is not publicly accessible, though the dock authorities have given permission for a number of private visits in recent years. Heading north from a junction just to the west of Ellesmere Port station, one branch curved east to Ellesmere Port Docks, where sand traffic was handled on a somewhat ad hoc basis until 2016. The line north to Eastham, on a significant upward gradient and serving storage facilities, was only opened in 1967; its date of closure seems unclear, but it may well have survived into this century. Manisty Wharf, on the ship canal itself, opened in 1931 and maintained a small amount of coal traffic right through to 2015; officially, at least, it is still considered a live line for potential storage of wagons.

Dee Marsh Junction–Mickle Trafford

Originally two quite different routes, this line, bypassing Chester to the north, was relatively unsuccessful in terms of passenger services but continued as a valuable through route for freight right into the 1990s. The eastern section was opened first, the Cheshire Lines Committee (CLC) reaching their new station at Chester Northgate from Mouldsworth in 1875, but it wasn't until 1890 that the Manchester, Sheffield and Lincolnshire Railway (MS&LR) completed their line heading west from Northgate to Hawarden Bridge. This facilitated passenger services from Chester Northgate, either north towards Bidston (then onwards to Liverpool, New Brighton or Birkenhead) or south to Wrexham. A few services bypassed Northgate: these served Chester's Liverpool Road station, just a few hundred yards to the north of Northgate. Passenger services declined quickly after the war, with Liverpool Road station and Mickle Trafford (East) closing in December 1951 and Saughall following three years later. Services to Chester Northgate, arguably closer to and more convenient for the city centre than the current Chester (General) station, hung on until October 1969.

Manchester Ship Canal Railway (Ellesmere Port section) Manisty Wharf seen in 2016. *Phillip Earnshaw*

In later years the line was kept busy as an access route from the east to the extensive Shotton Steelworks, together with United Paper Mills, built on the site of a blast furnace just to the north of the steelworks. This traffic kept the line open until May 1984, but two years later there was an unlikely revival, after the steelworks had closed, with further use of the line from August 1986 to October 1992 when use finally ended, and the track (but not the ballast) was lifted in 1996. Plans were announced for a guided busway from Mickle Trafford to Chester city centre, but nothing ever came of them and instead conversion to a cycleway took place, opening in stages from 1991, with the Mickle Trafford end finally being completed in 2009.

A surviving piece of track at Dee Marsh Junction, west of Chester on the Mickle Trafford route, in 2022. *Author*

Bridge carrying Dee Marsh Line over the Shropshire Union Canal west of Chester. *Author*

A good place to start exploration of this line is Hawarden Bridge station (just across the River Dee from Shotton, which retains regular services from Chester), from where a triangle is reached with a curve north-west towards Chester and another north-west towards Bidston. Both are accessible, with a small piece of track still in situ at the latter junction. Being an official path, the line is easily followed, on a solid tarmac service throughout. Quickly you reach the site (no remains) of Chester Golf Club platform, in use from 1890 to September 1927. This was the original Chester Golf Club, no relation to the current one at Curzon Park. The Second World War brought about the demise of the first club as apparently most of the younger members were serving in the forces and the removal of the civilian petrol ration meant that it was difficult for the remaining members to get out to the club at Shotton. A report on the 'Golf's Missing Links' website (an excellent resource for details of defunct golf courses) suggested that the clubhouse survived into the 1960s, long after the rest of the area had been built over by industrial premises.

Returning to the railway, stations pass in quick succession: only a pair of concrete lamp posts mark the site of Sealand station but at Saughall both platforms survive in an overgrown and degraded condition. Saughall and Blacon Stations had superb, mock-Tudor style station buildings that were both sadly demolished in the early 1980s; Saughall, in particular, situated in a rural location, would have made a superb dwelling. Blacon station has been redeveloped but with a clear nod to its history as a number of replica nameboard signs have been erected in the area. Heading into Chester, the Shropshire Union Canal is crossed by a sturdy iron girder bridge, then Liverpool Road station site is reached; just a widened formation now marks the site of this once substantial station. Chester Northgate station's site is covered by a leisure centre with just a small part of a wall remaining, so most people continue straight on towards Mickle Trafford, the trail ending just a few hundred yards before the former Mickle Trafford East station site is reached. The junction with the Helsby route was a wartime connection, put in place in 1942.

Helsby–Mouldsworth

Although short and only infrequently used by passenger services, this line was of importance to the CLC as a route into the key market of Birkenhead. Manley station, halfway down the line, was only officially open to passengers between 1870 and 1874 but retained goods facilities for many years afterwards. There was also a short branch running into Manley Quarry, just south of the station, which closed in 1910. Helsby & Alvanley station saw intermittent use, mostly for excursion or unadvertised workmen's trains, right through to January 1964 and the importance of this station is also demonstrated by the presence of an engine shed until 1929. In later years the huge Stanlow oil refinery and a power station at Ince (Cheshire) provided traffic, though the route's closure in 1991 was sudden and unplanned. A signal box fire at Helsby Junction in September 1991 blocked access to the Mouldsworth route and it never reopened, official closure taking place in May 1992.

Helsby to Mouldsworth line, bridge under A56 north of Helsby & Alvanley station. *Author*

Although both Helsby & Alvanley and Manley's station buildings became private residences, there is now little else left to see. The line's post-closure history is a classic example of an unofficial or 'desire' path that never made it to maturity. With tracks lifted but some ballast retained, the line became a popular local footpath, particularly along the embankment north of Manley, which gave fine views of the surrounding countryside. The route was walkable until at least 2002; however, sometime after that, the line was blocked at the Helsby end, where it was most accessible, and use declined until it was no longer passable. A local resident recently described the line as 'completely overgrown in most places with some flooding'. Given that many official paths start with unofficial use, the attention and, more importantly, funding of the relevant authorities might well have been attracted – very much a case of 'one that got away'.

Helsby to Mouldsworth line, bridge at Manley now without its decking. *Author*

Chester–Whitchurch

Built by the L&NWR, this line opened in 1872, effectively competing with the Great Western Railway's route from Shrewsbury to Chester via Wrexham. This route was about 14 miles long and was built as double track throughout, with aspirations of it becoming a valuable through route, linking Shrewsbury and South Wales with the busy Mersey Docks in Birkenhead. Never successful and serving no towns or villages of note, it became something of a backwater. Closure to passengers took place in in September 1957, with the last goods services running in November 1963. Track lifting took place a little later, around 1965, suggesting that there was some doubt about its permanent closure as, at the time, most closed lines were lifted within months, if not weeks, of traffic ceasing.

As a line that closed almost sixty years ago in a flat and largely rural area, it is not surprising that any remains are somewhat fragmented with very little trackbed easily accessible.

There is, however, one short section, east of Hatton Hall, which has been converted to a footpath for about 500m. Much has been lost altogether in the Tattenhall and Broxton area, though the station sites are still easily traced. At Tattenhall the station building survives as a private residence, although it has in recent years been substantially altered. The platforms have been removed to create a large lawn and the buildings extended and largely rebuilt. The whole site now looks totally 'un-railwaylike' and one has to wonder why people bother to buy up a former station if their intention is to eradicate any sign of its history. Broxton station – once with a handsome, solid-looking, station building, has vanished from the landscape with the site used as a car park; the base of a crane being the only railway-related survivor.

However, Malpas station, situated almost 2 miles north of the village of that name, remains in commercial use and is beautifully preserved, right down to the clock in the frontage and its signing; an absolute credit to its owners, the construction and surfacing firm Miles MacAdam Ltd. South of Malpas the line remains more intact with a short section north of Ebnal Farm now a footpath and potential to extent this further south, though two bridges north of Grindley Brook have been listed for eventual infilling by the Highways Agency. Nothing remains at Grindley Brook Halt, opened in July 1937, and situated in a small cutting just north of where the line crosses the Llangollen Canal. This halt seems to have been something of a mystery; no photographs, either before closure or afterwards, having ever come to light. All traces had vanished by the early 1970s; it might well be that the halt's platforms were of wooden construction and were simply dismantled when the track was lifted. Finally, Whitchurch station, where a disused bay platform survives at its north end, is reached; this was the starting point for most passenger services (though there were a few Hereford to Chester trains in the line's early days).

Chester to Whitchurch line, a modern view of Malpas station. *Author*

4
Mid and East Cheshire

Cuddington–Winsford & Over

Running south, then east, for around 6 miles from Cuddington, near Northwich, to Winsford, this line was promoted by the Cheshire Lines Committee (CLC) to reach the extensive and indeed lucrative salt works close to Winsford, on the opposite (west) side of the River Weaver from those served by the L&NWR. Opening to freight in June 1870 and a month later to passengers, sufficient land was bought for two tracks, but the second track was never needed and never laid. The line quickly became busy with salt traffic, but passenger traffic was not so successful. No services ran between January 1874 and 1886, nor between December 1888 and February 1892 before final (permanent) closure in January 1931. Many trains were mixed, basically freight services with a single passenger coach tacked on at the front or back. After 1931, salt traffic and general freight kept the line busy for some years, although the latter ceased beyond Whitegate in September 1958. The route's last use was to serve Falk's and Meadowbank Salt Works, traffic finally coming to an end in March 1967.

Whitegate station seen in the early 1990s. The bridge in the background has since been reconstructed. *Author*

Trackbed of Wallerscote Light Railway, west of Northwich. *Author*

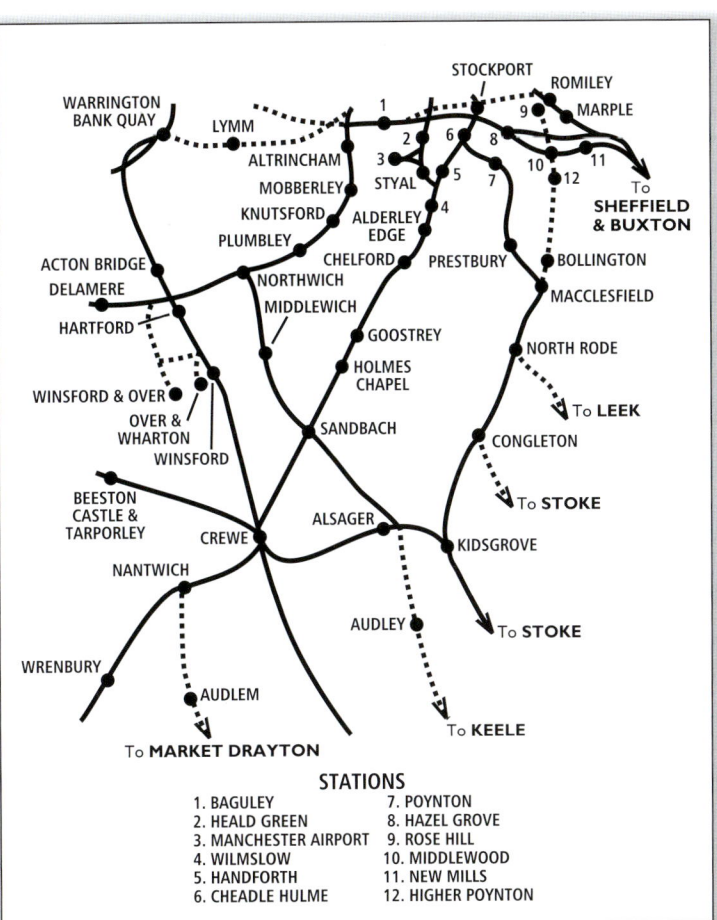

Map showing lines in the Cheshire area.

Unlike many lines closed at the time, the trackbed was not sold off piecemeal and was fortunate to be acquired by the local council in one single purchase. As a result, in the mid-1970s, it was an early conversion to a footpath and has remained popular ever since, being known as the 'Whitegate Way'. As such, access at either end of the line is straightforward with a (shorter) return trip possible via the River Weaver and the village of Sandiway. Winsford Junction lies about fifteen minutes' walk from Cuddington station and is easily accessible via minor roads and footpaths. At Whitegate station, over a mile from the village of that name, the station and platform remain intact, and the area is provided with car park spaces and picnic tables. The line continues east as far as Falk's Junction, where the line once split into spurs running north and south into different works. The northern spur can only be followed as far as the first minor road west of the River Weaver, where it disappears into industrial premises, but the southern branch continues as a path south to the site of Winsford & Over station. This station had just a single platform but extensive sidings for goods, however all has been swept away and the site now used for a road and adjacent car park; good for accessing the trail but a loss in terms of railway history.

Railways of Northwich

Northwich has a rich industrial history, going right back as far as Roman times where salt was mined, though at that time used as a form of currency rather than for seasoning of food. Salt was rediscovered in the late 1600s almost by accident when mines were sunk in search of coal. The railways reached Northwich by 1863, though arguably the town has suffered somewhat over the years with its station not situated on a major through route.

Much remains to be seen of Northwich's industrial railways, now silent since the last train reached the Winnington chemical works, via the Hartford Junctions, in January 2014. Probably the best line to explore is that of the Wallerscote Light Railway (though it is unclear if that name was ever used officially), which ran from Wallerscote sidings, on the West Coast Main Line, just over a mile north of Hartford station, to the west side of the huge chemical works. Joe Brown, in his 2021 *Liverpool & Manchester Railway Atlas*, had an opening date of July 1953 for this line, with the last train believed to have been an October 1980 railtour. The best point of access is by the approach road to Hartford Golf Club, a few hundred yards north-west of Greenbank station, where an embankment is clearly used unofficially as a footpath by locals.

Winnington Chemical works line, Northwich, May 2021. *Author*

A further line worthy of mention formerly ran north from Northwich East Junction, a few hundred yards east of Northwich station, to serve salt works at Marston and Wincham. Despite closure in March 1968, some short sections of formation remain, including a small bridge over the Wincham Brook.

Nantwich–Market Drayton

The Nantwich & Market Drayton Railway, the southernmost line to be considered in this volume, was an outpost of the Great Western Railway (GWR), who saw the line as a route to gain their share of traffic from the increasingly busy junction at Crewe. But to begin with, the line was merely a branch heading south to Market Drayton from Nantwich, opening in October 1863. It wasn't until four years later that it was extended south to Wellington, thus creating a through route. In 1870 the North Staffordshire Railway (NSR) also opened their line from Stoke, thus making Market Drayton a junction station.

Seen very much as a secondary main line, the route was notable for the paucity of the small village stations, serving scattered communities, that are seen on most rural routes: there were just two intermediate stations between Nantwich and Market Drayton, at Audlem and Adderley. In typical GWR style, though, Coxbank Halt, south of Audlem, was added in 1934 and Coole Pilate Halt, north of Audlem, opened the following year. The line had a brief period of activity as a diversionary route during electrification of the West Coast Main Line but after that a familiar story of decline set in and the line closed to passengers in September 1963 and to through goods traffic four years later in May 1967.

The towns at either end of this route are well worth visiting in themselves. Nantwich is an ancient town with a remarkable collection of timber-framed houses. Many of these were built (though a few survivors are even earlier) after a fire destroyed much of the town in December 1584. Market Drayton is, however, an even more ancient town: as its name suggests, holding a market every Wednesday as it has done since gaining a charter from King Henry III as early as 1245. The town also held what was generally known as 'Dirty Fair' in October each year when Welsh farmers, gypsies and other travellers gathered to sell horses and ponies. A fascinating account of a visit to the fair in the 1930s was included by L.T.C. Rolt in his classic travel book *Narrow Boat*, the name being apparently derived from the poor weather that invariably coincided with the event. 'Dirty Fair' was last held in 1973.

Heading west and then south-west, the line can be followed pretty much right through to the sidings, though much of the year there can be some surface water in the cuttings. Soon Wallerscote Exchange sidings are reached, accessible and securely fenced off from the adjacent main line. East of the golf club the line is less accessible but runs on an embankment of some length before the formation peters out close to a sewage works.

The short but once busy route from the triangle of Hartford Junctions into Winnington chemical works (once ICI and later Tata) has now been closed for over eight years but very little has changed on the ground. There is virtually no vegetation on the line (I cannot say whether or not weed-killing trains occasionally run) and it is securely fenced off throughout with no apparent access points for trespassers. Thus, as seen in the photograph, a pair of tracks still head up to the works, with rusty rails showing no sign of recent activity, perhaps waiting patiently for a possible resumption of chemical trains with the works still busy, albeit on a much smaller scale than ten or more years ago.

Any potential explorer of what remains of this railway will first notice on a map that the line closely parallels the Shropshire Union Canal. This has two implications: the first being that with a perfectly good towpath between the various communities already, there was never any momentum behind conversion to a railway path. The second implication is that the canal forms a valuable 'spine' from which it is easy to access what remains of the railway, though sadly that doesn't amount to a great deal.

Let us start at the Nantwich end and head south. The junction with the still-operational line to Whitchurch is about half a mile west of Nantwich station, with the first piece of formation visible where it is crossed by a pair of public footpaths. At Baddington Lane, the A530 Whitchurch Road crosses over the railway on a narrow bridge, controlled by traffic lights. Traffic here is often delayed, and one wonders the value of the bridge's survival. Little remains of the formation as it heads south past Hack Green, passing the well-signposted 'Secret Nuclear Bunker' (the irony is, I presume, intended), which is actually a fascinating place to visit and gives a real insight into military spying and surveillance from the Second World War through to the days of the Cold War in the 1960s. Returning to the railway, a crossing keeper's house is all that survives at this location.

South of Austin's bridge, the line crossed from the east side of the canal to the west side and while the abutments remain, the bridge itself is long gone. The crossing of the River Weaver a couple of miles south has met the same fate, though do be aware that it is still marked as intact on some modern OS maps – it certainly isn't. A little north of here a fine long cutting remains accessible with permission but there is nothing to see any more at the site of Coole Pilate Halt. All is lost for a good mile or so west of Audlem, including the station site, though more trackbed remains in place approaching Adderley. At Adderley station a good part of one platform remains, though much is covered by bushes and long grass. South of Adderley the trackbed is again fragmented, though becoming increasingly close to the canal. Approaching Market Drayton, the trackbed becomes an access road for various industrial premises, but the site of the junction with the Stoke line can still be made out, close to Sych Farm. Apart from a short cutting, nothing remains in Market Drayton itself at all now, and the station site has been long since built over by light industry.

Sandbach–Kidsgrove

This line was opened by the NSR, largely in 1852, although it did not connect with the main line in Sandbach until 1866. Around 6½ miles long, it had a local passenger service over most of its length between July 1893 and an early closure in July 1930, being a classic example of a line that didn't take people to where they wanted to go, whether that was Alsager, Crewe or Sandbach town centre (Sandbach station is situated in Elworth, almost 2 miles to the west). The line soldiered on until it was finally closed in January 1971, having been for many years of some value as an avoiding line for Crewe.

The northernmost part of the branch has today been lost under a new road to Ettiley Heath but a goods shed still survives near the start of what is now an established trail. Access to the former railway formation then extends from here to the east side of Wheelock. On the approach to Wheelock, the site of Wheelock Forge Junction can be

Junction of former Market Drayton line west of Nantwich. *Dave Coogan*

Nantwich to Market Drayton line, abutments of bridge over Shropshire Union Canal south of Hack Green. *Dave Coogan*

Nantwich to Market Drayton line, surviving platform at Adderley Station, seen in 2021. *Dave Coogan*

made out on the line's southern side. Here diverged a short mineral line to Wheelock Forge of which little remains; what is left is situated in a local property's back garden and as such is not readily accessible. A little further on, Wheelock station is reached, where a platform can be seen, once covered by undergrowth but now tidied up and with its former role clearly identifiable. The approach path, railway properties and main booking hall all survive, the latter being at road level and now in use by a local business as a tyre and exhaust centre.

The formation extends to the Trent and Mersey Canal west of Malkins Bank. After crossing the canal (the small bridge remains intact), the trackbed has been lost to development where it passed through the local salt works, now landscaped into a golf course. However, the canal towpath, running almost parallel to the railway and climbing gently through a couple of locks, makes a pleasant alternative. At Malkins Bank, a short siding carried freight to and from a large alkali works known as Brunner Mond after its founders; this company was to become ICI in the 1920s, but no trace of either railway or factory now exists. They later built a much modern and extensive works at Winnington, near Northwich, as described above.

Just before the M6 motorway is crossed the trackbed reappears and soon Hassall Green station is reached, in operation for just twenty-five years from 1905 to 1930. The station house, now a private residence, still stands adjacent to the former level crossing at this point. From here the path, known as the 'Salt Line', continues south-east; the official path ending at Lawton station, to the north of Alsager. Here a second station house still stands as a private residence, again next to a former level crossing. Nothing remains of the station itself. Although the line is largely intact as Lawton Junction is approached, no official access is possible here; for walkers it is back onto the Trent and Mersey Canal towpath for the hike back into Kidsgrove.

Macclesfield–Marple

This route was opened by 1870 by the 'Macclesfield Committee', a joint venture of the MS&LR and the NSR, although passenger trains did not gain access to the present Macclesfield station until July 1873. Originally built as single track, with just one passing loop at Higher Poynton, an early change to double track was made and by June 1871 it operated as such. The line was, however, always something of a backwater and it performed something of a duplicate function to the still extant line from Macclesfield to Manchester Piccadilly via Cheadle Hulme, albeit less directly. As such it was ripe for closure when economies were looked for and this was completed in January 1970.

The story of the abortive attempt to save this line is not especially well known. In May 1970 a local railway preservation society was formed, with the initial aim of postponing track lifting and raising £50,000 to purchase the line from British Railways. A month later a public meeting was held, attended by the local MP, but, overall, only about eighty people turned up and support for the railway was well below expectations. More crucially, British Railways demanded an immediate payment of £1,400 in return for not lifting the line, though even if this money had been forthcoming only three months' extra time was offered. This sum could not be found at short notice and the preservation scheme never made further headway. Track lifting then commenced and was completed by March 1971.

Now known as the Middlewood Way, this route has since become a popular, well-established trail. Opened between Marple Rose Hill and Bollington by Dr David Bellamy in May 1985, it was extended through to Pool End on the north side of Macclesfield in 1988. Today it is difficult to remember the lost southern part of the formation other than a large tract of land in Macclesfield that could be accessed before heading north-east past industrial units towards Bollington, passing a number of redundant signal posts en route. The temporary joint station, built in 1871

Sandbach to Kidsgrove line, Platform at Wheelock station. *Author*

Trackbed north of Macclesfield with signal post in 1988 – all now buried under a new road. *Phillip Earnshaw*

and remaining in use for goods until 1969, was situated here but all is now gone from where at one time a reassuring crunch of ballast added a touch of authenticity to proceedings that had been eradicated further north. The fact that the route was not converted in the same way as further north was not without reason. The reason, in the form of a new road, sadly became a reality and it is with this in mind that to depart from Macclesfield requires a roadside walk or a stretch of the Macclesfield Canal towpath to the north side of Macclesfield at Tytherington, where the trackbed re-emerges from its successor. The trackbed is largely uninspiring to Bollington and the station has long since gone, the buildings being demolished in December 1971 and the platforms following suit in the early 1980s.

Lineman's hut on Middlewood Way between Macclesfield and Marple. *Nick Melling*

Macclesfield to Marple line: A modern view of Higher Poynton station. *Nick Melling*

The first major feature on the line is Bollington Viaduct, a twenty-three-arch structure that barely survived demolition; Macclesfield Council only agreed to take over responsibility when British Rail offered a £20,000 grant towards its restoration. Happily, its future was secured in 1982, allowing that final stretch of the Middlewood Way to be completed.

Much of the route is split between a footpath and a bridleway and runs mainly in cuttings, under a string of overbridges, with the result that views of the surrounding countryside and distant hills and moorland are limited. At Higher Poynton a substantial station was constructed, but as with Bollington the buildings were an early casualty. Happily, though, the platforms are today still visible and intact, with the formation in between used as a picnic area, together with its access from street level above. Further north, the Middlewood Curve is still visible, open between 1885 and 1955 and connecting with the Buxton Line; indeed between 1920 and 1927 a direct service between Macclesfield and Buxton operated using this curve, though apparently with limited commercial success.

Its divergence from this route at Middlewood High Level Junction is on the approach to Middlewood High Level station, closed in 1960. Unusually, the up platform was considerably longer than the down platform, but it was the tiny down platform that outlasted its companion, still being in place in 1975 but long since dismantled. Its site can still be gleaned due to access paths that still exist in the vicinity, and the stationmaster's house, now in private use, has also survived. Useful access to the still operational Middlewood (Low Level) station for trains to Buxton or Manchester can be found here.

The path continues north and soon reaches High Lane station; here the station buildings were still intact in a derelict state as late as 1976. The platforms survive though and, as at Higher Poynton, picnic tables have been installed as a welcome facility for walkers and cyclists. It is then only another 2 miles or so to Rose Hill, where a single platform suffices for services into Manchester Piccadilly, these days taking a somewhat indirect route via Woodley and Guide Bridge.

5

Warrington & Altrincham

Warrington–Skelton Junction (Lymm Line)

The Warrington & Stockport railway (originally the Warrington & Altrincham Railway, though the name change took place before the line opened) very much fits the 'does what it says it does' model, linking the two towns in question, opening in stages from 1853, though initially it existed as an independent line not linked to the rest of the railway network. In Warrington a temporary terminus at Wilderspool served until a bridge was constructed over the River Mersey to reach Warrington's Arpley station (always the nearest of Warrington's stations to the town centre), the low-level platforms at Warrington Bank Quay and then on towards Widnes with connections into Liverpool. At the east end, a link through to Stockport via Skelton Junction was provided, as was access to Manchester via Sale from 1854 using a connection at Broadheath Junction.

Passenger traffic was never successful, there being two (arguably three) alternative routes between Warrington and Manchester and very little intermediate traffic. Both Lymm and Thelwall have grown in size only since their stations closed and Dunham remains a delightful and quite unspoilt rural location, with the deer park at Dunham Massey close by. Instead, the line became busy with middle or long-distance freight traffic, particularly with the line having easy connections via Stockport and the Apethorne Curve at Hyde to the Woodhead route, bringing coal and other goods from Yorkshire to Warrington, Fiddlers Ferry power station and the Port of Liverpool. Local passenger traffic ceased in 1962, Thelwall station having closed in 1956, but freight continued into the 1980s. The decline of the collieries in that decade, together with the closure of Woodhead and the condition of Latchford Viaduct, proved to be the final nails, and the line closed altogether in July 1985.

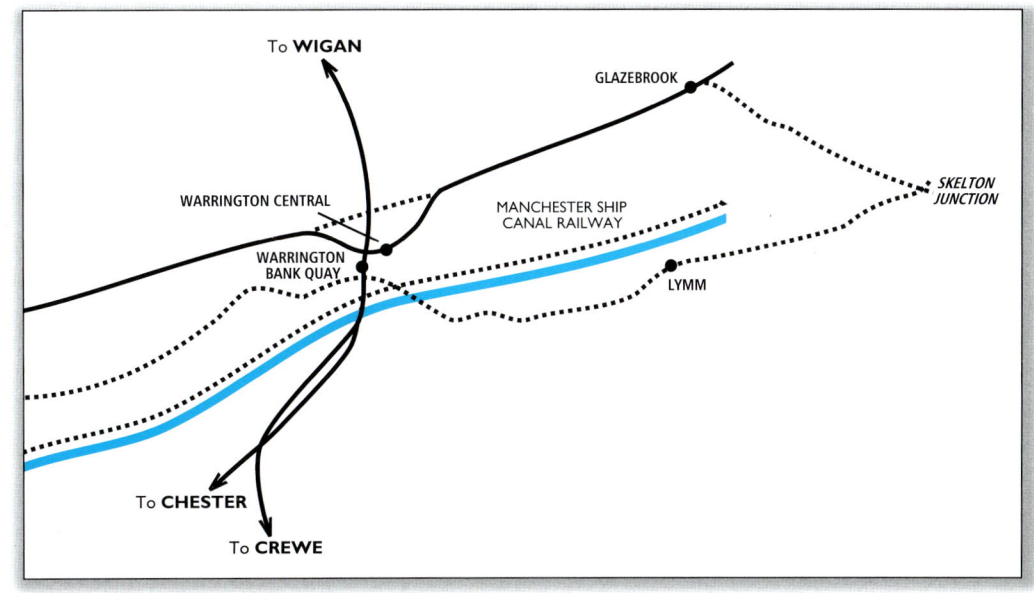

Map showing lines in the Warrington and Lymm area.

Warrington to Skelton Junction (Lymm) line, clearing the embankment at Latchford in 2015. *Author*

A look at a modern map shows a large part of the route, between Grappenhall and Broadheath, now forming part of the Trans Pennine Trail but, starting from the Warrington end, there is plenty to see before we reach the official path. At Warrington Bank Quay, a footbridge just outside the station entrance crosses the line and allows a view of the site of the long-gone low-level platforms, though road widening has taken place on the space taken up by the little-used former bay platform here. Moving a little to the east, Arpley Junction is reached, allowing access to the West Coast Main Line but also to an array of sidings and former access to the transporter bridge (see below). Returning to the main route, there is little left to see at what was once Arpley station, though a headshunt still runs through the site, over the River Mersey and into Latchford, where a footpath crosses just behind the buffer stops that mark the limit of operations. At this point it may be noted that there are now two levels of trackbed, one at ground level and one starting to climb on an embankment; these mark the original route and the later, post-1893 route, built with embankments to facilitate a high crossing of the Manchester Ship Canal at Latchford Viaduct. The old route north of the Ship Canal remained in use until the 1960s, retained through the original Latchford station to serve sidings on the northern bank of the ship canal; it was, however, singled through the station site. The signal box at Latchford (old) station was also demolished. The main station building survived well into the 1960s and the down platform building until the 1980s. Little is left to see now, though the site of a bridge at Wash Lane, close to Warrington Town Football Club's ground, can still be made out. On the south side of the Ship Canal the old alignment closed once the new one was ready, but a remarkable survivor is a crossing keeper's cottage on Bradshaw Lane; the old building standing out in a road otherwise occupied by modern housing.

Let us return to the new alignment, climbing steadily to gain the 75ft height it needed for a viaduct high enough for full-sized commercial shipping to pass below.

Warrington to Skelton Junction line, the decking of Latchford Viaduct.
Author's collection

For reasons unknown, the track was never removed here and in addition it was (and possibly still is) unofficially used by locals as a footpath, passing Latchford (new) station, though no traces remain of the wooden station building and platforms here. The embankment dominates the scene on the north side of the canal, crossing Knutsford Road on a high bridge and continuing behind the new residential development at Clearwater Quays. This huge embankment was scheduled for removal around 2016; indeed, the Railway Ramblers Club organised a walk to view it 'possibly for the last time' in September 2015, but in late 2021 it remains, though for how much longer is a matter for speculation. Let us now turn to Latchford Viaduct, now securely fenced off, the poor condition of which was cited as one reason for the line's complete closure in 1985. Having attempted to walk across the viaduct in the late 1990s and been put off by the alarmingly rusted away condition of the girders, I can only concur with this decision. The survival of the viaduct to this day is due more to the fact that the Ship Canal Company will not sanction the nine-day total closure of the canal that apparently would be needed to allow its demolition and removal.

A little further east, at Bradshaw Lane, the official path starts and the site of the eastern junction between old and new routes quickly appears. Soon the site of Thelwall station is reached; here the small station building is a remarkable survivor, quite derelict in the 1990s but in 2006 it was restored and now forms part of a small industrial premises. Continuing on, the second Thelwall Viaduct (opened in the early 1990s) of the M6 requires a slight diversion but the trackbed is soon regained, passing through Lymm station, where all that remains is the station house. At Heatley & Warburton the station building survives, as does the degraded remains of the eastbound platform. It is worth noting that, for an official path, the condition of the trail east of here is quite poor and almost impassable after significant rain; however, in December 2021, it was announced that funding had been obtained to carry out some much-needed improvements.

Warrington to Skelton Junction line, Heatley & Warburton station building.
Phillip Earnshaw

With quite possibly very muddy boots, the explorer of this line can continue east, past Dunham Massey, where a fine station building is now a private residence, until the trail leaves the trackbed at the outskirts of Broadheath. At Broadheath, isolated sections of trackbed remain but most is lost under roads or light industry. The station is long gone but the Railway Inn still overlooks the spot. A long, low viaduct, with the arches in commercial use, is the final point of interest before reaching the former bridge over the Bridgewater Canal, though by taking a train from Navigation Road station towards Stockport a bridge over the Sale line and Skelton Junction itself may also be viewed.

The Manchester Ship Canal Railway

The Manchester Ship Canal opened on 1 January 1894, but arguably the railway preceded it, as the line that ran alongside it can be considered to have effectively followed on from the canal constructors' railway. Strictly speaking, the system should be termed 'Ship Canal Railways' as no continuous route along the canal ever existed. From the Manchester Docks, where there were links to the public railways at Weaste and also across the canal to Trafford Park (see Chapter 10), a line ran west past Barton and Irlam as far as Latchford, where a connecting line allowed

The Manchester Ship Canal Railway passed under the West Coast Mainline at Acton Grange Viaduct, south of Warrington, using a separate small arch. *Author*

access to the L&NWR in Warrington. There was then a short gap before a line heading west from Acton Bridge Junction followed the canal north of Moore out to Wigg Island on the outskirts of Runcorn, with a siding heading east from Acton Grange to the former Laporte chemical works, just to the west of Warrington's erstwhile docks. For details of the Ellesmere Port section of the MSC railway system, see Chapter 3.

The scale of the Ship Canal Railway should not be underestimated. At its peak after 1948 it was the largest private railway in Britain, with over 230 miles of track, seventy-five locomotives and at one time almost 800 members of staff. Its busiest time was during the Second World War and the decade that followed, some years carrying over 8 million tons of traffic before rationalisation commenced in the 1960s.

There is plenty left to see, though this description starts at the Runcorn end. Here the railway explorer must first make their way to Wigg Island; this location is in effect a peninsula, lying between the Ship Canal and the Mersey and only connected by a swing bridge in Runcorn or a narrow spit of land west of Moore. It was the site of an acid works and then later, in the Second World War, a top-secret location for the production and storage of mustard gas. Today Wigg Island is a nature reserve, though some parts remain to this day out of bounds to visitors. From here onwards it is possible to walk along or alongside virtually the whole length of the Ship Canal Railway to Stockton Heath. The main remaining features are the rail-over-road bridge at Moore; this concrete overbridge was built in 1928 to replace an earlier wooden structure, and Acton Grange Viaduct, where the West Coast Main Line crosses both the Ship Canal and the adjacent MSC railway, which passed through a separate arch. Traffic to Wigg Island from Acton Grange ceased in 1968 but the Laporte's siding lasted until 1970; this route is still accessible as a narrow, often muddy, footpath. Warrington Docks had a somewhat peculiar history; despite being built with high hopes, it never developed into an industrial facility due to the Ship Canal Company and Warrington Council failing to agree financial terms. For many years a forgotten corner of Warrington, the dock area is now surrounded by modern flats.

The Latchford to Barton section has become less accessible in recent years. A good place to start is Knutsford Road, where the road swing bridge had to be moved to allow locomotives' passage as well as the ships on the canal. New housing development has obliterated any railway remnants here but shortly after passing under Latchford Viaduct (see above) a rough path can be accessed, its last railway use having been to serve the Alcan factory at Westy. Continuing east, the line passes the jetty for the Thelwall Ferry (do check times of operation if you wish to use it) with access ended by a large fence at Thelwall Eye. Twenty or so years ago, the Ship Canal Railway could be followed right through to Bollin Point, passing under the M6 Thelwall Viaduct and across the landslips along the way that were a key reason for the line's closure, but in the summer of 2021 this path was completely inaccessible.

Latchford Viaduct with the former Manchester Ship Canal Railway route in the foreground, 2015. *Phillip Earnshaw*

Manchester Ship Canal Railway bridge at Boysnope Wharf, north-east of Irlam, 2009. *Phillip Earnshaw*

Access to Bollin Point, also known as Rixton Junction, can still be gained from the east. Rixton Junction is where the ship canal took over the route of the River Mersey as far as Irlam and a delightful little bridge remains in situ over the river just north of here. Though in places somewhat overgrown, a path exists under the Warburton Bridge as far as Cadishead, where a new bypass route takes the course of the line. Crossing the new road, one can still see the Lancashire Tar Distillers works, with some sidings still intact, one of the line's last customers, whose rail access was via a link to Glazebrook (see below). Passing through Irlam, the line, hidden behind industrial premises, is inaccessible but after Irlam locks the track can be regained, a footpath squeezed into a narrow gap between the canal and the A57 road. At Boysnope Park, the railway crossed an inlet of the former course of the River Irwell on a short viaduct; there was also formerly a connection with a tramroad system that used to take nightsoil onto Barton Moss for use as fertiliser. Remains at Boysnope include a large shed, level crossing gates and a bridge carrying the Barton Moss line under the A57. This bridge was latterly used by Boysnope Park Golf Club for access between its clubhouse and the course but the golf club itself closed recently, so prospects for this area are now rather uncertain.

The Ship Canal Railway continues on, passing Barton Locks, the new rugby stadium and under the M60 motorway at Barton Bridge. The formation used to pass under the Barton swing aqueduct (which takes the Bridgewater Canal over the Ship Canal, just a few inches of the level of the water. The abutments of the Bridgewater Canal's original aqueduct, just to the east of the current structure, are also well worth seeing at this location. From here into the docks the line is mostly lost beneath new roads or redevelopment, though the Salford Trail does briefly run along the course of the old line. Let us instead return to Glazebrook and commence further explorations from there.

Manchester Ship Canal centenary plaque from 1994. *Author*

Cadishead Viaduct, seen in 2003 with access blocked by containers, a situation that remains today. *Gordon Suggitt*

Glazebrook–Skelton Junction

The Cheshire Lines Committee's route from Glazebrook to Skelton Junction was primarily an industrial line, with close links to the Manchester Ship Canal though arguably providing competition to the Ship Canal Railway as well as links to it. Passenger trains were of secondary importance; although there were three stations en route, these did not link directly to Warrington, Altrincham or Manchester, the places to which most people wanted to go. As with the 'Lymm Line' and also at Irlam, a couple of miles to the north, the railway was obliged to cross the Manchester Ship Canal on a 75ft-high viaduct. As a result, there are again two quite separate alignments for much of the route, the original low-level route, which continued in use after the new line was constructed, serving wharves and industries on either side of the canal and indeed on the north side, outliving the 'new' route across the viaduct.

The line had opened in 1873 but the 1893 diversion required the resiting of Partington and Cadishead stations. The high-level route, including the 'new' Partington station, as well as West Timperley station, closed to passengers in November 1964 but remained open across the Ship Canal as a through route for freight until August 1982.

With Cadishead Viaduct securely blocked off by a series of containers and no nearby alternative crossing point, any exploration must be done in two parts, either side of the Ship Canal. On the Cadishead side, both upper and lower alignments are walkable in part, as what nowadays seem to be semi-official paths. Access to the lower alignment can be made off Martens Road, just off Cadishead Way, which goes under a quite new, fully engineered bridge for the railway; built over ten years ago but one that has never carried a train. Just east of the two bridges that carried each alignment over Liverpool Road, access to the upper level from the lower one is possible. Close by can be found the degraded remains of Cadishead (second) station, with a few concrete platform supports visible, particularly on the westbound side. The upper alignment can be walked north-west for some distance, but after passing under a long and impressive footbridge (over both alignments) the path fades away and there is no access to the bridleway east of the Glaze Brook here nor to Glazebrook station.

Moving to the south-east side, at Partington it is possible to head north-west but only on the original, low-level route, the new alignment being on a high embankment and fenced off at the bridge over the A6144. On the lower route tracks used to fan off towards wharves that still jut out over the water to this day; these remained rail-served until 1966. Also, on the south-west side of the Ship Canal is the remains of a stone viaduct that once carried the original, pre-1893, alignment over the former course of the River Mersey, somewhat surprisingly having outlasted the once-adjacent metal bridge on the new alignment.

Returning from the Ship Canal and this time heading south-east from Partington, the high-level route is the better option, and you will soon reach the site of Partington station, where the westbound platform remains as does

Glazebrook to Skelton Junction line, remains of platform at Cadishead (second) station, 2021. *Author*

the tile-lined remains of an underpass that allowed access to the Manchester-bound platform. Continuing further, the trackbed is initially ballast covered but soon deteriorates and the site of Partington Junction, where the high-level and original routes joined, is now flooded and inaccessible. At Partington Junction a further route diverged north, leading to the extensive Shell Oil Works (between 1953 and 1991 also serving Partington power station), which kept the line from here to Skelton Junction in operation until *circa* 1997–98. On a Railway Ramblers event in 2003 this formation was still in situ but now the track has been lifted, or in places just dismantled and left where it is.

Just south-east of Partington Junction lies the site of exchange sidings with the narrow gauge Carrington Estate System, a 2ft 6in-gauge route that operated from 1887 to 1937 to help dispose of Manchester's nightsoil and allied waste. Some of these lines can be followed across the estate, particularly on what are now known as Dunham Road, North Road and Ashton Road, though only in a few places is there any feel of a former railway. The final section runs east towards West Timperley station, nowadays a narrow but passable path, prone to obstruction by fallen trees. West Timperley had concrete platforms, much of which survive but are somewhat covered in undergrowth now. It is possible to continue a little further on as far as the Bridgewater Canal, where the line is fenced off but the rails remain, and a colour-light signal still controls theoretical access onto the busy line at Skelton Junction.

Further Explorations Around Warrington

A number of other shorter sites or routes in and around Warrington are well worth time taken to explore them, the most notable being the Warrington or Crosfields Transporter Bridge. Built in 1915 to cross the River Mersey and used until around 1964, it was the only transporter bridge ever built to carry rail traffic anywhere in the world and as such it now has protected status. There is also now a 'Friends' group dedicated to the bridge, though it is hard to imagine money being found to restore it. Access to the bridge is possible on the east side via footpaths, though these take a somewhat convoluted route. The route passes a karting centre and continues on into a small, wooded area; there was a quite famous story a few years back about a transporter bridge enthusiast who travelled all the way from Japan to Warrington to see the bridge and couldn't find it, but once you reach the river you head north for about 200m and the bridge is in clear view. Unfortunately, the opposite side of the bridge, where the cradle permanently lies, remains inside a secure and private industrial area. Perhaps in the future it might be possible to arrange some organised visits to the 'far' side to view more closely what remains.

Also worthy of note in Warrington is the 'straight line' built by the Cheshire Lines Committee in 1883 as an avoiding route for Warrington Central; running, as it says, in a dead straight line from Padgate Junction in the east to Sankey Junction in the west. The best remains are at the east end, with formation visible as you head west from Padgate and south of Orford, where a pleasant path, albeit with bridges removed, can be found on an embankment in a residential area. East of Sankey Junction the line has not fared as well, the only point of interest being one surviving abutment from the former bridge over the West Coast Main Line.

Close by is the former route, originally a branch off the Liverpool & Manchester Railway, now a road, passing just to the west of Warrington RLFC's Halliwell Jones Stadium. The former Dallam Shed (8B) may still be seen here, long since turned over to non-railway commercial use. At the bottom of this road, on Tanners Lane, lies the Three Pigeons pub, of great railway history significance as effectively Warrington's first station. Though not of railway origin or appearance, it provided waiting and ticket booking facilities to early passengers. Close by is Warrington Central station, of course still open and busy, but with passengers all using the new facilities. Hidden just behind the ticket office is an absolute gem of a station building, with its own, quite separate entrance road. Another little-known railway in Warrington was the short branch to serve what became Winwick Hospital, one of three large psychiatric hospitals in Lancashire (as was) to have their own railway. Primarily to supply coal, the Winwick line was more an extended siding, accessed via further sidings north of Winwick Quay rather than directly through from the main line. Access to the former trackbed can be gained from the back of the hospital, at Hollins Park, where a footpath exists on a slight curved embankment through what is now a residential area. One final route to mention was the short branch to the RAF Burtonwood base, in operation from around 1940 to 1970. This line left the CLC route slightly to the west of Sankey Junction where the line through Central station and the 'straight line' rejoined. It was pretty much walkable throughout until the mid-1990s but today the site is almost totally covered by modern housing.

Above: Sidings leading up to Warrington's Transporter Bridge, 2004. *Phillip Earnshaw*

Left: The Warrington (or Crosfields) Transporter Bridge, seen in 2017. *Author*

6
Liverpool

The Liverpool Overhead Railway

It is not unfair to suggest that this early 'commuter' railway attracted a slightly less elite clientele than many others fitting the description. By the 1880s, Liverpool's dock network was virtually complete, but so too was the congestion along the Dock Road, as carriages, omnibuses, lorries, carts and drays all plied the route. Numerous railway crossings that connected goods stations and dockside lines only added to the confusion. With increasing trade, it became clear that passenger traffic had to be isolated from the cargo routes in the interest of efficiency. Among the many problems encountered was the decision around suitable motive power. Steam was considered too dangerous to the many flammable cargoes within range of locomotive sparks, so as early as 1893, an electric commuter railway was operating on Merseyside, the Liverpool Overhead Railway, always known locally as 'Dockers Umbrella'. Running originally from Alexandra to Herculaneum, the railway was extended by 1896 to run between Dingle and Seaforth, with a connection at the latter location to the L&YR added in July 1905. Having run mostly without incident for almost fifty years, extensive bomb damage was inflicted during the Blitz, but it was quickly repaired to maintain the smooth running of the docks. Modernisation of some of the nineteen three-car sets had begun as the war drew to a close and eight new units were in operation by 1955. But, in the same year, the curved deck plates that supported the track were reported as needing replacement at an approximate cost of £2 million. This was beyond the financial resources of the company, who looked to the City Council and the Mersey Docks and Harbour Board for assistance. No adequate solution could be found, and despite vigorous public protests, the railway closed in December 1956. Rescue attempts continued until September 1957, when the dismantlers moved in, and virtually nothing remains now except at Dingle station, the line's eastern terminus.

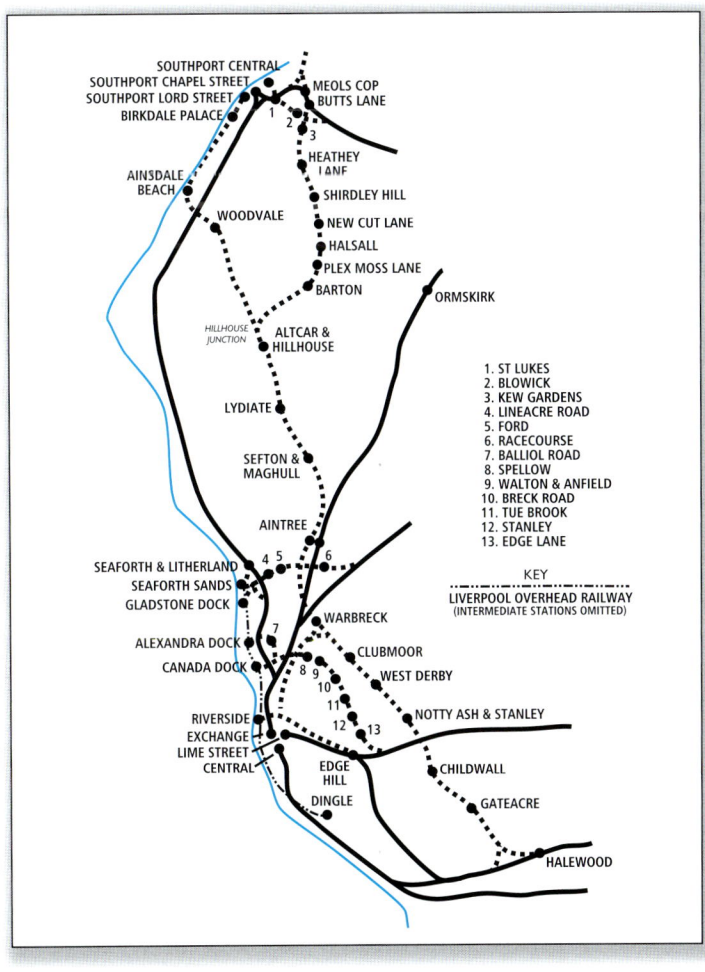

Map showing lines in the Liverpool and Southport area.

Above: Entrance to the Liverpool Overhead Railway's southern tunnel, 2003. *Gordon Suggitt*

Left: A 1950s view of James Street station on the Liverpool Overhead Railway. *Gordon Suggitt collection*

This station was accessed via a tunnel of some length, bored out of the cliff face at Herculaneum Dock to Park Road. The surface entrance is still standing, and the former platform and track area survive; they lie within the premises of an engineering firm. However, in July 2012, part of the tunnel near Dingle railway station collapsed. A number of homes above this section of the tunnel were evacuated but given the situation, the tunnel was repaired, and residents allowed back into their homes well over a year later, in February 2014.

Bootle's Midland Goods Branch and Aintree to Fazakerley

The Midland Railway's branch into Liverpool's dockland was a late arrival on a scene largely dominated by the L&YR and the L&NWR. Opening in 1885, it predominately served Langton Dock and Alexandra Dock on the north side of Bootle, closing in January 1968. A good place to start explorations is Bank Hall station, where there was formerly a second island platform for northbound traffic on the west side of the one in use today. It is then possible to walk north and view what is left of Bootle Balliol Road station, closed in May 1948. This station was situated in a deep cutting; only the degraded partial remains of a cutting survive, although the road-level station building was only finally demolished in the early 2000s.

Reaching the Midland goods branch out of Bootle, then passing under Rimrose Road, the line is hardly discernible, but its route inland becomes clearer. A deep cutting has been largely filled in, with a thoroughfare under Bootle New Strand station before reaching two single-bore tunnels just past Marsh Lane. Walls above the portals and separating the cutting from adjacent roads mark the formation. A line from Linacre Gas Works (reached by train until April 1968) converges slightly east of this point, having descended sharply from its source. Although largely intact, there is no official access to the formation between this point and where it joins the Liverpool loop line at Fazakerley North Junction.

The former Lancashire and Yorkshire line from Aintree to Fazakerley is worthy of a visit despite being of less than 2 miles long. Close by was Aintree MPD, which closed in 1967 but was only demolished in 1996. Here also was Aintree Racecourse station, last used on Grand National day in March 1961. This station was unusual in having running rails along its platform; being on an embankment, there was no room for normal platforms, so the up line was raised and filled with ashes to rail level. All trains that stopped had to use the down line but as it was only used on one day (Grand National day) per year it was not too inconvenient. Recordings of the race from the early 1960s show rows of special trains stored at Fazakerley sidings east of the station and south of the racecourse waiting to take racegoers home, but similar views from later years show empty sidings and vacated formation. East of this point the line forms an increasingly narrow path through modern housing, with occasional glimpses of the racecourse just to the north. The vast former site of Fazakerley sidings is, however, largely untouched but difficult to appreciate, these days being covered with trees and undergrowth. The last point of interest is the thrice-widened arch carrying the Kirkby Line and Aintree route over the River Alt close to Fazakerley Junction.

The Liverpool Loop Line (CLC Route)

The Liverpool loop line was another route constructed with the primary aim of reaching and profiting from traffic coming into or out of Liverpool's busy docks. During the nineteenth century, as ships increased in size, broader and deeper docks were built further and further north of the city centre where the River Mersey was more accessible. In particular, the CLC reached Huskisson Dock, close to the current Sandhills station. As with many busy freight routes, passenger services were of secondary importance but did at first have value in bringing dock workers into and out of their place of work. The line opened in December 1879 with an extension to Huskisson (including a single platform for passenger trains), the following year. However, passenger services on the 'extension' did not prove successful, being cut back from Huskisson in 1885 and from Walton-on-the-Hill in January 1918. The route did gain some more importance with the opening of the Midland Railway's Docks lines in 1882 and 1885 (see below) and a link to the direct route from Aintree to Southport (see below) that opened in 1884. The CLC had great belief in this route, buying sufficient land for four tracks although only two were ever laid, but evidence of the extra space and some preparation work may still be seen, as explained below.

A walk along the loop line starting at the south end is best started at Halewood station, which was opened in May 1988 on the site of Halewood East Junction. The original Halewood station (May 1874–September 1951) was a quarter of a mile further east but is now demolished. Trains for both Liverpool and Aintree could stop at the original station. Starting by following the east–north curve, within Halewood triangle was a raft of sidings and just before the north junction is reached it is possible to follow one such siding south to the main line, from where Hunts Cross East Junction and Hunts Cross station can be viewed from a footbridge.

From here the west–north curve is accessed, now part of the Trans Pennine Trail, with embankments and cuttings apparent. Leaving behind Halewood North Junction, walkers continue north on a long embankment, with wide views east to Tarbock and Cronton. Gateacre station (opened December 1879, closed April 1972) was, after closure of the through route to passengers in 1960, the terminus of a short stub from Hunts Cross and was situated just north of Gateacre Brow, but little trace of it remains.

Continuing onwards, Childwall station is passed, again with little trace. Next up was the Liverpool & Manchester Railway passing overhead at Broad Green. The L&M tracks were lifted at the south side when quadruple track was reduced to double track at nearby Broad Green station, but still had duplicated arches over the loop line. Thomas Lane Tunnel was soon reached, a twin-bore structure with one bore open for the trail and the other not apparently blocked but awkward to access. At Knotty Ash & Stanley station (December 1879–November 1960), it is still possible to pass through a gap in a former wall and walk down the ramp to the one remaining, grassed over platform.

Liverpool Overhead Railway. A signal survived inside Dingle Tunnel in 2009. *Phillip Earnshaw*

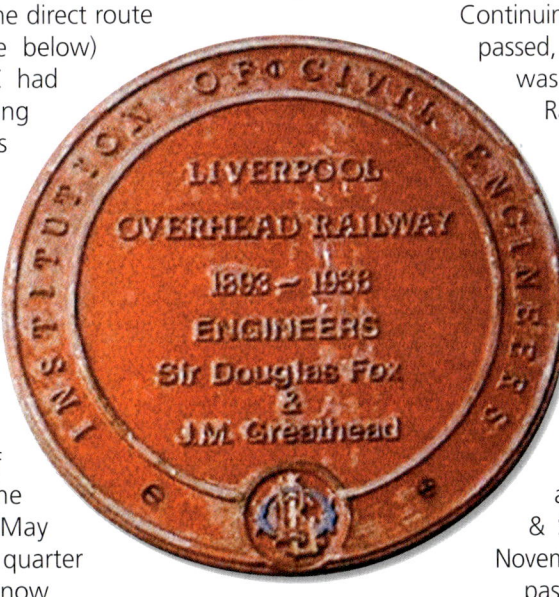

Liverpool Overhead Railway plaque. *Gordon Suggitt*

Liverpool Overhead Railway at Herculaneum, 1956. *Gordon Suggitt collection*

Former Liverpool loop line, bridge over the East Lancashire Road, 2003. *Gordon Suggitt*

Passing Alder Hey Hospital, a long, deep sandstone cutting is reached, cut vertically and smooth, with fascinating geology, formed by desert sands blown by dry winds millions of years ago. Here can also be seen the geometry of the skew arches on the road bridges and the spiral brickwork. Every bridge has twin arches; also clearly visible is the sandstone rock cut out for the duplicated arch that was never used as the cutting was never widened. The Cheshire Lines Committee (CLC) must have had grandiose visions and provided bridges for future widening of the route with anticipated freight traffic from the North Mersey at Huskisson and Langton Docks. All too soon this lovely stretch of line reaches West Derby station (again December 1879–November 1960), where the platforms, ramps and station buildings are all intact. Heading on to Clubmoor station (April 1927–November 1960), the degraded remains of the platforms can just about be made out. Also of interest here are two original lattice girder bridges, best viewed from below. After Fazakerley North and South Junctions an enjoyable break from the railway can be made by heading a short distance west to view the former Hartley's jam factory and its associated 'purpose-built' village. Continuing along the CLC route, the Trans Pennine Trail leaves the former line at the former site of Aintree MPD (27B).

Liverpool loop line, Knotty Ash & Stanley station seen in March 1983. *Maurice Blencowe*

Turning to the former Huskisson branch, very little of this line is directly accessible but there are three tunnels, Walton Hill, Breeze Hill, and Hawthorne Road. These can be viewed with some difficulty from adjacent roads; a Railway Ramblers Club visit to the area some years ago is remembered fondly as, without any prompting, at two quite separate locations, different local people brought out stepladders for us to peer over bridge walls and get a better view of the cuttings and tunnels. A unique feature of these tunnels was the preparation for quadrupling of the track, which never occurred. Parallel tunnels were built, though they have no portals (except at Kirkdale) and the only access is through the recesses of the original structures. As a result, these 'blind' tunnels are apparently unstained and appear brand new. Reaching Kirkdale station, the south portal of Hawthorne Road Tunnel may be viewed, with its blind tunnel alongside, as can the deep level L&NWR Bootle branch to Seaforth Docks. The Huskisson branch can be unofficially followed south of here for a while, though there are no signs left of the bridge that took the line under the Leeds & Liverpool Canal. Finally, a large industrial area is reached, the former site of Huskisson goods station and the small and long-closed passenger station.

Liverpool loop line; West Derby station building, 2003. *Gordon Suggitt*

Liverpool-bound train crossing the former CLC route near Aintree, 2003. *Gordon Suggitt*

Liverpool's Stations

Liverpool Exchange station, opened in 1850 on a viaduct and almost completely rebuilt in the 1880s with the station moved to ground level, was for many years a serious rival to Lime Street as the city's premier station. Owned by the L&YR, the station had ten platforms situated behind a stunning frontage. This was a four-storey structure, very much in keeping with the stature of the city's impressive older buildings, consisting of a station frontage combined with the impressive Exchange Hotel. Facing north, Exchange was served by suburban trains from Southport together with longer-distance routes via Ormskirk to Preston, Blackpool and Scotland, and services to Manchester via Kirkby and Wigan. The hotel, an early user of electricity, was considered a pioneer in many ways, not least with its hairdressing salon, famously equipped with an overhead driving belt that powered mechanical hairbrushes! Closing in July 1971, the hotel was converted to offices and remains in that form to this day. The station hung on until April 1977, but was effectively replaced by the below-ground station at Moorfields just to the south. The platform area is still an open space, with pretty much all remnants swept away, and used only as a car park, but the glorious station frontage remains, with its original signage, an impressive and appropriate memorial.

Liverpool Central was perhaps the poor relation of the city's termini but was still impressive in its day. With a single arch trainshed, a rather smaller version of the survivor at Manchester Central, it offered services, mostly by CLC and Midland Railway routes, via Manchester to Yorkshire, the East Midlands and, for a time, London St Pancras. Local services ran to Southport (via Aintree), Stockport and Manchester Central, though after 1966 until closure in April 1972 the only trains left were local services to Gateacre. A separate low-level station acted as a terminus for trains from Birkenhead and the Wirral. The station was demolished, though the name 'Central' continues in use for the Merseyrail station built below ground. The platform area remains an open space, with some boundary walls intact, but although the Bold Street entrance remains in place for access to the modern station, no other buildings survive.

The Liverpool & Manchester Railway's original station was at Crown Street, though locomotives never reached the station, trains instead being hauled up from Edge Hill by cables and lowered back by gravity. Unlike its contemporary in Manchester, nothing remains of the station; the site now being a grassy public space with the only railway feature being an air shaft for Wapping Tunnel. Just to the east of Crown Street can be found Edge Hill station, opened in 1836 when the first, still cable-hauled, lines reached Lime Street, Crown Street's replacement. The steep cutting between here and Lime Street was originally one double-track tunnel, with a large fan and chimney in use to clear the smoke when steam haulage commenced in 1870. Later on, part was opened out and widened, giving space for four tracks but retaining seven short tunnels. The engine house at Edge Hill is now used by 'Metal Culture', an arts organisation, so hopefully its future is assured. Only just to the north is the east portal of Victoria Tunnel, still in use for a short distance as a headshunt. It is possible to try and follow the tunnel from above using its air shafts, though at least two seem to be no longer visible. The western portal of Waterloo Tunnel can be seen from a car park just off Pall Mall, after which the line reached Waterloo goods station, an impressive site in its day particularly with the L&Y lines above fanning out into Great Howard Street goods station. From Waterloo goods a line formerly ran along the east bank of the Mersey to Riverside station, opened in 1895 for use by boat trains. The dock bridges were insufficient for main-line locomotives until strengthened in 1950, but the line was gone by 1971, with the station site now built over by modern office accommodation. Today the remains of bridges over dock inlets and a short stretch of rails and pointwork encased in concrete and cobbles may still be viewed.

Huyton–Cronton Colliery

Cronton Colliery was one of the very last pits to close in the north-west of England and as such its railway lasted longer than most and is well worth a visit. Also known as the Willis branch after the owner of the land over which it ran, the line had a remarkably long life for a short goods branch. Opening soon after the Liverpool & Manchester Railway (L&M), around 1832, it initially served Halsnead Colliery, south of Whiston, and an adjacent landsale yard. In 1916, Cronton Colliery, owned by the Hulton Company of Chequerbent, was opened with the Willis branch extended south-east. Workmen's trains operated between 1916 and 1926 between the colliery and a point just south of Hall Lane Crossing, close to its junction with the L&M. Coal production ceased on 3 March 1984 and salvage traffic had ceased to use the line by the end of that year; the track was reported lifted by June 1991. Exploration is best started at Hall Lane Crossing, until around 1970 apparently operated by a man with a flag rather than with signalling and gates. To the south-east of Hall Lane, the trackbed occupied a very narrow and now overgrown piece of formation between factories and a residential street but becomes accessible on reaching Stadt Moers Park. This is also the site of the junction with the Seel branch, discussed later. Though still a little overgrown in places at first, the line can be followed on the south edge of the park, under a bridge carrying the M57 motorway, reaching as far as the south-east entrance to the park. This was the end of the line until 1896; there is an excellent information board here, giving relevant history and a selection of photographs.

The entrance to Liverpool Exchange station, 2003. *Gordon Suggitt*

Liverpool Exchange station Platform 5 in 1963 with No 45698 *Mars* ready to depart with a Windermere train. *Gordon Suggitt collection*

Trackbed of former Cronton Colliery Railway passing through Stadt Moers Park. *Author*

The 'extension' to Cronton Colliery takes a more southerly route, first passing through a rather wet but just about passable cutting, then a delightful, wooded section with a clear path on an embankment right up to the fenced off bridge over the M62 motorway, just to the east of junction 6. This bridge poses something of a conundrum: the northernmost part was a non-railway replacement built when an additional eastbound slip road was provided for the motorway but the remainder of the bridge, apparently the original, appears to be noticeably higher than the trackbed either side of it. The colliery site itself is rather overgrown, with the trackbed petering out before the pit area and no original buildings apparently survive.

Returning to the Seel branch; this line was believed to be operational by around 1832–33, shortly after the opening of the Willis branch. It first served Huyton Hey Colliery but was subsequently extended further east to serve Whiston Colliery and Tushingham's Brick Works on the outskirts of Whiston. Last used around 1930, it was reported to be padlocked out of use by 1932 and access pointwork had been replaced by plain track by 1936. The brickworks continued in operation, latterly served only by road transport, until 1943. Although the approximate course of this line can be followed and there are remains of buildings at the brickworks, much of this route is now unrecognisable, lying within the landscaped Stadt Moers Park.

Two Routes to Southport

Despite, or perhaps because of, the success of what became the L&Y route from Southport to Liverpool – still busy today and electrified as early as 1904 – the Southport & Cheshire Lines Extension Railway (S&CLER) opened their alternative route via Aintree in September 1884. Successful for a time with excursion traffic to Southport from Manchester, the route served virtually no centres of population at all between Maghull and Southport (some writers have wondered whether this was, in fact, deliberate) and was therefore an early candidate for closure. This took place in January 1952, though some goods traffic reached Gorehouse sidings, north of Sefton, until 1958.

Today there is virtually nothing to see south of Maghull, with the road largely built over apart from short stretches of flooded cutting. North of Maghull, 5½ miles of trackbed have been reclaimed and converted into a path, now forming the final part of the Trans Pennine Trail. Unfortunately, nothing survives of any of the intermediate stations, even though at places such as Lydiate and even Mossbridge (the one station not to reopen after temporary wartime closure of the line in 1917) quite substantial buildings were provided. Approaching Birkdale, the line crossed the dunes and is now converted into a road; though do note that this road is quite narrow in places and is not ideal for walkers and cyclists.

Soon the site of Birkdale Palace station is reached, at one time serving a large hotel of that name. It once had a long, wide, island platform and a covered walkway to the nearby road. Since closure the whole site has been demolished and now lies next to the road, which occupies the trackbed as it heads west from Birkdale. The hotel fared little better, closing in 1967 and suffering demolition just two years later. Heading east into Southport, the formation can be seen passing through a caravan park and picked up for a short distance as it curved round to the line's terminus at Southport Lord Street. Very much the highlight of a day exploring this line, Lord Street was an impressive station in its day; four platforms behind a red brick Italianate-style structure with an impressive clock tower. Fortunately, the frontage survives, the station having suffered rather mixed fortunes over the years since its 1952 closure. For some years the platform area served as the town's bus station, but in recent years a supermarket has taken over the inside of the site, while the main building is now a Travelodge. The impressive clock tower, with its 'S&CLER' stone panels, also survives and can still be admired to this day.

Curving north at Hillhouse Junction, north of Altcar & Hillhouse station on the S&CLER route, was an arguably even less successful line. The Liverpool, Southport & Preston Railway built a line that reached Southport via Meols Cop station. Opening in September 1887, the line was initially operated by the West Lancashire Railway (WLR) then the L&YR after the latter had taken over the former. The WLR at one time operated semi-fast services from Preston to Liverpool, using this route to avoid Southport, but other traffic was very meagre indeed. Local services from Altcar & Hillhouse ended in November 1926 and from then until closure, passenger services were effectively run as a branch line with trains terminating at Barton (renamed Downholland after June 1924) until September 1938 when the 'Altcar Bob', as the line was informally known, finally stopped running. Freight hung on until the early 1950s while the last three quarters of a mile south of Meols Cop became in January 1911 part of the L&YR route from that station towards Burscough, a role it still performs today. Very little remains to be seen, the line being now quite fragmented and in places built over, or entirely returned to nature, although a path remains from Hillside Junction towards Downholland. Remnants are scanty other than a few bridges, but perhaps worthy of note is the surviving brickwork of a goods platform at Downholland. Halsall station building also survives, much altered and extended, and these days surrounded by modern bungalows.

Right: Southport Lord Street station, 2002. *Gordon Suggitt*

Below: Site of Sherdley Hill station, near Downholland, 2002. *Gordon Suggitt*

7
Wigan and St Helens

The Great Central Railway to Wigan and St Helens

Originally promoted by the Wigan Junction Railway (WJR) and later the MS&LR, the two branches in question later became somewhat remote outposts of the Great Central Railway. Coal traffic was the clear target with, as was so often the case, passenger services being of secondary importance.

Very much a latecomer to the scene, the route opened to a temporary station at Darlington Street to all traffic in 1884 and was extended to Wigan Central in 1892. It retained a passenger service until November 1964, though Wigan Central remained accessible by way of Bickershaw Junction until November 1967 for goods traffic. The route since closure is much changed but can still be followed, though in places with a good deal of imagination required. In modern Wigan you would not know that a third station ever existed. The station's approximate site is under a modern shopping complex, which can be figured out with the archive ordnance survey map that conveniently adorns a wall as you exit it. It is not only the station that has gone, however, as much of the route through Scholes to Darlington Street has also vanished, although a short piece of embankment can be made out beyond some high-rise flats. The first remnant of interest is the overbridge that carries the still open L&YR line across our formation in Ince. At the site of Lower Ince station, all has been totally lost as the cutting where it used to stand has been filled in and the open ground beyond is also under threat to a proposed industrial development scheme. Whilst much of the railway has gone in this area it eventually emerges as a long watercourse that has been deliberately created; with the cutting dammed off at both ends, the water has nowhere to go. The bridge of a mineral railway first crosses it on a skew; this used to connect with a route to the former Ince Waggon and Iron Works. The embanked remains of the Pemberton loop (see below) come next, followed by a bridge carrying the Springs Branch as both lines curve round the east side of Wigan. It is proposed to infill the Wigan Junction Railway with the Pemberton loop at this location, effectively one railway formation wiping out another.

Beyond the 'watercourse' the railway is lost to landscaping on Amberswood Common, the site of the former Strangeways Hall Colliery. Today, not only the colliery has gone but everything else that went with it including a raft of mineral lines, the Whelley loop, our route and the relevant connecting lines. A large lake has been developed out of the lagoons that existed and it is impossible to appreciate what things used to look like. Archive film in this area shows a scene so different that you would be hard pressed to know you were looking at the same location.

Beyond the next main road stood Hindley South station (at one time Strangeways & Hindley, then Platt Bridge), which has been completely eradicated, but south of here the formation finally becomes more distinct. It is then possible to follow the WJR, beyond Strangeways East Junction, to the bridge carrying the L&NWR route from Springs Branch Junction to Eccles Junction via Tyldesley, through a slowly deepening cutting. The connecting lines to Bickershaw Junction can also be accessed. The up connection is easy to view, whereas these days the down connection requires a degree of pushing through vegetation to get to the bridge under the aforementioned L&NWR, before the climb beyond that is far easier to negotiate. However, all this could disappear, dependent on the route taken by a proposed South Hindley Link Road, should this ever come to fruition.

To continue further it is necessary to walk round the perimeter of Hindley Prison to the site of Bickershaw & Abram station. As with the railway around here, the station has long since gone and little remains of the formation

Map showing lines in the Wigan and St Helens area.

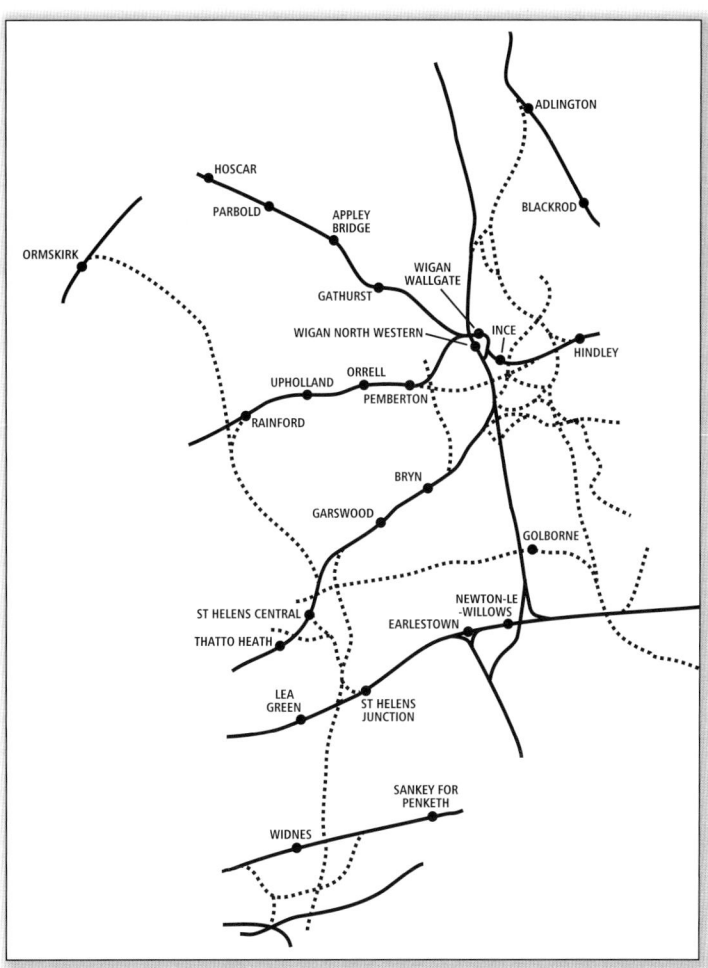

either, as it headed further south. The stretch of formation between Strangeways East Junction and Lowton Junction closed to all traffic in January 1965, although vans were apparently still stored on this stretch for a further two months at the Lowton end. A little further on, the Wigan Junction Colliery System is crossed, and north of this point stood Brookside Colliery. It was here on 13 April 1945 that Ludovic Berry and his charge, 0-6-0ST *Dorothy*, complete with thirteen wagons, plunged into a collapsing mine shaft that opened up beneath the train. The accident, attributed to underground water courses, took place at the New Zealand Shaft (Brookside No. 7 Colliery), which had ceased to be used in 1919, but had been used for ventilation until 1931, after which time it was infilled. A little further south can be found the site of Maypole Colliery, which closed in 1959. This is now a housing development, but the mineral railway from here down to the Leeds & Liverpool Canal is now a public footpath.

Wigan Central station after closure in 1964.
Gordon Suggitt collection

Former Wigan Junction Railway (Great Central) line near Hindley, passing under bridges for lines to Low Hall Colliery (foreground) and Wigan–Eccles line (background), 2003. *Gordon Suggitt*

Returning to the WJR, the trackbed can be regained and a further, sometimes rather muddy, footpath can be followed that reaches Westleigh & Bedford station, the site of which is the most interesting station on the entire route these days. Where the signal box used to stand is clearly apparent. The former down platform may gradually be rotting away but the fence behind it stubbornly clings on. While the up platform has gone, the access track south to Crankwood Road is still evident. Continuing south, the next feature is the abutment of the crossing over the Leigh branch of the Leeds & Liverpool Canal. Beyond here, the former railway can be followed on and off to Lowton St Marys, much of the route being a footpath, although no overbridges survive. On the approach to the latter location, a line of bushes marks the convergence of the line from St Helens Central, at Lowton Junction. From south of here the route remained in operation until April 1968, until a new link was put in from the West Coast Main Line for the line that survived towards Haydock.

Lowton St Marys station has today vanished without trace; a large light-industry building has been constructed on its site. However, the trackbed can be regained a few hundred yards to the south and followed on a clear if narrow path to a point slightly beyond where the line passes under the A580 East Lancashire Road. Here, the formation becomes overgrown and is no longer accessible between this point and the former crossing of the Liverpool & Manchester Railway west of Kenyon Junction. After a diversion around local footpaths, the trackbed can be regained south of the L&M; this forms the end point of the long-established Culcheth Linear Park and can be followed for almost 2 miles to the site of Culcheth station. All traces have long since been eradicated from the station's location but using old photographs and track plans it is still possible to visualise the site of the platforms, station buildings and goods shed. This line opened in April 1884 and closed to passengers in November 1964.

As mentioned in the introduction, south-east of here the trackbed has deteriorated in recent years and a formerly well-used unofficial path is now flooded and inaccessible where the A674 road passes over it. However, the formation can be regained a few hundred yards prior to Newchurch Halt. This halt only opened on in February 1943, largely to serve the nearby ROF factory but did at one stage in its short

Great Central Railway's St Helens branch, abutment of former bridge over the St Helens Canal. *Author*

life offer a regular service into Manchester. Here, rather oddly, an ex-Great Eastern Railway carriage provided shelter on the Manchester-bound platform but the only remains now are two sets of steps climbing up from the former platforms to either side of a minor road bridge above.

Just a little further on, the site of the junction with the short-lived ROF Risley branch can be seen, but most of this line has long been ploughed into oblivion. The main line continues south eastwards on a long embankment, entering private land, which is partly walkable if granted permission. Either side of the M62 the trackbed has vanished, and only a flooded cutting is visible before the triangle of junctions with the CLC line west of Glazebrook station is reached.

Returning to St Helens, the MS&LR had proposed building lines from St Helens towards Southport and the docks around Bootle. But nothing ever came of these plans other than an 8-mile branch from Lowton to St Helens, opening throughout as late as January 1900. Never able to compete with faster and more direct routes eastwards, it closed in March 1952 to passengers, though coal traffic continued into the 1960s. The line closed in stages from the St Helens end; but, as detailed below, a small section has recently reopened. St Helens Central's site is now a car park, but its location is identifiable from photographs by reference to surrounding buildings. Heading north, a short section of embankment is accessible, this area including a junction with a short branch that once led into the south side of the Pilkington Glass Works. Abutments over the LUR line towards Wigan and the St Helens Canal remain (in this area the canal towpath was rebuilt with stone sleeper blocks bought second hand from the Liverpool & Manchester Railway) but much is built over east of here. Haydock station is long gone and only Station Road identifies the location; just beyond, the remains of a small tunnel that once carried upon it a splay of tracks towards Haydock and Leigh Pits, as well as a waste tip, can be seen crossing what is now a filled in and landscaped cutting. Soon the East Lancashire Road (A580) is reached where the railway has been converted into a road and the bridge under the dual carriageway remains in good order. The GC route continues, though rather fragmented, through an industrial estate and under the M6 motorway to Ashton in Makerfield. Here the line survived until 1983 to reach an oil depot; the platforms of Ashton in Makerfield station remained until the 1990s, but all is built over by modern offices now.

Former GC St Helens branch, remains of footbridge near Haydock Park Racecourse station, 2003. *Gordon Suggitt*

GC St Helens branch siding to Kelbit works *circa* 2000. *Author*

The section through and past Haydock Park Racecourse is more attractive. The line runs in a cutting just north of the approach road into the course, though is often too wet to walk. On a race day it is possible to follow the trackbed through a field used for car parking and out of the racecourse environs but on a non-race day these fields are kept locked, and a diversion round is required. At Haydock Park station (opened February 1899, last used for race traffic on 4 January 1965) the wooden platforms are long gone but the remains of a nearby footbridge can still be seen. There follows a pleasant stretch of trackbed with just enough ballast to stop too much undergrowth blocking the way; though one bridge is in some disrepair and needs a degree of care to cross safely. Eventually a set of buffer stops is reached; these mark the end of a headshunt serving the spur that heads into the Hanson Aggregate (formerly Kelbit) works, opened in 1987 (though earlier industry, including Edge Green Colliery, on the same site

Great Central Railway's St Helens branch, line to Hanson Aggregate (formerly Kelbit) works, (left of picture) out of use in 2015. *Author*

was rail-served until 1967), which, after a lengthy period of closure, has been back in use since October 2018. The GCR east of this point towards Lowton had been replaced by a north–east chord from the WCML in 1968 and this chord is also occasionally used by engineering trains. Edge Green Colliery was first rail-served by a route to Dover Basin on the Leigh branch of the Leeds & Liverpool Canal, this line (known as Richard Evans' Railway) opened around 1860 and closed by 1933, and though not walkable here it is possible to see its junction with the modern route. Golborne's GC station, latterly termed Golborne North, has long been built over but a fine section remains walkable, on an embankment, eastwards from this point towards Lowton until modern housing blocks the route.

Widnes–St Helens

Close to the large lock on the River Mersey at Spike Island, south of Widnes (originally known as Runcorn Gap), that forms the start of the St Helens (or Sankey) Canal lies what was the world's first ever purpose-built railway-served dock, something arguably worthy of much wider recognition than it currently has. This was built by the St Helens Railway in 1833, but soon proved too small for the size of boats required for coal transport and was replaced in the 1860s by a new dock at Garston. As an early railway geared up for freight traffic, with inclined planes rather than gradients, the St Helens Railway initially struggled with passenger services, which were notoriously slow; one passenger who had just missed his train was famously told 'just run after the train; you will surely catch it up' But the line endured and prospered, providing a local passenger service until June 1951. The route remained in use for freight, diverted passenger services and the occasional excursion train until April 1982, with a ballasted trackbed remaining in place for a further ten years. However, in the early 1990s, part of the formation was used for a new link road to the M62 around the east side of Widnes, and thus nothing remains of either Ann Street or Appleton stations.

Further north, when the new road curves away west, it is then possible to walk a lengthy section of the St Helens Railway north from the site of Farnworth & Bold station almost to the L&M line west of St Helens Junction, with just a short diversion required at the site of Clock Face station. Trains reached Sutton Manor Colliery from the north until August 1987; it is also possible to explore the former route to Clock Face Colliery (closed August 1957) and the triangular junction that led to it. Unfortunately, there are no station remains along this part of the route. The bridge that carried the St Helens Railway over the Liverpool & Manchester, a replacement for the first ever bridge in Britain to carry one passenger railway over another, has sadly been demolished in recent years but its site can be viewed both from below and from an adjacent footbridge.

Dismantled bridge carrying the St Helens Railway over the L&M, the first bridge carrying one railway over another ever to be constructed in Britain. *Nick Melling*

St Helens Junction to St Helens line, siding to Hays Chemicals (right) out of use in August 2003. *Gordon Suggitt*

St Helens Junction–Ormskirk via St Helens and Rainford

Continuing north from at St Helens Junction, the next point of interest is the 'dive under' junction, under which traffic from St Helens Junction joined the former St Helens Railway's Widnes route until 1965. Moving north, past the site of Sutton Oak station, the remains of a short siding to Hays Chemicals can be seen. This minor line is notable for being one of the last closures in the north-west, its declining traffic finally ceasing to operate in September 2002. Two sets of rusty rails remain in situ, on what is now a fenced-off, overgrown and inaccessible formation, until the St Helens Canal is reached, just south of the junction with the former L&NWR Wigan to Liverpool line.

North of St Helens, the line to Rainford Junction, again closed to passengers in 1951, can be followed in part. At the site of Gerard's Bridge station, closed as early as 1905, ramps still lead up from the roadside to the trackbed on both sides of the line. Here, it can also be noted that the last part of the Rainford line to see traffic, that from Gerard's Bridge Junction to Pilkington's Plate Glass Works, appears rusty (but clear) but has apparently been out of use since around 1986. No access to the trackbed is possible at this point.

Gradually moving into more rural surroundings, the sites of Moss Bank and Crank stations are reached, the latter now beautifully restored by a loving new owner, with the southbound platform dug back out, together with a nameboard and a signal box base visible on the opposite side of the former crossing. North of the site of Old Mill Lane Halt, the line becomes an official footpath almost the whole of the way to Rainford Junction. The sites of Rookery and Rainford Village stations may be identified, but there is nothing of railway origin left to see at either location. Rainford Junction had an unusual arrangement in that the two main-line platforms continued for some distance alongside the two branches as they curved away, allowing trains to reach these platforms without blocking the main Liverpool–Wigan route. Evidence of both of these 'extensions' may still be seen, as can the now somewhat uncommon site of a signalman exchanging a token with the driver for the single-line section west to Kirkby.

North of Rainford the route was originally a separate concern, opened by the East Lancashire Railway and later the L&YR. Open to passengers between March 1858 and November 1956, the line also reached a number of collieries, with a quite extensive system of branches to the east of Skelmersdale. Beyond Rainford there is less to see but a section of trackbed south of Heys Crossing Halt (still marked on OS maps) including the junction with a short branch to Ferny Knoll Colliery is still intact. Nothing remains of the site of the junction with the freight-only line to Bickerstaffe, however, but a little to the west there is a pleasant, unofficial walk of over a mile along this formation, ending north of Wash Farm. However, north of the M62 the fare is very meagre indeed, Skelmersdale

St Helens to Rainford line, Crank station nameboard in 2019. *Author*

St Helens to Rainford line, Crank station platform in 2019. *Author*

Eccles to Wigan line, guided busway at Newearth Road, with the cycleway on the eastern part of line in background, 2022. *Author*

Bickershaw Junction 2003; the line to Hindley Green straight ahead and (then recently lifted) line to Bickershaw Colliery heading south (to the right). *Phillip Earnshaw*

new town having wiped out almost every trace of a railway, and just odd bits of bridge abutments and overgrown embankments are encountered past Westhead. Only on the approach to Ormskirk do things improve somewhat, as an official path of just under a mile long follows the line as it curves south into the north side of the station, the site of extensive sidings until the 1960s.

Whelley loop line, decking of Douglas Viaduct; a 2021 view. *Nick Melling*

Roe Green Junction–Wigan via Hindley Green

The L&NWR already had access to Wigan from Manchester via the L&MR to Parkside Junction, then north into Wigan North Western station, but by September 1864 had opened this much more direct route. Despite serving a number of quite substantial centres of population, as well as providing access to the large town of Leigh, this line was considered surplus to requirements, thought to be a duplication of other routes, and the whole route lost its local passenger service in November 1964, though most intermediate stations had closed prior to that time.

From Roe Green Junction an official and obviously well-used path heads west, as far as Ellenbrook. Here the main part of the formation is now used for a guided busway through Tyldesley (no station remains) and onto the Leigh branch, which closed later, in May 1969. From Tyldesley Junction a narrower, less official, path reaches Hindsford and a junction with the branch that formerly ran eastwards to Chanters Colliery. The two pits here closed in 1964 and 1966 respectively. This line ceased to be a through route after the withdrawal of goods traffic in January 1969 between Tyldesley Junction and Howe Bridge West. The loss of coal traffic to Parsonage Colliery in 1974 saw the line cut back further after the section between Howe Bridge West and Bickershaw Junction was taken out of use in February 1975, some six months after the last train over this section was believed to have run. The west end of this line closed after the last traffic reached Bickershaw Colliery in July 1994.

Since closure the formation in places was partly destroyed, open cast mining east of Howe Bridge resulting in the loss of several large embankments and adjacent bridges. The site of Howe Bridge (at one time Chowbent) station, closed in July 1959, is also now just a memory. Howe Bridge East Junction can still be discerned but most of the chord to the Bolton & Leigh Railway at Atherton Junction has been lost, in recent times, to housing. At Howe Bridge West sidings site, little of the former yard survives, although the junction with the former Parsonage Colliery route is still readily apparent. After the next major road is passed the route once again feels more like a railway formation to Hindley Green, although evidence of the mineral lines that once crossed it on their way to Eatock Pits and Swan Lane Colliery have more or less gone.

Of Hindley Green station, closed in May 1961, both platforms remain, as do part of the entrance/exit ramps. In recent years a hardcore path has been laid through the station site; mud and underlying water having previously been a serious issue. Beyond Hindley Green station site, however, the route is not well maintained and only likely to be a pleasant experience after a good period of dry weather. Former occupation bridges are marked today by infilled strips. On this section can also be seen the abutments of the bridge that carried a mineral line into Hindley Green Collieries over the main line, though the pit was generally accessed from a junction a little further to the west.

Whelley loop line, Douglas Viaduct showing damage to a pillar. *Nick Melling*

Whelley loop line, the northbound line, dives under the West Coast Main Line south of the former Standish station. *Nick Melling*

The 'second' Douglas Viaduct: pillars on Boar's Head to Adlington line. *Nick Melling*

It is also possible to see the junction with the main line of this branch at Scowcrofts sidings, where another line headed south towards Bickershaw Colliery.

A section of inaccessible formation follows to Bickershaw Junction, where the branch from the colliery of that name joins from the south. Beyond it is still possible to see the divergence of the up and down connections to the Wigan Junction Railway (see above), which ran from Glazebrook to Wigan Central. The down connection is crossed a little beyond before the Wigan Junction Railway is similarly passed, adjacent to a bridge that once carried a mineral line into Low Hall Collieries, just south-west of this point. The trackbed is still heavily ballasted west of Bickershaw Junction, reflecting its relatively recent closure, although the route is getting progressively choked by trees and as a result becoming harder going. A last mineral railway used to pass underneath the line east of before Platt Bridge, where the formation beyond is effectively a cul-de-sac since the removal of the bridge over the A573 to the north of the town. A little further west the bridge that carried our route over the Whelley loop line remains in place.

The Whelley Loop, Boars Head to Adlington and the Pemberton Loop

The Whelley loop was originally built by the Lancashire Union Railway as part of its Blackburn to St Helens (via Chorley and Red Rock) route to enable their trains to bypass the busy routes through Wigan. Opening in 1869, the line was extended by 1886 to form a north–south bypass road for Wigan on the West Coast Main Line, at Standish Junction to the north and Bamfurlong Junction to the south, together with a connection at Boar's Head Junction (south of Standish) onto the route into Adlington via Red Rock station. A further connection west of Hindley on the L&YR line, at de Trafford Junction, provided a fast route for passenger trains from Manchester to Blackpool and the north that avoided both Bolton and Wigan. At its busiest in the early 1970s, during electrification of the West Coast Main Line, the route saw its last train in 1976, the Adlington line having closed some six years earlier.

Plenty remains to be seen. Starting at the south end, the line passes under the LNWR route at Platt Bridge and disappears into the landscaped area south of Amberswood described above, before suddenly emerging as a public footpath to the west of Hindley. This path then continues for almost 4 miles, with just slight diversions required where bridges have been removed over the A577 road and over the Leeds & Liverpool Canal, about halfway up the long flight of locks. The most attractive section is through the 'plantation' of Haigh Hall Park, where there was once a cut and cover tunnel, opened out in the 1880s.

The 'loop line' continued north-west, crossing the River Douglas on a viaduct, still in place but securely fenced off and with clear signs of wear to at least one of its pillars. It then splits, the northbound track passing under the West Coast Main Line with its own small bridge before joining the main line just south of the former Standish station. The line from Boars Head heads east; it also had a viaduct over the Douglas but only the pillars remain, still impressive in their own way. Joining the Whelley route at Haigh Junction, the formation is hard going south of the B5239 (Red Rock Lane) but an official path for the 2 miles or so to the

White Bear station (Adlington) shortly before the final train, January 1960. *Gordon Suggitt collection*

outskirts of Adlington, though this path is not well maintained and is very muddy after significant rain. The last section is now landscaped into a public path before White Bear station is reached, where a small station building inside a commercial premises is the sole survivor, but still a surprising and welcome one.

The Pemberton loop, Wigan's east–west avoiding line was built by the L&YR to create a faster Liverpool to Manchester route, bypassing Wigan Wallgate, in conjunction with the opening of their (still open) main line via Atherton. Opening in June 1889, its design for 'inter-city' traffic is demonstrated by the fact that it had no junctions with other lines nor any spurs to local collieries. Closing in July 1969, some trackbed is accessible to the west of Hindley No. 3 Junction, but much of the western part of the route has now been converted into a new road and while still walkable on pavements has largely lost any 'railway' experience.

Pennington–Platt Bridge

This L&NWR built line was another latecomer on the scene, reaching Bickershaw by 1885 and opening throughout in 1895. It was clearly intended as competition for the WJR route into Wigan Central, which is closely paralleled for some distance. Passenger services were brief and unsuccessful – the only intermediate station at Plank Lane in operation just from October 1903 to February 1915 (do note that the quite separate Westleigh & Bedford station on the WJR route was known as Plank Lane until 1894). The route continued to be of value to freight, however, until land subsidence and the emergence of Pennington Flash (a 'flash' is a Lancashire term for a lake or lagoon caused by flooding of low ground due to subsidence) took its toll. The last train was a LCGB special in 1963, which crossed a section that had apparently by then became almost permanently under water. With ground levels much altered in this area and mining waste dumped in places, virtually nothing of the old formation survives here.

The northern section of the route, that which served Bickershaw Colliery, is of more recent interest. Known for its use of industrial steam locomotives on site until the late 1970s, the colliery remained in operation right through until September 1993. Rusting track continued down to the increasingly derelict site before it was lifted around ten years later, and the formation remains in the most part accessible as a footpath from the colliery site as far as Bickershaw Junction, where it once joined the line from Hindley Green referred to above.

8
Bolton and Bury

The Bolton & Leigh Railway

The Bolton & Leigh Railway, the first public railway in Lancashire, opened in part in 1828, two years before the Liverpool & Manchester Railway, with a connection made between these lines by 1831 at Kenyon Junction, north-west of Culcheth. As was the way in those early days of railway construction, the line was built on minimal gradients together with two inclined planes, at Daubhill and Chequerbent, and with a terminus at Great Moor Street in Bolton. As the line developed and the L&NWR route from Eccles was completed (see Chapter 10), which also needed facilities in Bolton, the original station began to prove inadequate. Eventually as traffic increased, Bolton Great Moor Street was rebuilt in larger form, completed by 1874. The grades were then eased, with two deviations at Daubhill and Chequerbent avoiding the original inclines; these opened in 1885. But with increasing competition from both buses and other railway routes, the passenger service between Bolton Great Moor Street and Kenyon Junction via Atherton was withdrawn in March 1954, though the terminus station was still used by excursion traffic until 1958, as it was ideal to serve destinations to the west such as North Wales. Goods traffic hung on much longer, the last traffic being to bring construction materials for the M61 motorway, which was to permanently sever the line.

At Bolton, a visit can begin by viewing the site of Deansgate goods station. This opened around 1829 and was to close in February 1930. The building remained until 1963 and today an external wall still survives to mark its former presence. A little to the south, Great Moor Street station stood at the corner of Great Moor Street and Black Horse Street. It was demolished in October 1966, although its site was used as a car park into the early 1970s. After that time, the site hosted a swimming pool for some years but this in turn closed in 2003 and the land is now buried under the car park and petrol station of the nearby Morrisons.

Beyond Fletcher Street, the formation can be traced by means of the route's overbridges, even though the formation is infilled, as far as its junction with the Eccles line. Here there were two tunnels; though neither have any identifiable remains. The Bolton and Leigh tunnel apparently collapsed and was infilled in the early to mid-1980s, while the Eccles route tunnel may have gone a little earlier. The original formation of 1828 can also be traced nearby by walking up Lumsden Street and beyond. Some of the wall that separated the railway from the road can still be seen. The old route from this end served High Street Coal Yard until 1947 and other sidings until 1965. The incline beyond High Street closed in 1885 and was soon afterwards built over with terraced housing.

Returning to the later route, a section of trackbed with a path, but very much a rough and ready affair, can be followed from the back of Vernham Walk as far as Higher Swan Lane. However, most of the route beyond has been lost to industry or to a housing development, until just prior to the site of (the second) Rumworth & Daubhill station site. South of Daubhill things get rather fragmented; what hasn't been built over still remains but mostly in the form of long since filled in cuttings. As stated above, the line today is broken by the M61. On the south side stands Chequerbent embankment, engineered by George Stephenson, the most complete section of trackbed remaining of the Bolton & Leigh. This formation is on two levels; the new alignment is the lower one, which descended to Chequerbent goods yard, before passing through Chequerbent (for Hulton Park) station and going under the A6. Both embankments are unofficially walkable, although the higher route is overgrown in part, but its recent scheduling as an 'Ancient Monument' should hopefully ensure its survival. The old route was relegated to a colliery railway in 1885 to access coal mines, which eventually found it extended to serve Chequerbent Bank Pits 3 and 4. Today, the crossing keeper's house still exists on the A6, albeit extended, with a blue plaque confirming its provenance.

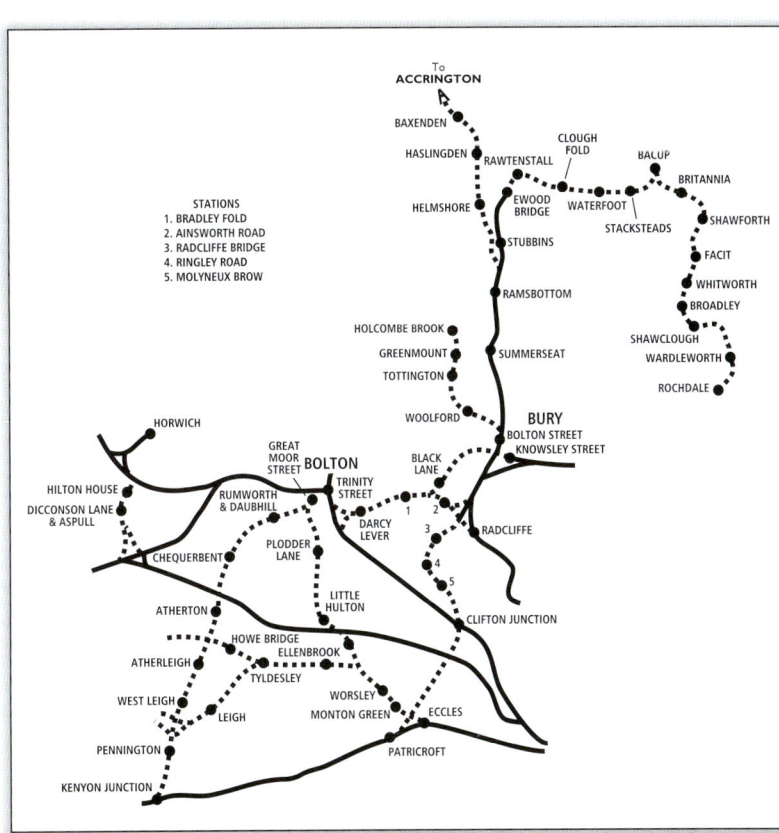

Map showing lines in the Bolton and Bury area.

Bolton & Leigh Railway, Chequerbent crossing keeper's house, 2003. *Gordon Suggitt*

Bolton & Leigh Railway passing under Wilton Lane, north of Kenyon Junction, 2003. *Gordon Suggitt*

Chequerbent station, closed in 1952, was largely removed before the line closed. There are no remains visible and its site is now overgrown.

South of the A6, accessed by walking around the side of an electricity sub-station with green fencing, a path of some distance can be followed. This appears to be semi-official, with access provided but no signposting and with little maintenance, leaving it quite muddy and slippery in places after significant rainfall. This path ends a few hundred yards north of the railway between Daisy Hill and Hag Fold stations, though access by separate footpath down to Atherton's L&YR station is straightforward enough. From Atherton southwards, much less remains. The platforms at Bag Lane station survived into the late 1970s but all is now buried under industrial premises, though the former Railway Hotel still oversees the site. South of Atherton, just a small section of formation remains intact, heading down to the A577 road at Howe Bridge. From here, the line was converted in the mid-1980s into the A579 Leigh bypass road, leaving no trace of either Atherleigh or Westleigh stations, though another former Railway Hotel remains at the latter location. This road was extended south to the A580 East Lancashire Road in the 1990s, leaving just a short distance left towards Kenyon Junction, securely private, where until 1954 you could arrive from Bolton and change for trains to Manchester or Liverpool. With Leigh the largest town in Lancashire without a railway and nearby Culcheth a large and growing village, a parkway station near Kenyon Junction to serve both communities might well be of value; perhaps something that might come to fruition in future years.

Horwich–Blackrod–Crow Nest Junction (Hindley)

The Horwich branch was opened by the L&YR to passengers in February 1870 but became of significantly greater importance with the opening of that company's huge locomotive works in November 1886. Just 1½ miles long and closed in September 1965, the Horwich branch is very much an example of a once walkable line that is no more. The station site 'Old Station Park', marked with an axle and wheels mounted on a short piece of track, still has its stone sett access road, but no buildings or platforms remain. Heading out of Horwich, where extensive sidings once stood at the junction with the Locomotive Works, housing development has taken place in recent years but without inclusion of a footpath to allow a through walking route. The works site itself has had approval in 2021 for over 200 houses to be built on it, so it is not clear how much of the original building will survive. At Blackrod station part of the Horwich platform, separately sited to the north of the still-extant main-line platforms, may still be found behind industrial buildings.

Horwich Locomotive works, 2011. *Phillip Earnshaw*

Heading south out of Blackrod, the most sensible way of accessing the Hindley line is by following the south end of the eastern part of the triangle that used to connect Horwich to the route between Bolton and Preston. This curve had opened in 1887; the two apexes being Loco and Horwich Fork Junction respectively. Today a footpath follows some of this curve, though the actual line is largely enclosed in an industrial premises. The site where the line met the Bolton to Preston line at Horwich Fork Junction is evident. On the other side of the overbridge at this point the Hindley route (or Aspull cut-off line) used to diverge from the Bolton to Preston route, though its original junction was at Red Moss until 1891 but after that time the two routes ran parallel for a short distance to Horwich Fork Junction.

The line south was opened in 1868 between Red Moss Junction and Crow Nest Junction, closing to passengers in January 1960, the same date as the route between Wigan and Chorley via White Bear and also the Chorley to Blackburn line. Similarly, all three also closed to all traffic on the same day in September 1968. The Aspull line curves away from the Bolton to Preston line in a deep cutting that still exists to this day with a number of attendant telegraph poles. After a flooded section, the route climbs onto an embankment, which continues to near Hilton House. It is possible to get to where the formation ends abruptly, prior to the A6, where it has been lost to development. In the 1970s you could see the empty trackbed from the A6 and the ghostly remains of a bracket signal. However, in more recent times, this signal has been cut down and its constituent parts are just strewn around; the base, parts of the main shaft, the gantry section and supporting metalwork can all be found lying in the undergrowth hereabouts.

Before the passenger railway arrived, a mineral line extended from Red Moss Siding to Scot Lane Collieries. This original route was retained to serve Red Moss Colliery 1 and 2 and now forms a pleasant public footpath through woodlands east of the hotel at Hilton House. To the south of the A6 further connections were required to join this mineral system here. Hilton House station itself opened in 1889, became a halt in 1945 and was to close in February 1954. Nothing remains of this site today and the railway beyond has been wiped from the face of the map as far as Brinsop Hall, where it first reappears as an overgrown, flooded and messy cutting. Much of the rest of the route to Dicconson Lane and beyond has been lost; on the main line just one crossing gate survives near Brinsop Hall.

An equestrian centre has been built across the trackbed prior to Dicconson Lane; preventing any view of the site of Dicconson Lane & Aspull station, although nothing is believed to have survived. It had varying names during its lifetime and closed as a halt in 1954, in tandem with Hilton House. But on the other side of Dicconson Lane, things improve, and the formation then makes an excellent walk for over a mile to the last former overbridge prior to Crow Nest Junction. En route is the site of Hindley and Blackrod branch Junction, where the base of a signal box can still be found. Further down the branch a sizeable base of a signal post still stands proudly, high on the top of the cutting. A little further south there is a short stretch of private land before Crow Nest Junction is reached; some parts are walkable, some overgrown and some flooded. From the junction it is an easy walk along roads or paths south into Westhoughton or west to Hindley station.

Clifton–Radcliffe (East Lancashire Main Line (South) and Lines Through Radcliffe

The East Lancashire Railway (ELR) opened between Clifton Junction and Rawtenstall in September 1846, a busy main line but a casualty of Beeching in December 1966. While Clifton station is the obvious starting point for a day exploring this route, unfortunately it is today one of the poorest-served stations in the area, with just one daily train in each direction. Clifton Junction station, as it was, was reduced to two platforms after closure of the Bury line and renamed Clifton in May 1974. However, its former importance can be gleaned on the East Lancashire Line, where two further large disused platforms still slumber in the undergrowth. Access to the old platforms is unofficially possible from a road leading into industrial premises just to the north; you can squeeze through a set of rusty gates then quickly head up a narrow path onto the East Lancashire Railway's formation. It is then just a couple of minutes' walk up the trackbed before the platforms come into view

The line is lost briefly across industrial premises but emerges before crossing the River Irwell on Clifton Viaduct. This structure is 80ft high, with thirteen stone arches. It can still be accessed unofficially from the north end but gets quite overgrown when summer vegetation is at its peak. The aqueduct of the Manchester, Bolton & Bury Canal can be seen below, whose towpath is the best way to cross the river and access the route on the north side. The viaduct acquired Grade II listed status in 1987 and it is a little frustrating that it does not form part of the footpath at present. A sizeable underbridge can be seen prior to the M60 and after crossing the motorway on a footbridge the formation is easily regained. Just north of the motorway used to stand Molyneux Brow station, closed in 1931, not that you would know this today. The trackbed to Radcliffe now forms part of the Outwood Trail. It used to have a lot of concrete railway furniture on route such as mileposts/gradient posts and catch point sign but on a recent visit just one surviving decaying catch point sign and milepost were noted. The route passes through the woods to Ringley Road station, closed in 1953, which still retains one of its platforms. You can see where the station building would have stood, and the station approach path is still in use. North of the station, the abutments of a bridge that formerly carried a tramroad to Outwood Colliery (see Chapter 19) may also be viewed.

Clifton Junction–Bury line, northbound platform of Ringley Road station, 1998. *Gordon Suggitt*

Clifton Junction–Bury line, Outwood Viaduct under restoration, 1998. *Gordon Suggitt*

Clifton–Bury line, decking of Outwood Viaduct, Radcliffe, in poor condition prior to restoration, 1996. *Phillip Earnshaw*

The formation then followed passes the site of the aforementioned Outwood Colliery together with its washery and also Radcliffe power station, last supplied by rail in 1959. Near the end of this path is Outwood Viaduct. This structure was designed and built by Andrew Handyside and Co. of Derby in 1881 at a cost of £4,225. It is built of cast iron and stands 70ft above the Irwell Valley. It has five graceful spans and is now Grade II listed. In 1987 British Rail wanted to demolish it but fortunately consent was not given; at the time it was fenced off, heavily rusted and had lost much of its decking. The transformation to a modern-looking, well-surfaced bridge is impressive and supports the argument that with almost any piece of engineering, if the will and the appropriate funding can be found, the structure can be saved.

Crossing the River Irwell on the viaduct, the trail ends in Radcliffe, before the site of Radcliffe Bridge station, whose last remains were lost to a road scheme; nothing is left. It is better instead to resume exploration at what is now Radcliffe's Metrolink station. This was once the site of Radcliffe South junction, where a line diverged towards Bolton, and where two further, long gone, platforms were situated. The line to Bradley Fold Junction opened in December 1879; it had a triangle at its eastern end that allowed connections northwards to the Bury line at Radcliffe North Junction, opening on the same date. The passenger services were lost on these lines in September 1953, before total closure in November 1964. Part of the route to the Manchester, Bolton & Bury Canal is identifiable, as are the abutments of the bridge that formerly crossed the old canal. A little further on was Radcliffe West Junction. The north curve can be followed unofficially along the alignment towards Radcliffe North Junction for some distance, though there are no remains of the line from Clifton Junction east of this curve. The section is particularly interesting as rails still survive as the route nears the junction; though these days they are buckled and contorted and with trees growing between them. A quite fascinating spot to visit. As what is now Metrolink is approached, a concrete catch point sign can also still be viewed.

Heading north from Radcliffe West Junction, the formation is a path before becoming overgrown alongside a newer road. At the end of this stretch lay Ainsworth Road Halt. This opened in 1918 and closed with the line. The only point of note today is the bricked up access to the Bolton-bound platform but today the halt's site lies under housing, as is also the case for the rest of the route beyond to Bradley Fold Junction.

Bury–Bolton

The Bury to Bolton line opened in 1848 and survived into the 1960s; as a well-used route it was notably not on the Beeching Report list of closures but was put aside for further appraisal. The led to a closure proposal for the route in 1964. It should have closed in 1965 but such were the objections that the line was reprieved in 1966. Unfortunately, British Railways persisted and after further decline in provision of services, closure took place in October 1970.

Rather than using Bury's main Bolton Street station, the Bolton line could only be accessed from the smaller and less well-situated Knowsley Street station. When Bury Interchange station was built in 1980, the route from Heywood crossed it on the level, though this unusual arrangement was only operational between March and December 1980 when coal trains from Castleton to Rawtenstall stopped running. The formation on the curve from Bolton Street heading out towards Heywood still passes through the site but at a higher level, now passing over the Metrolink line on a bridge. Nothing remains of Knowsley Street station nor of the now built-over goods facilities to the north. The bridge under the East Lancashire Railway south of Bolton Street can still be made out from above and the formation can be picked up beyond,

Bolton–Bury line, Darcy Lever cutting, 2005. *Phillip Earnshaw*

Burnden Viaduct, Bolton, before conversion to trail, 2003. *Gordon Suggitt*

crossing the low-arched Wellington Street Viaduct, which takes the formation across the River Irwell. This structure is notable for some interesting corbels within its stonework. A little beyond was Bury Gas Works sidings, in use until 1966, which reached the works in question via a short tunnel under Bolton Road. The Bolton line, initially on a metalled path, becomes less distinct as Bury is left behind and is little more than a muddy path at the side of the formation by the time Radcliffe (Black Lane) station is reached, now buried under a large, grey, industrial shed.

From here to Bradley Fold Junction the trackbed has been built over by housing in recent years, though a new footpath has been provided just to the north. Nothing remains at Bradley Fold but the trackbed can be picked up from here, and with only a few short deviations, followed all the way into Bolton. On this stretch a solitary milepost survives near the former site of Bradley Fold West signal box, and the base of a footbridge that once existed near this point can still be seen. After this, the route crosses Darcy Lever Viaduct, the first of two box girder viaducts, passing some 80ft above the River Tonge. Since 2014 it has been open for the public to cross, albeit in a metal 'cage' for the protection of people and property below. Its survival is down to its Grade II Listing. Once off the viaduct, the site of Darcy Lever station (closed in October 1951) is reached, of which nothing remains other than part of the back of the up platform. A further short piece of trackbed brings walkers to Burnden Viaduct, a smaller version of Darcy Lever with a similar Grade II Listing and given the same 'cage' treatment as its compatriot. The viaduct crosses the A666 (St Peters Way), the River Croal and the former Manchester, Bolton & Bury Canal. Once over the viaduct, the rest of the route has been lost. The triangle at the west end of the route was retained as a turning point until the late 1970s but even this became surplus to requirements at that stage.

Bury–Holcombe Brook

This short branch was originally built by the Bury & Tottington District Railway; it opened in November 1882 and had an unusual history of periods of both overhead (1913–18) and third rail (1918–51) electrification. After a final year of steam haulage, it closed to passengers in May 1952. The line closed to all traffic beyond Tottington in May 1960, with the remaining section passing into history in August 1963. Setting off from the Bury end, the trackbed

Right: Holcombe Brook branch, new Viaduct at Woolfold. *Chris McFarlane*

Below: Holcombe Brook branch, Tottington Viaduct, 2005. *Chris McFarlane*

Above: Holcombe Brook branch, platform at Tottington station. *Author*

Left: Bury–Bacup line, a now demolished bridge at Lee Road, west of Bacup, 1999. *Phillip Earnshaw*

can be accessed just east of the sturdy Irwell viaduct, the short stretch of trackbed between Tottington Junction and this point having long since been built over by light industry. An official footpath crosses the viaduct, built as a single-track structure but with pillars wide enough for a possible doubling that never proved necessary. The trackbed can be followed past Woodhill Road Halt (no traces left) but has been built over by new houses between this point and Brandlesholme Road.

At Brandlesholme Road the former road bridge and much of its adjacent cutting have long since been filled in, taking any remnants of the halt with them. From this point a new footpath/cycleway has been built, using what had previously been private and gated off land. This path leads to a new, concrete, viaduct at Woolfold, opened officially in May 2012 by Sustrans at a cost of £650,000 using part of their 'people's millions' fund. It is an impressive structure, only slightly lower than the old formation; the original viaduct having been demolished in 1974. The line continues north, taking a slight diversion past gardens that were extended over the former site of Woolfold station. From this point onwards, a number of the former concrete catenary bases from the overhead electrification era (last used in 1918) may be viewed next to the formation. Reaching Tottington station, the single platform has largely survived and the outline of the goods yard behind it is also still clearly apparent.

The path continues north to cross Tottington Viaduct, again with single track but foundations wide enough for doubling. There were no catenary bases on the viaduct itself, resulting in a noticeable 'sag' of the wires that can be seen from contemporary photographs. The official path ends at Greenmount station (no remains) and north of here residential developments have obliterated the formation. At Holcombe Brook station, the line's terminus, the site of the station has been built on by a small precinct of shops, but a stone retaining wall and a former ramp leading down to the platform also provide some remaining identifiable features.

Ramsbottom and Rawtenstall–Bacup

At Stubbins Junction, north of Ramsbottom, the ELR built a branch line heading north then east, reaching Rawtenstall by September 1846 and Bacup in October 1852. Situated in the narrow, industrial Rossendale Valley, the line quickly became profitable with coal and brickworks traffic together with stone traffic from the numerous quarries higher up on the moors (see Chapter 19). This justified doubling of the line, which included the construction of Newchurch No. 3 Tunnel (known locally as Thrutch; tunnels 1 and 2 were on the original line), opening in March 1881. Closure of the Bacup line was one of the more controversial closures of the 1960s, having for some years enjoyed a well-patronised and frequent DMU-operated service, but nevertheless all passenger trains east of Rawtenstall ceased to run in December 1966.

Services to Rawtenstall hung on until June 1972, however, and coal traffic kept the line in operation until December 1980. This comparatively late closure meant that the line stayed intact and available for the 'new' East Lancashire Railway to take over operations, though it was over ten years later, in April 1991, that the preserved line first ran services back into Rawtenstall. Now very much in the Premier League of such lines, the station buildings at Rawtenstall and Ramsbottom are impressive but are reconstructions of the sadly demolished originals. The 'new' ELR chose not to reopen the somewhat inaccessible Ewood Bridge & Edenfield station (opening Irwell Vale station, a little to the south instead) but some platform remains are still visible here.

LYR goods warehouse at Waterfoot.
Gordon Suggitt

Walking the Rossendale Valley line, you quickly realise how the route had to be squeezed into the narrow valley, between older buildings and crossing and recrossing the River Irwell. Starting at the Bacup end (see Chapter 11 for Bacup station), much is inaccessible, buried under industrial buildings, including Stacksteads station, with an island platform built right onto a bridge over the river, though this bridge is one of the few that survives. Waterfoot station had its building on the main road itself, looking more like an office than a station; the platforms were at first-floor level. Although the building was demolished in the 1970s, part of the site remains in use as a coal yard and an entrance to the goods sidings from the south can still be made out. An impressive goods warehouse west of the station remains intact. Further west, the authorities have converted as much of the line as they could to a footpath and cycleway, with two significant sections in use. The first of these includes (and runs east of) the two accessible and now fully lit, tunnels on the line. Newchurch No. 2, the longest and easternmost of the two, has always been open but prior to remedial work was rather unwelcoming, being particularly damp in places. Newchurch No. 1 was blocked for many years, but in 2019 was reopened as part of this route, with a new footbridge at the western end put in to allow access. Newchurch No. 3 (Thrutch) Tunnel remains blocked at both ends and is reported to be in poor condition.

After a short period of road walking a further section of trackbed can be accessed that runs as far as Clough Fold, crossing the river one last time on a sturdy low viaduct. Clough Fold station (a later opening, in 1870) was another island platform, next to the town gasworks, but both station and gas establishment have long gone, though another, still walkable, incline linked the location with a number of stone quarries high up on the moors (see Chapter 19). The last section into Rawtenstall is now a bypass for the town and, lacking a pavement in parts, is not ideal for walking.

Bury–Bacup line, Newchurch Tunnels; photograph taken from inside No. 2 tunnel viewing east portal of No. 1 tunnel. *Nick Melling*

Bury–Bacup line, east portals of Thrutch Tunnel (left) and Newchurch No. 2 tunnel. *Author*

9 Stockport & Tameside

Chorlton and East Didsbury to Reddish and Bredbury via Stockport

The former Midland Main Line from Manchester Central (Chapter 10), through Bakewell to Derby and St Pancras was one of the more controversial closures of its time, though presumably it was considered a duplicate to the Hope Valley route via Chinley at a time when such duplications were frowned upon; we will pick up its story after it dived through a tunnel below the Altrincham line close to what is now Trafford Bar Metrolink station. After closure the track was kept intact and, with most but not all ballast removed, it became a well-used but obviously unofficial path. However, in 2008 work started on conversion of the route as far as East Didsbury into a tramway and this extension of Manchester's Metrolink system opened in July 2011. At St Werburgh's Road tram station the Fallowfield loop (Chapter 10) branched off to the east. Reaching East Didsbury, the formation continues for a further 500m or so but access ends at a point where the main Buxton route and the Stockport line diverged. South of here there are two missing bridges over the River Mersey: the first carrying the Buxton route south, where it soon formed a junction with the line heading west from Cheadle Junction, still in use for freight traffic. The second bridge carried the CLC's route from the latter location, joining with the Midland Railway at Heaton Mersey East Junction, then forming an east to west route through Stockport. There have been proposals to extend the tramway into Stockport, which would make use of this formation, but Stockport already has a fast and frequent service by train into Manchester city centre and there are legitimate questions around the value of a significantly slower and less direct tram service.

Approaching Stockport from the west, much has been obliterated by the M60 motorway, but some abutments of bridges remain that help to identify the route. A little further, on the east side of town, there were two tunnels, Wellington Road and Tiviot Dale. In 1980, during construction of what was then the M63 extension from Cheadle to East Stockport, British Rail monitored movement in Tiviot Dale Tunnel, leading to a series of rock anchors being installed over most of the tunnel to ensure the stability of the sandstone face of the new road. Unfortunately, during this work, a mobile site crane fell into a void that existed between the tunnel and the rock lining. While the crane did not penetrate this lining, the line was considered unsafe from then on and a temporary closure became permanent as from 1982. Both tunnels were just about accessible in 2004, subsequently they were partially filled in and accessible only by crawling on hands and knees, but nowadays they are both securely fenced off from either end.

At Stockport Tiviot Dale (opened December 1865, closed January 1967) the fine station building apparently cost a remarkable, for its time, £8,000 to build. Impressive from the outside but described as 'almost permanently gloomy' and 'dark, dank and foreboding' on the inside, the building was demolished soon after closure, but a bay platform, covered in trees and bushes, is a surprising survivor. The site can still be viewed below Wellington Road North on the north-east side of Stockport. East of Tiviot Dale was Portwood, the line's original Stockport station, relegated to goods duties in 1875, with its site now buried under a supermarket. After passing in front of an impressive surviving mill building, the line can be regained just north of Junction 27 of the M60 through Reddish Vale to Brinnington Junction and towards Reddish Junction. This is a delightful official path, particularly when autumnal colours can be enjoyed. The connection towards Bredbury can be followed through Brinnington Tunnel (less obvious is the steep cutting on its west side, once the site of a second tunnel until this structure was opened out in 1931) and for a short distance afterwards before this line also disappears under the orbital motorway.

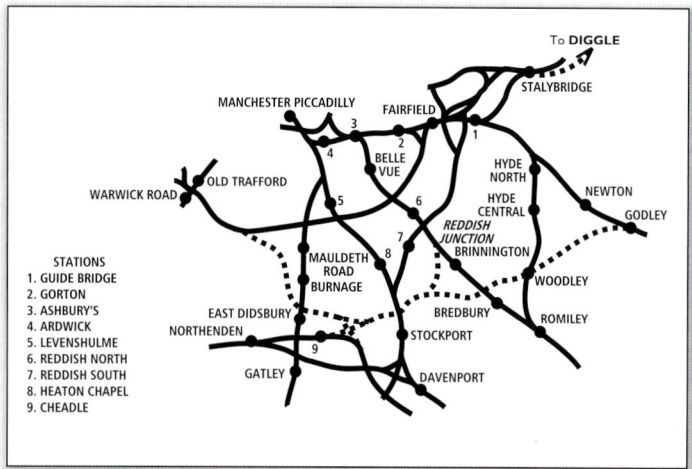

Map showing lines in the Stockport and Tameside area.

Trackbed at Chorlton (Midland Railway main line) during tramway construction. *Author's collection*

Stockport Tiviot Dale Tunnel, west portal partly infilled. *Phillip Earnshaw*

Brinnington Tunnel, north of Stockport, between Brinnington Junction and Woodley. *Author*

Former turntable west of Godley Junction, 2022. *Author*

Audenshaw station building (left) and stationmaster's house Denton to Droylsden line, 2003. *Gordon Suggitt*

Trackbed of Crowthorn curve, north of Guide Bridge, facing north. *Phillip Earnshaw*

The Apethorne Curve and Bredbury to Romiley (Low-level Line)

At Godley Junction on the still-open section of the Woodhead route between Guide Bridge and Hadfield a four-platform station could be seen until its effective closure in July 1986 (a token once-weekly service continued until May 1995). It took two stations to replace it: one to the north-west (Godley) and one to the south-east (Hattersley). In the late 1980s Godley Junction was a scene of dereliction with abandoned platforms, a derelict, dangerous looking and securely blocked-off footbridge and waiting shelters more like piles of detritus, though the site has long since been cleared. But the key to Godley Junction's importance was the 2-mile Apethorne curve south-west to Woodley, from which a further, wider, range of destinations could be accessed. From Godley Junction's Apethorne curve platforms, the CLC at one time provided services right through to Liverpool, but most trains were locals and these services ended in 1962. Of much greater importance was freight, and when the Woodhead route was electrified in 1954, Godley Junction became an important point of exchange between steam and electric traction. As a result, a locomotive turntable was provided, the abandoned pit and basic structure of which can still be seen (with its history helpfully detailed on information boards), together with coaling and watering facilities.

The Apethorne curve's working life ended with the closure of the Woodhead route in July 1981, the source of virtually all its latter-day traffic. Until the late 1990s things were pretty much left as they were on the curve, but by 2000 Sustrans had purchased and converted the line into a footpath. It remains in use as such today, though it of course blocked off at Godley Junction; indeed, currently the Godley end is something of a cul-de-sac with no access from the south end of Station Road at the Godley end and only a steep, slippery, grassy public footpath provides access from Brookfold Lane, just west of Station Road. However, access via Apethorn Lane (note the lack of an 'e' at the end of the street name; the former public house in that area was also similarly spelt) at the Woodley end is straightforward enough. From Apethorne Junction it is less than half a mile south to Woodley station, still served by services to Rose Hill (Marple), and just south of Woodley lies Woodley Junction, where freight still travels along a stub to a tarmac works, though the sliproads of Junction 25 of the M60 have long since blocked access to Brinnington.

A further closed line ran south from Bredbury Junction, close to the tarmac works site, as far as Romiley between February 1875 and March 1967. Curving south from Bredbury Junction, most of the way it ran parallel to, but separately and at a lower level to, the line from Reddish North. Generally freight only, no platforms were provided at Bredbury despite the line running just on the south side of the station, though on opening it formed part of the route of the Midland Railway's short-lived St Pancras to Liverpool Central Pullman service. South of Bredbury two parallel tunnels were provided: high level for the Reddish route and low level (162 yards) for the former Bredbury line. The former remains in use; the latter is believed to remain intact; it was unofficially accessible some years ago but the approach cutting from the north is now too flooded and overgrown to get within view of the tunnel. Further north towards Bredbury station, the trackbed is unofficially accessible as far as Stockport Road, but has been subject to infill and landscaping that, it is fair to say, has not added any scenic value to the location.

Routes from Denton Junction to Droylsden and Stalybridge

Denton Junction, just north of Denton station, which, somewhat infamously, has just one train calling in each direction per week, is situated on the still-open line between Stockport and Guide Bridge. At one time, though, it had also connections with lines heading north-west towards Droylsden, north to Ashton and north-east towards Stalybridge. The former line at one time provided the shortest and easiest route from Manchester Victoria to Stockport and the south but was deemed surplus to requirements after the modernisation of Piccadilly station was completed. It was opened by the L&NWR in November 1883. At Ashton Moss Junction a further route headed towards Ashton; here it made a link with the Oldham, Ashton & Guide Bridge Railway (OA&GBR), where it was joined by the Crowthorn curve from the west side of Guide Bridge station. The formation of this curve remains largely intact.

North of Ashton Moss Junction, the Droylsden line closed in May 1969 and was quickly lifted. Passenger services here were always very limited; the only intermediate station, Audenshaw, had services only until May 1905. In terms of what remains, the M60 obliterated the line in Audenshaw itself and though the crossing point over the Ashton Canal is recognisable, neither bridge nor abutments remain. However, Audenshaw's station building is a remarkable survivor, a small, square, hipped roof building, now in commercial use. Behind this building is a short piece of inaccessible embankment but on the opposite side of Manchester Road, the line is an official footpath that can be followed pretty much all the way to the site of Droylsden station. This station, at the junction of the Audenshaw and Ashton lines, had opened in 1846 and closed in October 1968, though the Audenshaw platforms had been unused for some years previously, and has now been almost entirely obliterated. A footpath links this site to the towpath of the long-disused Hollinwood branch of the Ashton Canal, which in turn gives access to the public park at Daisy Nook.

Exploring the former railway that once ran from Denton Junction to Stalybridge, popularly known as the Hooley Hill line, is a task for the railway rambler who relishes a serious challenge. Opened to Dukinfield in 1882 by the L&NWR, it was extended to Stalybridge Junction in 1893. After the extension, the connection at Dukinfield became surplus to requirements and was removed in 1903. The passenger service over this line perished in 1950 and the whole line was to close in 1968; as with many such places, the general rundown of the railway system meant that duplicate lines were expendable. At Denton Junction, the formation now forms an access road to the still-operational signal box. Beyond Stockport Road, the route curved towards Hooley Hill and is today walkable, but so landscaped that you would not know a railway had existed. Hooley Hill Tunnel (176 yards) is today buried, the retaining wall at road level being all that now exists. Hooley Hill station is also a distant memory.

The formation then passes into an industrial area, then a new housing estate blocks off any access beyond. As such it is better to utilise the towpath of the Ashton Canal towards Portland Basin. Just south of the basin, the Peak Forest Canal crosses the River Tame on an aqueduct. In turn, just south of this point, the Guide Bridge–Stalybridge line of 1845 also crosses the River Tame on a small viaduct; behind this viaduct a girder bridge used to carry the Hooley Hill line over the river, but this has long since gone. The one piece of interest lies next to the canal; what is believed to the remains of the original Dukinfield line of 1882, which was removed in 1903.

There is nothing left of Dukinfield & Ashton station, nor of Dukinfield Central on the main line north of Guide Bridge that closed in May 1959, but beyond the former station, a large piece of masonry on the formation can still be appreciated. The Hooley Hill line was heavily engineered, and it is therefore not surprising that little remains as bridges were removed and the large, low, viaducts completely demolished once the line closed. It takes a good deal of imagination to see, or indeed work out, where the line once ran; only the base of a bridge abutment next to the River Tame in Ashton remains, such has been the success of removing the railway from the landscape, until the two lines came together at Stalybridge Junction, just to the west of the station.

Micklehurst Loop

The Standedge route between Manchester and Leeds is today the most important of the trans-Pennine rail crossings. Indeed, the twin-tracked route is again close to capacity and there has been talk of a further two tracks being laid along sections of the route and the possible reopening of the two single-bore Standedge Tunnels. The line between Stalybridge and Huddersfield was opened in 1849 and such was the success of this route, together with the gradient profile, that it eventually became apparent that two tracks were not enough; in particular, express passenger trains and slow-moving freights did not mix. While most of the route was expanded to four tracks, this was not possible without considerable expenditure between Stalybridge and Diggle. These issues led to a second formation being built on the other (east) side of the valley, which was unusual in being considered as part of the main line but situated some way away from it. This line, the Micklehurst loop, was heavily engineered with a number of major structures, but was still considered preferable to expanding the existing line. The line was to open to goods traffic in December 1885 and passenger traffic used it as from May 1886. Whilst a local passenger service existed, it was a short-lived affair, ending with the last of the local station closures in May 1917.

Butterhouse Tunnel on the Micklehurst loop line. *Phillip Earnshaw*

Latterly the 'Loop' was seen purely as a capacity enhancement for the original route, but the contraction of traffic and the loss of much slow freight meant that by the 1960s a four-track main line was no longer required. The loop finally closed to through passenger traffic in September 1964 and to through goods in October 1966. The southern part of the loop line, to a point north of the former Staley & Millbrook station, was retained, in much rationalised form, to serve Hartshead power station, opened in 1926 by the Stalybridge, Hyde, Mossley & Dukinfield Tramways & Electricity Board. Trains brought coal to the power station until its closure in July 1972, though it is believed that material was still being removed from the site by rail until 1976.

Exploration of this route is best started at Diggle, which had platforms on all four running lines and closed in October 1968. Despite the buildings and platforms having long since vanished, some clues to its former existence still remain on the ground. Prior to 1963 the new, twin-track tunnel carried the slow lines and the original single-track tunnels the fast lines, but following rationalisation the single-track tunnels were closed and the tracks lifted. These tunnels remain intact and can be used by road vehicles for maintenance of the existing tunnel and also for the Standedge Canal tunnel, which runs parallel but at a slightly lower level to the railway tunnels. The area to the south of the closed tunnels is now overgrown but in among the foliage can still be seen an abandoned water tank.

The junction with the loop line was a mile or so south of Diggle, with the towpath of the Huddersfield Narrow Canal providing convenient access. Almost straight after the junction, Butterhouse Tunnel is reached, effectively burrowing through the hillside to gain a course on the other side of the valley. The tunnel still remains and is unofficially walkable from the north portal, but the far end is currently infilled and therefore it forms a sort of cul-de-sac. A broken concrete catch point sign still stands where the formation leaves today's busy running lines.

To reach the former southern portal of Butterhouse Tunnel a minor road and footpath slightly east of the tunnel can be followed, which links easily onto the trackbed heading south towards Greenfield. One feature to look out for on this stretch is the former station house at Uppermill, which now serves as a private residence. Uppermill station was dominated by a large and impressive two-storey goods shed but this has long since vanished along with the platforms. Access ends at a large void where a viaduct once crossed the Chew Valley. Friezland station House, just to the south, still stands as a private residence but where once were platforms now lies an equestrian arena. At the goods yard, a little way further south, some cobble setts still remain, as does the base of a small crane.

Heading further south, nothing remains of Royal George Tunnel, which is buried in the depths and no remains are visible, though the nearby public house of that name makes an attractive alternative option. From here the next section to Micklehurst is once more an official path, though access effectively ends at the former station house at Micklehurst, which again serves as a private residence. Much of the formation beyond Micklehurst has been lost to development and the Huddersfield Narrow Canal towpath is again the best option to follow here, through the short and well-lit Scout Tunnel. The next accessible piece of trackbed is an unofficial path through the ruins of the buildings that were associated with the former Hartshead power station, including what appears to be an engine shed with its coaling stage. It was served by coal from Millbrook sidings via an underground hopper and overhead conveyor, part of which can still be seen today. Today this hive of activity is silent, the power station being now but a memory. Beyond the power station was the site of Staley & Millbrook station, of which nothing now remains except a derelict goods shed a few hundred yards to the north.

From this last station the railway formation is once again a footpath, known as the Tame Valley Way, to the site of the demolished Knowl Street Viaduct on the eastern side of Stalybridge. This led directly to Stalybridge New Tunnel, whose east portal, whilst blocked, is these days on a hillside with no easy form of access. The same is true of its western portal as only a short deep cutting exists before an infilled overbridge. Within Stalybridge New Tunnel, it is understood that there is a poster giving notification of a construction shaft. It is believed that these notices were produced following the inquiry into the Clifton Hall Tunnel (Chapter 10) collapse of 1953. Just west of the tunnel, the Micklehurst loop ended as the route re-converged with that of the 1849 formation through Mossley. A little further on is Stalybridge station and, for many, an opportunity to slake their thirst in the well-known station bar.

Micklehurst loop trackbed converted to bridleway, north of Micklehurst. *Author*

Micklehurst station, 1998. *Gordon Suggitt*

10 Manchester

Eccles–Bolton

Originally a coal line branching off the earlier route from Eccles to Wigan at Roe Green Junction (Chapter 7), this L&NWR route provided an alternative service between Bolton (Great Moor Street) and Eccles from November 1874. With most of the locations served by other routes, the line was an early target for closure and the last scheduled passenger trains ran in March 1954. As goods traffic declined, the line closed in stages from 1960 until the last section, in Bolton, accessed via Atherton, closed in 1967. Starting at Eccles, the station still survives, almost reluctantly it seems, now the first stop out of Manchester, with an hourly service to Liverpool, though there is little to see at Eccles Junction. A footbridge still crosses the live line but also passes above industry, which now stands on the former closed line; but there is little to be seen of interest as far as Monton Green as the line's route has been built upon. The station at this location is also no more. However, from this point, a cycle path follows the formation almost to the M61 motorway without interruption, save for the odd infilled overbridge.

The first point of interest is Worsley station, where both platforms still survive but the buildings are long gone. A short distance further on was the site of Sanderson's sidings; here the Bridgewater Collieries system used to pass overhead on its way towards Sandhole Colliery, although there is little trace of this. The connecting chord that converged with our line is still visible, as is the space where the sidings were situated adjacent to the running lines. The signal box is also long gone. It is also possible from here to reverse and follow a colliery branch south-west towards Worsley. Most of this line is today a footpath as far as the A572 road; only the final stretch, close to the Bridgewater Canal, has been built upon. The position of the canal tip can still be established by archive photographs.

Roe Green Junction marks the point where the Wigan and Leigh lines (see Chapter 7) diverged west. A signal box existed at this location but has long gone. A succession of cuttings follow, heading north-west towards Walkden, where the next station was located. Walkden Low Level, once a delightfully well-kept station as photographs from the 1930s testify, has been totally eradicated from the landscape, although the approach path to the down platform still exists from the A575. Within Walkden the high and imposing bridge carrying the still open L&YR Atherton line overhead is also worthy of note. On leaving Walkden, our line once also passed under a bridge carrying lines to Mosley Common and Astley Green Collieries from Walkden Workshops, once crossed on a bridge, not that you would know it today. Moving on to reach Little Hulton, again the station is long since gone and the formation is infilled and not walkable, though the converging connecting line from the Bridgewater Collieries system, south of Brackley, is now also a footpath at this point.

The M61 motorway was driven through the formation north of Little Hulton, destroying embankments on either side. However, a convenient footbridge exists a couple of hundred yards to the east and the formation can be rejoined via yet another arm of the Bridgewater Collieries system east of Brackley Colliery. It is then possible to walk the formation north to the site of Plodder Lane station. En route can be seen, to the right, the mineral line overbridge under which ran a line off the Bridgewater Collieries system into Dixon Green Landsale Yard. Plodder Lane station is today no more, with the cutting in which it was situated partially filled in. Of more interest is the surviving outer wall that used to run around the former motive power depot, though the depot site and goods facilities have largely been developed for housing. Plodder Lane Shed was opened in 1875 and became a sub-shed of Patricroft in 1885, before later coming under Springs Branch control. It was to close after the final withdrawal of passenger traffic from Bolton Great Moor Street in October 1954.

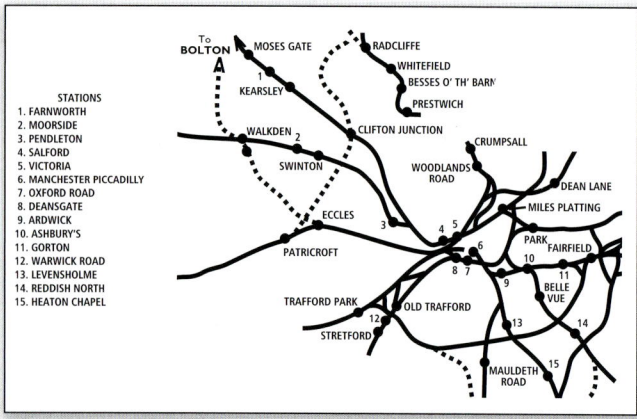

Map showing lines in the Manchester and Bolton area.

Patricroft–Clifton

Patricroft station is a shadow of its former self, with the engine shed long gone and only minimal remains at the west of the disued northernmost pair of what were formerly four platforms. The line heading north-east from Patricroft towards Clifton was termed the Clifton branch by the L&NWR but was more generally known as the 'Black Harry' line. The route opened in 1850 but passenger services were withdrawn after a matter of months; subsequently the line settled into its role as a useful but minor freight or diversionary route. It closed in 1939, before reopening in 1947.

Much of the line can be followed on official or semi-official paths from north of the M602 motorway to a landscaped cutting leading to the south portal of Clifton Hall or Black Harry Tunnel, a structure of 1,298 yards long that took the route under Swinton. It was a notoriously wet structure that had been hard to construct, with quicksand causing numerous problems. It had no ventilation shafts but did have eight construction shafts that had been filled in after completion. The land above the tunnel was originally clear but had been built up as Swinton developed. During the Second World War the line had been closed, and the tunnel was used to store tankers of liquid chlorine, used in the manufacture of batteries. The plans for the tunnel were partially lost in the Manchester Blitz of December 1940 and the rest lost in a fire of 1952. During the war, the tunnel's maintenance would have been limited.

It is then possible to walk adjacent to former railway land past Bolton's hospital and then on the formation to a point just before the route vanished underground, under the Recreation Ground in Bolton. Beyond the tunnel, quickly fenced off after closure and rumoured to have become filled with methane gas, there are only scant remains of former infilled cuttings and overbridges to the site of Fletcher Street Junction, where the line joined both the Bolton and Leigh Railway for the short distance into Bolton's Great Moor Street station (Chapter 8).

Worsley station platform, 2003. *Gordon Suggitt*

Patricroft to Clifton line, Clifton Hall sidings, 2004. *Phillip Earnshaw*

The line had reopened on 6 October 1947 but in early April 1953, a ganger on duty noticed some brick rubble on the up line within the tunnel, observing on closer inspection that the brickwork above was peeling. The line was closed straight away as a result on 7 April 1953. There was clearly a concern, and rail ribs were ordered from Gorton Works to strengthen the structure. On 26 April 1953 these were ready for installation, but the profile of the tunnel was not regular, and the rings did not fit. What had not been considered, with all the delays, was that the problem lay within the tunnel, not the rail ribs. This was to prove fatal on 28 April 1953 as, at 5.35am, the tunnel collapsed below a construction shaft. Sand that had filled the void then fell into the tunnel. Sadly, a pair of semi-detached houses and the best part of a third house collapsed into the space left by this sand, far above the tunnel, leading to the loss of five lives. The resultant gap in a row of semi-detached housing on Temple Drive may still be seen, though garages have in more recent times been erected where the houses once stood. Above the tunnel, explorers must take a diversion over a bridge that does allow a view of the site of Pendlebury station on the Atherton line, which closed in 1960 and whose island platform was removed in 1978 but with running lines still curving round the platform's outline.

After the tunnel collapse the line obviously closed as a through route, and the tunnel itself was infilled in 1959, but in recent years the top of the northern portal has begun to re-emerge due to erosion. The trackbed can be unofficially walked north to Clifton Hall sidings, which served a number of adjacent collieries and kept this section open until 1961. This is still a wide expanse of land that can be passed through until the formation regains its normal size but the last stretch to the road close to Clifton station is not worth the difficulty. Beyond this point, access is difficult to the now infilled bridge where the line used to pass under the main Lancashire & Yorkshire Railway. On the other side of the main line the route reaches Molyneux Junction, where it joined the Clifton Junction to Bury ELR route (see Chapter 8).

Fallowfield Loop

Loop lines around many major cities, other examples being Liverpool and Edinburgh, were built with great hopes that remained unfulfilled. The Fallowfield loop, opened in May 1892, is another example; the obvious problem being that such lines do not provide a direct link into the city centre where the majority of people want to go. Starting at Chorlton Junction on the former Midland Main Line, close to the modern St Werburgh's Road Metrolink station, this loop headed east until it reached Fairfield Junction, just west of the station of that name. A curve, completing a triangle, ran a little to the west from Hyde Road Junction to Gorton Junction on the east side of Gorton station. By 1958 only three or four daily services from Manchester to Guide Bridge took this route; these ceased in July of that year when the intermediate stations closed. The loop remained of value as a diversionary route or a bypass for freight around the city centre but as use declined it was singled in the 1970s. Closure of the eastern section from Hyde Road Junction to Fairfield Junction took place in October 1983, with the rest of the route seeing its last train five years later. Although the line was subsequently lifted, ballast remained, and the author can remember walking this loop in its unconverted state in the early 1990s. By 2001, conversion by Sustrans to a footpath and cycleway had been completed and since then the route has become increasingly popular for leisure use.

Fallowfield loop line, trackbed east of Fallowfield, 2000. *Phillip Earnshaw*

Fallowfield loop line, Levenshulme South station building, 2000. *Phillip Earnshaw*

Fallowfield loop line, Levenshulme South station platforms, seen in 2000. *Phillip Earnshaw*

Let us start from St Werburgh's Road; the 'Loop' is a straightforward line to follow almost throughout, but a few pointers will be of value. The original Wilbraham Road station is quickly reached, once known as Alexandra Park; sadly, the handsome street-level building is long gone but small parts of the platforms survive alongside the cycleway. Fallowfield station had a similar arrangement: here the road-level station building does survive, with part of it in use as a bar, but all is gone at rail level with a supermarket and car park occupying the site. The next station, Levenshulme South, is well worth a visit as what was formerly a pretty much derelict building, once used by a fireplace company, has been patiently and carefully restored and is now in use as a cycle café with its own outdoor garden space. Both platforms remained until the route was converted to a path and, given that a change in level can clearly be seen, it is thought that the platforms may have been covered over with soil rather than destroyed. Hyde Road station had been completely demolished by 1982 when the line was still in use, but the former entrance road to the goods facility may still be seen.

North of Hyde Road, neither of the routes can be followed right through to their respective junctions: if you are headed for Gorton, the towpath of the abandoned Stockport Canal just to the west provides an interesting alternative. Towards Fairfield the trail ends south of Boothdale Drive but is signposted on footpaths and estate roads through to Fairfield station. Also of interest here is an unusual Moravian settlement; effectively a self-contained village founded by immigrants from Eastern Europe in 1795 with a church and an impressive array of Georgian houses and other buildings.

Trafford Park and its Railways

As the name suggests, Trafford Park was once truly a park, consisting of 1,200 acres of farmland and meadowland surrounding Trafford Hall, an environment frequented by deer and other smaller wildlife. Surrounded on one side by the Bridgewater Canal, after the construction of the Manchester Ship Canal the park became quite isolated, almost an island, and was sold to a financier named Hooley who, in collaboration with a Mr Marshall Stevens, was quick to begin developments. Marshall Stevens was to oversee its transformation into what was to become the first purpose-built industrial estate in the country. A railway connection between the park and the docks was put in place by 1898 and, as various factories were constructed, the railway was continuously being added to and extended. The Co-operative Wholesale Society (CWS) developed a major food packing factory and a flour mill there; it also had a soap and candle works further up the canal at Lower Irlam, served by the Manchester Ship Canal Railway. The Ford Motor Company produced the Model T Ford at Trafford Park, The British Westinghouse Electric Company (which later became Metropolitan Vickers) made turbines and generators there and Rank Hovis McDougall built its wooden grain silos there.

Trafford Park expanded rapidly during the First World War and was used extensively for war work by the Ministry of Munitions but after the Armistice, development of new factories resumed. The British Alizarine Co. set up production in Trafford Park in the 1920s, later becoming part of ICI. Other residents included W. & R. Jacob & Co. Ltd., biscuit (more famously cream cracker) manufacturers,

Trafford Park, locomotives stored at Trafford Park depot, outside Kellogg's, August 2005. *Nick Melling*

Returning to the railways, several difficulties were encountered because of the size and diversity of the different premises. Some buildings could be built in neat rectangular rows, but because they all required rail access, some had to be built at what now seem rather odd angles. The laying out of the roads was straightforward but with the railways it was more complex. A minimum curve radius of 200ft was agreed upon but this still required a special breed of engines. The MSC's steam locomotives were designed to negotiate the tight-radius curves of the tracks on which they ran; the middle wheels of the 0-6-0 arrangement were flangeless, and the coupling rods had a hinged central section that permitted several inches of lateral play. Eventually a fleet of diesel locomotives was purchased between 1959 and 1966, but gradually decline set in and the last operational section of the railway at Trafford Park was closed in December 2012. Much remains in place to be explored, though the lines than ran out of the still extant Trafford Park sidings, used by DB Cargo, are securely fenced off. The western end of the line that formerly the served the Barton Dock Containerbase can still be unofficially accessed and much of the rest of the system, sitting next to existing streets, can be followed, with track still in situ at a number of locations.

Manchester's Lost Termini

Although not a 'railway walk' in its usual sense, a tour of Manchester's former terminus stations still makes a fascinating day out, albeit with less to see than ten years or so ago.

Mayfield station was opened in August 1910 by the as an additional facility alongside London Road (later Piccadilly) to handle the increased number of trains and passengers following the opening of the in 1909. Four platforms were provided together with a high-level across to London Road. Mayfield suffered the effects of bombing during, when it was hit by a on 22 December 1940. After the war, Mayfield was largely a relief station mainly used by extra trains and suburban services to the south of Manchester. It came into its own for a brief period during the electrification and modernisation of what was to become Piccadilly station in the late 1950s, when many services were diverted into it, but was closed to passengers in August 1960. Between 1970 and 1986 Mayfield had a second life as a parcels station but the tracks were finally lifted in 1989. The roadside building was gutted by a fire in 2005 but on a 2008 exploration, the platform canopies still remained in their original form but have since been removed. The station is these days best enjoyed from one of the official tours of Mayfield that run at intervals, but proposals exist to develop the site with homes, office space, a hotel and other leisure facilities.

Manchester Central station was built between 1875 and 1880 by the Cheshire Lines Committee (CLC) and was officially opened in July 1880. The Midland Railway, one of the CLC's partners, used Manchester Central as its terminus for services, including express trains to London St Pancras.

Trafford Park redundant level crossing signals near Cerestar works, 2021. *Author*

and the Lancashire Dynamo and Motor Company. But when hostilities resumed, many of the factories in Trafford Park were quickly returned to war use, an example being the Metrovick factory, which was rapidly adapted to manufacture munitions. During the Second World War, employment in Trafford Park rose from 50,000 to 75,000. After the war, Brook Bond moved its tea packaging factory to the canal side in Ordsall, Kellogg's started producing cereals, while ICI built its first purpose-built factory for the mass production of penicillin. The Guinness company began brewing 'authentically Irish stout' in the park, too. Employment held up well in the 1940s and '50s, but the '60s brought the first closures.

Manchester Central station as 'G-Mex', 2003. *Gordon Suggitt*

Manchester Central station clock, 2022. *Becca Norton*

The Cheshire Lines Committee (CLC) was keen to have its own station in Manchester; between 1875 and 1880 they constructed the impressive, single-arched Central Station, which was open and ready for use by July 1880. One of the key partners of the CLC was the Midland Railway who wasted no time in developing a London to Manchester service from St Pancras to Manchester Central via Derby and Matlock. Between 1960 and 1966, during the electrification of the West Coast Main Line, Central Station was as its busiest, notably as the terminus for the Midland Pullman, a streamlined blue six-coach diesel multiple unit. Services through Millers Dale and Bakewell finished in July 1968 when the line was closed as a through route. The station also provided local services to Chester and Liverpool but closed to passengers in May 1969, when the remaining services were switched to Piccadilly Station. During the decade after closure, Central Station fell into a dilapidated state, was damaged by fire, and became little more than a rough area used merely for car parking. But the property was then acquired by Greater Manchester Council and in 1982 work began on converting it into an exhibition centre, opening in 1986 as the *Greater Manchester Exhibition and Conference Centre* or *G-Mex*. It was subsequently renamed *Manchester Central* in honour of its railway history. During the covid pandemic Manchester Central was set up as an overflow or "Nightingale" hospital but fortunately was never required to fulfil that role and since 2021 it has returned to hosting conferences and exhibitions. The stately and impressive Midland Hotel still sits opposite, unlike many such buildings very much serving its original purpose.

Exterior of Manchester Liverpool Road station, 2003.
Gordon Suggitt

Platform side of Manchester Liverpool Road station, 2003.
Gordon Suggitt

Manchester's first station was, of course, Liverpool Road and with its incorporation into the Museum of Science and Industry (MOSI) much has been preserved and is accessible for viewing. The station itself comprised a slightly curved brick viaduct that terminated in the slope that led up from Water Street to, alongside Liverpool Road. The viaduct fronted a solid brick warehouse, a construction that owed much to similar canal buildings, and the station's location itself was well placed in the midst of the canal and warehousing complex. Provision for passengers was something of an afterthought; one of the most curious features being the positioning of a sundial over the first-class entrance. The railway only carried first- and second-class passengers, not third class, and each class

Manchester Mayfield station platforms (with canopy fully intact), 2008. *Author*

Manchester Mayfield station building and ramp, 2008. *Author*

had an office for buying tickets and class-based waiting rooms in which a bell was rung to announce that the train was ready for passengers to board. After the Liverpool & Manchester Railway built an extension of their line from Ordsall Lane to Hunts Bank in May 1844, passenger services were transferred to the newly open Victoria Station. Liverpool Road was retained as a goods depot, right through until 1975, then in 1980 was largely restored as part of the 150th anniversary celebrations of the L&M. Now forming a key part of Manchester's Museum of Science and Industry (MOSI) its future seems secure. However, the connection with the national rail network was severed in 2016, not without controversy, by the new Ordsall chord that was built to link Victoria and Deansgate stations.

Manchester Exchange station was built by the London & North-Western Railway, opening in June 1884, after the latter company was given notice to quit Victoria Station by the Lancashire & Yorkshire Railway, with whom they had shared for over 40 years. The station had five platforms, with Nos 1 and 2 being bays and Nos 3, 4 and 5 being through.

Sign at Manchester Mayfield station. *Author*

Platforms Nos 4 and 5 were reached by a footbridge from near the station entrance. The opening of Exchange allowed the L&NWR to vacate Victoria, which it had shared with the L&YR (and its predecessors) since 1844. From April 1929, Exchange had a platform link with the adjacent Victoria, when an eastward extension of platform No. 3 over the Irwell bridge was opened, meeting Victoria's platform No. 11, thus creating Europe's longest platform at 2,238ft; it could accommodate three trains at once. In addition to the L&NWR, the Great Western Railway also operated a service from Chester General station via Frodsham, Warrington Bank Quay and Eccles to Manchester Exchange between 1884 and 1943.

The station suffered hits by several German incendiary bombs during the Christmas 1940 Blitz. On 22 December of that year, the station roof was severely damaged, portions of which were never replaced. The station thus took on a rather neglected appearance until closure in May 1969, when all remaining services were redirected to Manchester Victoria. After many years of remaining relatively intact (with trains still running beneath the train shed) the site became a car park and in 2014 just a footbridge across the site remained. Since then, however, the whole area has been taken over for redevelopment with tower blocks of apartments and office space.

Manchester's Oldham Road station was the original terminus of the Manchester & Leeds Railway. Built on a lengthy viaduct about 30ft above its surroundings, passengers and goods were kept strictly separate. The passenger facilities were apparently well regarded, accessed by 'a flight of spacious stairs'. Opening in July 1839, at first with services only as far as Littleborough, the station remained in use for just four and a half years, when an incline was built from Miles Platting, originally operated by rope and stationary engine, down to the new station at Victoria. Now all in commercial and Post Office use, the site was still rail-served until the 1980s. There are only a few remnants as the main buildings were demolished after goods traffic ceased in October 1968, with the best survivor being the still extant boundary walls. At Livesey Street, the remains of the viaduct as it left the goods depot area can be seen, but nothing remains of the 1874 ramp down to the ground level of what became a very large site. Further viaduct arches can be seen closer to the junction with the Victoria route, as can piers of a former bridge that took traffic from the Oldham Road branch across the new main line to sidings and a brewery on the north side.

11

Oldham and Rochdale

Oldham has no railways at all these days, with the loop line from Rochdale having been converted, in much altered form, to tramway use, providing a much more frequent, if slower, route into Manchester or Rochdale. This conversion was discussed in Chapter 1.

Oldham–Ashton

This line formed part of what was known as the Oldham, Ashton & Guide Bridge Railway, (OA&GBR), though here we will only consider the route north of Ashton; the lines around Guide Bridge having been discussed in Chapter 9. Opening in 1861, this railway was straight away more valuable for freight than passengers, the towns in question sharing an active and prosperous cotton industry. The line also served, via a short branch, the large Park Bridge ironworks and its textile machinery manufacturing facility. Passenger traffic peaked at the end of the nineteenth century, when Oldham's Clegg Street station was rebuilt as an island platform with a full roof and a separate bay for the Ashton services, although some of these continued to Glodwick Road (see below) and there was also a connection that allowed access into Oldham Mumps station. Ashton was not so well served as the line had a west-facing connection and therefore could not easily serve the existing station; a separate facility, Ashton Oldham Road, therefore had to be provided. Being paralleled by the A627 road, the line was always vulnerable to tram and, later, bus competition. With there being little natural flow of people between the two places, the passenger service was a relatively early closure, the last service running in May 1959. Parcels traffic kept the line in business until 1967, though the tracks were not lifted until 1970.

Let us start at the Oldham end. As previously noted, Oldham once had no fewer than five main stations, but not one has survived in any recognisable form. The line south of Clegg Street is lost under a rather sad-looking and largely empty retail park but can be picked up south of Park Road as it curves round close to the west side of Kings Road. Although somewhat rough and ready, this track can be followed through to the north side of Park Bridge. Here, the viaduct over the River Medlock was demolished in early 1971 and the void in which it stood is quite clearly defined. Park Bridge is well worth a visit, with a heritage centre (opening hours vary) and the remains of various workshops, mills, and forges to be seen.

Heading south from Park Bridge, there is effectively a choice of three routes. The original route into Park Bridge was via a tramway that ran into the works from the terminus of the Fairbottom branch of the Ashton Canal at Fennyfield Bridge. The tramway lay on the west side of the approach road here, with much of the old formation now used as car parking space. Another option is to head directly south to access the formation south of the former viaduct.

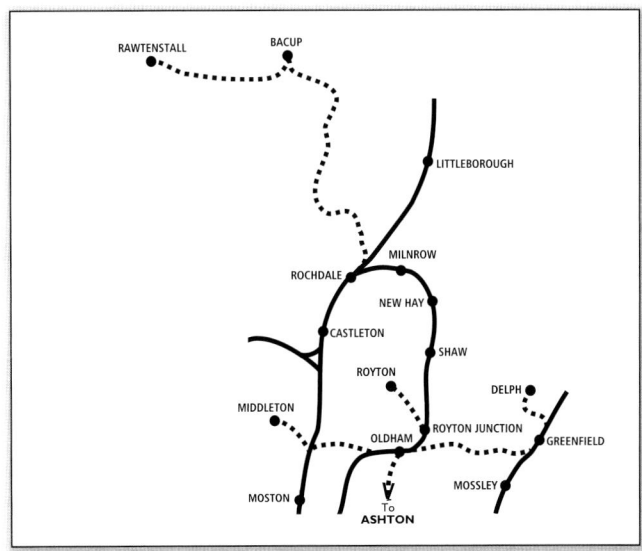

Map showing lines in the Oldham and Rochdale area.

Oldham to Ashton line, Smallshaw tunnel, north portal, north of Ashton. *Phillip Earnshaw*

Oldham–Ashton line, Ashton Oldham Road station, after closure. *John Fiander*

The station house, privately owned and some distance from the railway, lies close to the access road, but there is no trace of the station itself, which was an unpretentious wooden structure built directly onto the embankment. The third, and probably best, option is to take the sharply curved branch railway out of Park Bridge, which served the works and also at one time Rocher Colliery, slightly to the east. Regaining the trackbed from whichever route you chose, the line south continues as a very pleasant footpath, with deep cuttings and high embankments, through gentle countryside before reaching more urban surroundings at Limehurst. Some small bridges have been removed but these can be diverted round without difficulty.

Eventually the footpath ends at the east portal of a now-blocked short tunnel under Lordsfield Avenue on the north side of Ashton. From here the line has been built over by light industry and there is nothing to see at the former Oldham Road station site. The junction itself can be best viewed from the A627 where it formerly crossed the formation just north of the current line west of Ashton station. To the west can be seen the junction site and, to the right, the footprint of the now built-over line can be identified as a row of modern buildings sited between older ones.

At one point an extension of Manchester's Metrolink system along the old line was proposed, linking the two tram-served towns together. However, traffic between Oldham and Ashton is limited and perfectly well served by the existing, regular, bus service, so it is to be expected that the railway path will remain in place to be enjoyed for many years to come.

Oldham–Middleton Junction, Middleton and Royton Branches

Oldham, despite its close proximity to Manchester, lies on higher ground and, consequently, early railway engineers

Middleton Junction in the 1980s with track towards Oldham (Werneth) still in situ. *Nick Melling*

Middleton Station, just before closure. *Author's collection*

did not believe that a conventional rail route into Oldham town centre was possible. The first trans-Pennine route, originally serving Manchester Oldham Road station (Chapter 10) had opened in 1839, bypassing the town to the west, but it soon became clear that a way into Oldham had to be found. The solution arrived at was to build a branch from what was originally Oldham Junction, later Middleton Junction, just under 2 miles long, to a point of lower ground south of the town known as Werneth. Three quarters of a mile of this route consisted of a 1 in 27 incline, on which trains were hauled up or let down by a rope and pulley system. Had the line been constructed ten or so years later, the climb would almost certainly have been more gradual and spread over more of the route. However, around 1850, the story goes that a rope failed and a locomotive was forced to attempt the climb up the incline unaided. This, at the second attempt, it did, and though it always posed a significant challenge to locomotives, the incline became part of the local network with regular services running from the junction into Oldham until 1958. Even diesel multiple units, using this route as a diversion on certain Sundays in 1960, struggled themselves at times with the climb. However, by 1880, a direct route from Failsworth had opened to Werneth, and from then on, the bulk of the traffic had taken this more gently graded, though still quite challenging, route.

Middleton, situated to the west of Oldham, was also a substantial town and soon needed a branch of its own. It was originally served by a station at Mills Hill, on the main line from Rochdale, but within three years this station had been replaced by Middleton Junction; in modern times the original arrangement has been resumed with the 'new' Mills Hill station having opened in March 1985. Opening in 1857, the Middleton branch was busy enough by 1886 to justify rebuilding with a second platform, both with extensive canopies, and several extra sidings for goods. As with many short branches, the inconvenience of changing trains contributed to a decline in usage, with the last passenger train leaving in September 1964 and freight lasting just a year longer. As one of the largest places in the Manchester area not linked to the city centre by either rail or tram, Middleton is not a particularly popular commuting town, and it retains a rather independent-minded and slightly old-fashioned feel.

The final branch to be considered here was that built to serve Royton, situated to the north of Oldham but nowadays pretty much part of the same conurbation. Curving away west from the Oldham to Rochdale line about a mile north of Oldham Mumps station, a short branch of just under 1½ miles was provided in 1863. The usual story of early popularity and later decline ensued, though this branch did act as the terminus for many Manchester–Oldham trains and had an increased service in the early 1960s, provided by DMUs. But freight traffic was halted in 1964 and the last passenger service, watched by thousands despite teeming rain, departed in April 1966. Royton Junction station survived until 1987 until it was replaced by a more accessible station at Derker, less than half a mile to the south.

There remains a certain amount, though not that much, still to see for explorers of these routes. Let us start at Werneth, or perhaps arrive from Manchester by tram at the new Freehold tram station, just a short distance to the south-west. Werneth tunnel and the trackbed immediately south were briefly used by Metrolink services between 2012 and 2014, but the platforms at Werneth station are long gone and the tunnel is in private, commercial use. The incline can be accessed just west of the former junction and, though not an official right of way, paths exist parallel to the line and the gradient heading down away from Oldham can still be appreciated. A better path exists on a short branch built slightly further north in 1914 to serve a coal depot at Chadderton. The Chadderton line saw its last official service in June 1987, although a branch Line Society brake van tour may have run slightly later (Joe Brown has the last train to reach the depot as late as 8 August 1993). An official footpath now runs from the east side of the former crossing of the Rochdale Canal east of Middleton Junction through to the coal depot area, though this is now built on with modern housing.

The Middleton branch is mostly landscaped but its basic route can be followed with little difficulty for the most part, though the station area has long been built over by industrial premises. The Royton branch is less accessible; there being no way of getting to the former junction station site. From a passing tram nothing remains visible anyway other than overgrown formation at the start of the route west. North-west of where the line formerly passed under the B6194 Oldham–Shaw road a path runs parallel to the course of the former road, though this quickly becomes an anonymous urban footpath and the station site itself is covered by a small estate of modern flats.

Oldham–Greenfield and the Delph Branch

These two lines were originally built quite separately but traditionally came as a pair as generally they were served by the same trains. The Huddersfield to Manchester main line through the valley had opened in 1849 and it was only just over a year later that what became the L&NWR opened its branch to Delph, where a number of textile mills also benefitted from a rail link. The line into Oldham, much more challenging to build, came along five years later with services starting from Oldham's Clegg Street station, also serving a station at Glodwick Road, before heading out of town to the east. The line was briefly extended beyond Delph station in the 1880s to supply materials for the construction of Castleshaw Reservoirs, though no trace of this route survives. It should also be noted that until the 1974 local government reforms, Delph and the townships of Saddleworth were actually in Yorkshire (further examples of this 'transfer' will appear later in the book), though Oldham was always the nearest town to visit for shopping and other facilities. Just west of the Delph line junction a halt opened at Dobcross in 1912, though it was not designated as such until 1938 and there is some confusion over whether or not it started as a staffed station. Measurements Halt followed in 1932; with two intermediate stopping points on such a short branch, locals never had a long walk to get to their train. But Delph to Oldham by train was a circuitous route and other nearby villages such as Denshaw had no railway at all, so the area was better served by buses. Closure of the Delph line to passengers came in April 1955, though freight, eventually down to one train a week, clung on for a further eight years.

The Oldham–Greenfield line lasted just a few more weeks, closing in May the same year. Heading east out of Oldham, the landscape becomes hilly, necessitating a series of cuttings, ledges, and embankments as well as the 1,332-yard Lydgate Tunnel (unusually for a tunnel, built at a 1 in 100 gradient, inclined down towards Greenfield). Having closed to all traffic in 1964 and with track having been lifted by the end of that year, a process of infilling cuttings and overbridges, together with general landscaping of the

Grotton station, Oldham–Greenfield line, 1997. *Gordon Suggitt*

surroundings, started to take place. Between 1964 and 1986 much was lost, and it wasn't until July 1986 that a linear path was completed along the route from a point just south of the former Oldham Mumps station as far as the station site at Grotton, with the result that, although it follows the route, much of the path lies above the level of the original formation. So, whilst still a very worthy effort, the path doesn't really compare for authenticity with others built on the actual formation.

Delph station, terminus of the eponymous branch line.
Author

Nothing remains at the sites of Glodwick Road and Lees stations, with no sign either of the old engine shed at the latter location. A couple of underbridges survive, and the route when explored by the author on a cold, sunny, late autumn day in 2021 was a very pleasant walk indeed. At Grotton, the stationmaster's house survives along with the eastbound platform, though much of it is now hidden under bushes and brambles. The cutting that leads to the west portal of Lydgate tunnel, once quite accessible (as reported by Gordon Suggitt in 1997), is now very wet and, without a proper footpath, the blocked up tunnel portal cannot be reached. Perhaps it is still possible after a prolonged period of dry weather. East of Lydgate Tunnel, the landscape has a quite different feel, with transport arteries squeezed into the narrow valley of the River Tame and Saddleworth Moor brooding darkly just opposite. The blocked up east portal of the tunnel can just about be viewed from the A670 road at Grasscroft but there is virtually no accessible trackbed between there and the junction with the main line just before Greenfield station.

Turning to the Delph branch, despite its short length of only 1½ miles, it is very much worth a visit. The line can be picked up at the first underbridge to the east of its junction with the main line and can be walked, virtually in its entirety, to the terminus. Delph station is beautifully preserved by its loving owner with a clock and other railwayana on display, indeed at one time housing a small museum, but these days is surrounded by a small estate of modern houses.

Rochdale–Bacup

Bacup was first served via the line from Rawtenstall through the Rossendale Valley (see Chapter 8) and the later Rochdale line was always known as the 'New Line' to the extent of a parallel road in Bacup being given, and still retaining, that name. The L&YR's route to Bacup was driven through quite unpromising territory and the severe gradients involved were a key factor in its early demise. The climb to over 900ft at Britannia, together with a steep descent back down into Bacup, meant that through freight traffic was very limited and this summit was indeed the first part of the line to close completely. Opening in its entirety by 1881, but with a main road parallel, from the beginning it was in competition with more frequent trams, and later buses, operating on effectively the same route. Passenger trains ceased as early as 1947, though freight hung on as far as Facit until 1963 and Whitworth in 1967.

The history of this line after closure is quite complex, with some sections faring much better than others, and if you wish to explore both the 'new line' and its tramroad offshoots onto the east side of the Rossendale moors (Chapter 19), a couple of days are needed to do it justice. A notable early post-closure feature was the use of Britannia Tunnel as a setting for the film *Whistle Down the Wind*, made in 1961 and starring Hayley Mills. The story revolved round the discovery of a bearded man, in reality an escaped killer, who is found hiding in the tunnel and is mistaken for Jesus by some young siblings.

Let us start, though, at the Rochdale end. The junction with the main line lay just east of that with the former Oldham loop line, and a short section of trackbed leading down to the junction can be accessed from the north via the B6266, Entwistle Street. The viaduct over Yorkshire Street just north of here was an early casualty, demolished in 1972 though not without incident – a supposedly controlled explosion to demolish one arch led to a chain reaction taking out a further ten. From Yorkshire Street, the line heads north then west with a path either on or to the side of what are long since filled in cuttings as it heads out of Rochdale. Nothing is left of the station at Wardleworth nor at Shawclough, where modern housing occupies the site. But shortly after Shawclough, one of the best accessible sections of trackbed, covering around a mile and a half of trackbed, is reached. Climbing steadily, mostly on a ledge with higher ground to the east, the views become increasingly rural and offer a sense of heading up into unspoilt country.

This terrain was not easy to push a railway through, and evidence of the problems encountered can soon be seen. Around 400 yards north of Healey Dell is a remarkable 'double bridge'. The original one, together with a short section of embankment on either side, slid down the hillside during construction but was left in place to help support a second bridge, one that went on to carry the formation without incident throughout its time as a working railway. Healey Dell viaduct, striding 105ft over the eponymous Dell, owes its survival to having had gas pipes laid across it and can provide two quite different experiences; in summer a feeling of being up amongst the treetops of the surrounding woodland and in winter

Rochdale–Bacup line, Broadley station platform. *Author*

Rochdale–Bacup line, Healey Dell Viaduct, 2003. *Gordon Suggitt*

stunning views of what are often snow-capped moors to both the east and the west. Carrying just a single track, the viaduct has a sense of elegance not matched by many of our region's other large viaducts and is very much worth seeing from below as well as at track level. North of Healey Dell lies Broadley station, which had just a single platform though a passing loop was provided for goods traffic. The platform still stands, together with a noticeable square-shaped 'gap' at the north end where a signal box once stood. Just past Broadley the courses of two narrow-gauge lines can be seen heading west. Here two tramways used to head west: first the Bagden Quarry Tramway, of 3ft gauge, in operation between around 1871 and 1900. Apart from a short section that lies within walled off water board property, most of this line can be followed, the main features being a long self-operated incline and the remains of an engine shed close to the quarry. The later Spring Mill Tramway (1910–1950s) was a much smaller affair of around half a mile long and served the eponymous mill.

Access ends at the south side of Whitworth, where a residential care home occupies the site of the station, though the approach down from a bridge just to the north can still be seen. North of here the former line has been converted to a residential road, with modern housing either side, though the sites of former level crossings, their roads lined with older terraces, still stand out. At Facit, the road ends but there is little to be seen other then another incline, with an industrial chimney still standing at its side, that led up to a further series of tramways on the moor to the west. North of Facit the line is partially built over until the trackbed can be regained at Millgate and followed to Shawforth.

With two such similarly named stations as Shawclough and Shawforth on the same line I have often wondered if any travellers ever confused the two and got off at the wrong place. But having reached Shawforth, the modern explorer finds a quite unusual remnant; no platforms or station buildings but an underpass still intact and used as a right of way to link two parts of the village. After a short diversion past another street of modern housing the trackbed can be regained, climbing steadily, and soon a superb, latticed footbridge is reached, a remarkable survivor. Approaching the line's summit, a cutting has been filled in next to the A671 road, taking with it any remains of the former island platform at Britannia, closed as early as 1917. The line continues north as a public path heading west, with yet another quarry tramway incline heading up onto the moors, though this one is private and almost entirely inaccessible.

Passing under the main road, the south portal of Britannia Tunnel is reached; this tunnel is privately owned these days, in commercial use and not accessible, though in previous years organised visits from the Railway Ramblers Club have been permitted and indeed conducted by the friendly and knowledgeable owner. North of here, the trackbed is lost under an industrial estate and nothing remains of the former engine shed,

Rochdale–Bacup line, footbridge north of Shawforth, 2003. *Gordon Suggitt*

situated half a mile south of Bacup station. A short, unofficially accessible section can be walked before large industrial premises cover both the throat of the junction with the Rossendale line and the station itself, although again an approach road survives.

Rochdale–Bacup line, east portal of Britannia Tunnel, 2005. *Phillip Earnshaw*

12
East Lancashire and Blackburn

The East Lancashire Main Line– Stubbins Junction to Accrington

It was noted in the previous chapter how the towns of Oldham and Ashton grew quickly as the result of rapid development of the cotton industry. The same situation very much applied in east Lancashire with a string of towns from Blackburn right through to Colne, all originally served by the Leeds & Liverpool Canal, which brought coal and other raw materials in and took the finished produce outwards. Bury became a railway centre, as discussed earlier, and from there the East Lancashire Railway drove a line through Ramsbottom and Haslingden to reach Accrington by August 1848, though the still-open line from Blackburn, owned by the same company, had arrived two months earlier. Accrington, as a town, has always been slightly in the shadow of its two close neighbours, Blackburn and Burnley, and indeed only became a municipal borough in 1878. Nevertheless, for many years the town prospered, with profitable cotton mills and brickworks providing plentiful employment and goods of all kinds to be found for sale in the splendid market hall.

Returning to the railway, cotton and coal kept this route profitable for many years but it never gained traction as a trunk passenger route and local trains became less patronised, as they so often did elsewhere. Baxenden station closed in 1951, followed later by Haslingden in November 1960, and the whole route north of Stubbins closed in December 1966, though goods traffic reached the goods depot at Scaitcliffe Street, on Accrington's south to west curve, for a further year. Although the East Lancs line could have been considered a duplicate of the Bolton–Blackburn route, the latter line has since those days rarely had any direct services heading into east Lancashire. Indeed, with the effective closure of passenger traffic into Yorkshire via the Copy Pit route towards Todmorden in 1965 the line east of Accrington was, in operational terms, pretty much a dead-end branch to Colne. On the subject of Copy Pit, it is worth taking a moment to reflect on how close that line came to its own closure: regular freight traffic had ended in 1982 but by then plans to reintroduce a passenger service had been given the green light, commencing in October 1984, although Burnley Manchester Road station, serving what was obviously the largest town en route, did not open its doors again for a further two years. What Accrington and indeed Burnley had lacked after closure of the Haslingden line was a direct service into Manchester, leaving the two towns effectively quite isolated from the main rail network. After many years of campaigning and a wholly unnecessary further two-year delay, the west curve at Todmorden was finally reopened in 2015, allowing direct trains to reach Manchester via Rochdale. Whilst this provides a passably direct service into Manchester Victoria from Burnley, from

Bury to Accrington line, decking of Lumb Viaduct prior to restoration, 2012. The gap in the security fencing is clear from its shadow! *Author*

East Lancashire Railway at Helmshore station, 1970.
Author's collection

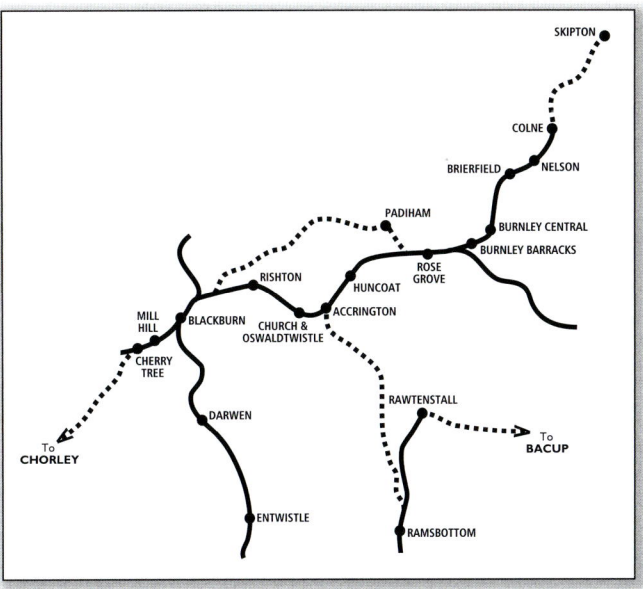

Map showing lines in the Blackburn and East Lancashire area.

Accrington it represents quite a roundabout route and one that does not compare well timewise with either driving or catching one of the frequent express buses.

Much of the old ELR remains to see and explore; unlike several other lines discussed in these pages, access has improved in recent years, with additional sections of track being opened up for walkers. Stubbins station, on the Rawtenstall line just north of the junction (curiously the Accrington line never had platforms here), is a second example, after Ewood Bridge & Edenfield, of a station on the current preserved East Lancashire Railway that was never reopened. However, the subway that provided access to the platforms remains open and views of the blocked up stairways to the platforms may still be seen; the platforms can be also viewed from an overgrown former car park on the west side of the former main line. The closed line is quickly picked up from here, unofficial but still well-used at first, then an officially designated path north of Strongstry. For some distance the line runs parallel to the Rossendale line, whilst gaining height, so on occasions a walk can be enlivened by the passing of a steam-hauled train. North of Alderbottom Viaduct, the first of two over a loop of the River Irwell, the trail used to end, but with the help of Railway Paths Ltd the formerly inaccessible and overgrown Lumb Viaduct has been cleared, resurfaced and was reopened to walkers in 2015. From here, another half a mile of trackbed has been provided with a hard-wearing material before access ends at a former bridge just north-west of Irwell Vale.

The section south of Helmshore, mostly in a deep cutting, though nowadays private and overgrown, is notable as at one time a miniature railway operated along the formation. This was certainly in use in the late 1990s but was closed around 2010 or possibly a little earlier. The track has been taken up in recent years and only the foundation of a turntable remains. The three-arched Ravenshore Viaduct remains intact though, if gently rusting away in a secluded spot where it crosses the River Ogden.

The next point of interest is the site of Helmshore station. After the line closed, a group of local residents and enthusiasts came together to try and save the line in the form of the Helmshore and District Railway Preservation Society. They took on the lease of Helmshore station in May 1967, but in April 1968 they gave up after their attempts had failed and the society was disbanded. However, from this meeting the East Lancashire Railway Preservation Society was born, with a more modest remit of reopening Stubbins Junction to Haslingden (Grane Road) as a preserved railway for enthusiasts, tourists, and schoolchildren. Discussions dragged on with British Rail until 1971, when they were given notice that the line would be lifted; indeed, this was to take place in October of that year. Now isolated in Helmshore, the preservation group were forced to cast their eyes elsewhere and found their forever home further south. Helmshore station survived until the mid-1980s, the signal box lasted until 1989 and the wooden goods shed was demolished in 2002. Today the stationmaster's house survives as a private residence, as does a concrete lamp post in front of a replica signal box-style building that was completed in 1990; but the site of the station itself, on the north side of the former level crossing is now a housing development.

Beyond Helmshore, another footpath follows the railway formation, crossing two low, seven-arch, viaducts which are separated by a large retaining wall. These viaducts cross the River Ogden and the reservoir that served Higher Mill and Whitakers Mill; these two mills now forming part of the Helmshore Mills Textile Museum. Both Lumb Viaduct and the Helmshore Viaducts are Grade II listed structures.

Above: East Lancashire Railway, in the 1990s a now abandoned miniature railway was laid on the trackbed south of Helmshore, 2002. *Author*

Left: East Lancashire Railway, Baxenden station, northbound platform, 2022. *Author*

The railway walk ends at Grane Road, Haslingden, and north of this point much of the formation beyond has been lost to the A56 dual carriageway, which was constructed in the early 1980s. This included North Hag Tunnel (146 yards) and the entire site of Haslingden station. The formation only emerges from the A56 in Rising Bridge and access resumes at the north end of the Holland Pies factory at Baxenden. Both platforms of Baxenden station survive, but curiously, whilst the northbound platform remains lie within the factory grounds (still visible through a metal fence), the remaining stub of the southbound platform lies open next to a path. A fine surviving goods shed also lies in the pie factory premises. From here the line descends a challenging 1-in-38 gradient down Baxenden Bank to Accrington and can be enjoyed as it forms an official path. The trail ends

Right: Former viaduct over Accrington Mill Pond, 2002.
Phillip Earnshaw

Below: From the same viewpoint as the previous photograph, with a causeway now laid along the base of the Mill Pond Viaduct, but the pillars remain, 2017. *Author*

beyond a Mill Pond at Accrington, which was crossed by another structure in the past, the piers of which still stand. The triangular arrangement with the Colne route has long been swept away and the existing Accrington station is a shadow of its former self. Gone are the buildings, though a new ticket office has been provided in recent years, but the footbridge still survives, albeit without its original top, along with the Colne line platforms.

The North Lancashire or Great Harwood Loop

The East Lancashire Railway's original route east of Blackburn served many but not all of the area's growing mill towns. In particular, Great Harwood and Padiham were not rail served, despite their increasingly busy cotton mills and the need to both bring in and take out supplies. It was not until 1877, having opened from the west in stages, that the railway was completed, in the form of a loop from Blackburn, north of the existing line to Padiham Junction just west of Rose Grove station. Although as a passenger route, traffic remained local apart from occasional diversionary and excursion trains, goods traffic developed beyond its original purpose to serve a coal mine at Martholme, and, more importantly, a large power station on the west side of Padiham. There were actually two power stations, Padiham 'A' in operation from 1927 to 1969 and 'B' from 1962 to 1993. Regular passenger traffic ceased in December 1957, but excursions continued until 1963, with the loop west of the power station(s) closing the following year. As noted above, coal traffic from Padiham Junction up to the power station ceased in 1993 but track remained in situ for more than ten years until funding was found and permission given for construction of a greenway.

The post-closure history of this line is of more interest than most and is worthy of quite detailed discussion. It is also ongoing, with a local group campaigning and gradually restoring sections of trackbed back into private use: search on social media for 'Martholme Greenway' for further updates. So let us start our visit from the Rose Grove end. Visitors walking down to the line from Rose Grove station pass the site of Rose Grove Shed, one of the 'final three' (along with Lostock Hall and Carnforth) to survive until the end of steam traction on 5 August 1968. The site was demolished in February 1975 and much of it now lies under the M65 motorway that runs parallel to the existing railway, though two rusty gates that gave road and pedestrian access into the back of the shed remain in place. Padiham Junction is fenced off, but a short section can be accessed unofficially just off the canal towpath underneath the motorway bridge; until recently a permanently red-coloured light signal guarded the now non-existent junction. The official path, opened in June 2010 and

Left: East Lancashire loop line, track at Padiham, prior to lifting in 2002. *Author*

Below: East Lancashire loop line two years later (2004), with track lifted at Padiham. *Author*

Great Harwood loop; Martholme Viaduct, 2002. *Gordon Suggitt*

known as the Padiham Greenway, starts a little to the north, at the end of Molly Wood Lane, and continues, on a noticeable 1 in 40 gradient down into Padiham. Padiham station is long gone but its site, on a curve above the town, remains identifiable though in recent years modern housing has been built behind it on the former goods yard. West of the station the path continues across a three-arched bridge over the River Calder, though this bridge, together with a smaller adjacent footbridge, was closed in June 2021, apparently needing quite substantial repairs. Just a little further on, the power station site is reached, with a short section of track together with a buffer stop marking the location and two rusty gates guarding the former entrance. The power station site itself is now built over with modern light industry but the greenway continues past, the official path ending at the crossing of the A6068 road. This road post-dates the railway, so there was never a bridge or level crossing here.

Accessing the trackbed on the west side of this road, we enter a wholly different environment. This marks the point from which the Martholme Greenway organisation has been given permission to access the trackbed and within a few yards a new footbridge built on former abutments gives a safe crossing over Dean Brook. Improvements to the trackbed west of here towards Simonstone Lane are very much work in progress, though at the time of writing no exit onto the lane has yet been built. However, the new path does allow access to the remains of Simonstone station for the first time in many years; part of the westbound platform remains in place, as does a now rather dilapidated goods shed on private land just to the north. On the west side of Simonstone Lane, on the south side of a former rail over road bridge, steps lead up onto the first of two sections that have been fully restored by the Greenway. Former bridges have been replaced and the line provides very pleasant walking indeed for the best part of a mile into Gooseleach Wood. West of here the line remains intact, but in private hands, and there is no immediate likelihood of access.

Let us now turn to Martholme viaduct. Prior to the 2001 outbreak of foot and mouth disease the viaduct was unofficially open and, together with the paved trackbed to the east, was a regular route for locals. However, by 2002, the viaduct was securely fenced off at both ends, together with the adjacent section of trackbed close to a caravan park. The viaduct later came into the care of Railway Paths Ltd and fortunately has remained in excellent condition since closure with only minimal maintenance required. In recent years the viaduct has been opened, but with access from the south end only as negotiations for access with the landowner of the trackbed beyond have not been successful. Hopefully, readers of this book in future years will be able to reflect on a successful resolution to this issue. South of the viaduct is an official path as far as Mill Lane, together with a path on a short branch to Martholme Colliery, used between 1900 and 1921. Approaching Great Harwood, the trackbed is rather fragmented, and the station itself was demolished in 1965, though the site can be identified without difficulty at the south end of Station Road.

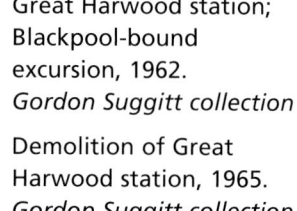

Great Harwood station; Blackpool-bound excursion, 1962. *Gordon Suggitt collection*

Demolition of Great Harwood station, 1965. *Gordon Suggitt collection*

West of Great Harwood station the route can be followed for some distance without difficulty although generally on top of or just to the side of filled in cuttings; this operation having taken place between 1972 and 1976. After passing Norden, on the north side of Rishton, one last section of trackbed is accessible before all trace is lost. The cuttings here were filled in as early as 1969–70 and returned to agricultural use, whilst the final section just to the east of Great Harwood Junction has long since been lost under light industry and large retail units.

Blackburn (Cherry Tree)–Chorley

Blackburn's other closed line, heading south-west through a series of villages to Chorley, effectively formed part of a series of lines linking the coalfields around Wigan and St Helens with the cotton towns of east Lancashire. After protracted negotiations, these lines were eventually developed jointly by the L&NWR and L&YR and indeed both companies, forming what became known as the Lancashire Union Railway (LUR), took responsibility for operating Blackburn to Chorley services. There were two separate routes from Chorley to Wigan (see Chapters 7 and 8), and it is notable that all three lines closed to passengers at almost the same time in 1960.

The Cherry Tree line opened to passengers in December 1869 but never really developed as a route for through traffic, the route up the West Coast Main Line and along the curve at Farington via Bamber Bridge to Blackburn being a faster and more straightforward alternative.

However, local goods traffic was plentiful and varied, with a brickworks, a quarry and a mill at Withnell, printworks at Brinscall and bleachworks at Heapey all having their own sidings. Perhaps the most interesting offshoot, however, were the sidings that served the ROF works and storage facilities north of Heapey, like many such lines not marked on OS maps until after closure. The use of these sidings for storage of condemned steam locomotives, even after the through route had closed, added to the intrigue. Although the Heapey Bleachworks branch closed in 1952, a number of the other facilities still required rail access and the line remained in use throughout for freight and diverted traffic until January 1966. The eventual closure of the line was, in part, a result of a need to create space for the new M61 Manchester to Preston motorway, which was to run past the east side of Chorley; it is also worth noting that this motorway also severed and led to the closure of the Walton Summit Arm of the Lancaster Canal. The nine-arched Botany Bay Viaduct was the main obstacle, and a crowd of over 3,000 gathered to see its demolition by controlled explosion one cold morning in November 1968.

Exploring the Cherry Tree to Chorley line makes a fascinating day out; even though as a route it is now quite fragmented, there is plenty left to see. Let us start at Cherry Tree station, where a goods shed remains, in private use, and look over the bridge at the west end of the station. It can be seen that Cherry Tree Junction was more a deviation of height than direction as the Chorley and Preston lines remain parallel but the former immediately starts to climb away before it turns south. The formation here is private and inaccessible but the railway rambler cannot fail to miss the three-arch viaduct, striding over the A674 road east of Feniscowles. In the early years of this century the top of the viaduct could be accessed via a path leading north of the former crossing of the Leeds & Liverpool Canal, but this has long since been blocked off. Little is accessible for the next mile or so, but the issue of access at Stanworth, where a short siding formerly led into the Withnell Brick & Terracotta Works, is worthy of note. Current OS maps show a path north from New Close Farm, alongside the old line, but ending without access to other routes. In 2021 the landowners gained permission to close this path, presumably once used by brickworks employees living in Abbey Village, and signage indicates that public access here is no longer permitted.

South of New Close Farm the old formation can be clearly on the west side of the access road to the farm and soon Withnell station is reached. This station has been in private ownership, indeed the same ownership, since being bought from British Railways in the late 1960s and retains both platforms and the main station building. At one time the owner laid a miniature railway along the platforms and around the site, and remnants of this can also be seen.

Blackburn–Chorley line, Withnell station. *Nick Melling*

Blackburn to Chorley line, nameboard of Withnell station. *Nick Melling*

Blackburn to Chorley line, wartime storage sidings for perishable goods at Brinscall with their outline still identifiable between the trees. *Author*

South of Withnell station the line forms an official path as far as Brinscall, at first a path in a deep cutting, now designated a nature reserve, then in a more landscaped area as far as Brinscall, where only the approach road and part of a loading bay survive at the station site.

West of Brinscall the line is built over by housing but can be seen again at a former occupational level crossing, south of Brinscall Hall. Soon the site of the former ROF sidings is reached; this area maintained an aura of secrecy right into the second decade of this century with locked crossing gates and 'no photography' signs, but apart from a couple of small bridges remains of the sidings are now minimal. At Heapey station, the main building remains but now forms part of a much larger residence with the platforms now removed and replaced by boarding kennel facilities. The former Railway Inn opposite the station can still be identified as such, but sadly it stopped serving liquid refreshment in 1999. West of Heapey, a short branch headed south to serve a bleachworks, passing over an embankment between two reservoirs that makes a pleasant short walk, though the works themselves are long gone and the site built on by modern housing. Approaching Chorley, the line remains mostly intact but not publicly accessible until reaching the Leeds & Liverpool Canal and the M61 motorway where the viaduct once stood. The descent to the Preston line has short sections accessible, but much is now built over or used for commercial purposes here.

Colne to Skipton and its Offshoots

Colne was originally the end-on junction of two quite separate lines, that from Skipton (originally the Leeds & Bradford Extension Railway, later the Midland Railway) arriving in 1848 and the East Lancashire Railway's branch from Accrington opening the following year. Despite happily sharing the station, no timetabled through trains ran until 1876, by which time other cross-Pennine routes had become more established. In 1880, the opening of the Hellifield route to the west reduced the Colne line's importance even further, and it is fair to say that traffic, on what was gradient-wise the easiest of all the Pennine crossings, never reached its full potential. This line also served the small town of Earby, moved from Yorkshire to Lancashire by boundary changes in 1974, which, as can be imagined, was not the most popular of such moves.

Local, intermediate, traffic was never numerous and Elslack station, serving a small, isolated community, was the first to close, in March 1952, with Foulridge, a much smaller place then than it is now, following in January 1959. School traffic from Barnoldswick and Earby was an important factor in keeping the line going as long as it did; a somewhat amusing early 1960s account exists of the efforts that the railway made to make to keep the teenage boys and girls apart from each other as they travelled to and from their respective grammar schools in Skipton. Closure, in February 1970, has never been fully accepted locally and hindsight suggests that it was a poor decision, severing a key link between east Lancashire and Yorkshire.

Close by was the larger town of Barnoldswick, proud producer of Rolls-Royce jet engines and terminus of its own short branch from Earby, which closed in September 1965. The Barnoldswick branch, always known locally as the 'Barlick Spud' (Barlick being the town's shortened name/nickname) had opened as an independent line in 1871 but traffic was operated from the start by the Midland Railway, who took the line over formally in 1899. Despite being a larger town than any settlements on the main route, Barnoldswick never had more than a couple of daily services beyond Earby to Skipton. Although it is right and proper to include this line in a book on north-west railways, it should not be forgotten that Barnoldswick was very much part of the West Riding of Yorkshire during the life of the line and thus looked to Skipton and beyond for shopping and other services. Accordingly, the junction with the Barnoldswick branch was built facing north and there was little expectation of significant traffic from either Barnoldswick or Earby heading south to Colne or Burnley.

So let us start our explorations at Colne station, perhaps having ridden up on the train from Burnley. It says a good deal about how unpromising the future of local railways was judged to be in the early 1970s that Colne station was demolished altogether in 1971 and its generous facilities were replaced by a small 'bus shelter'. The abandoned northbound platform, now quite degraded, lies next to a grassy area fenced off from the current running line. The closed line can be picked up from the north end of the surviving platform, and after crossing the A6068 Colne bypass enters a long cutting as it heads north. Quite walkable after dry weather though generally at least slightly wet underfoot, most of the way an alternative path exists on the west side of the cutting. Continuing north and passing the Foulridge Canal Tunnel, the trackbed can be followed right through to the outskirts of Foulridge.

Little remains at Foulridge other than a mound of earth where the platform used to be; the station building does survive but now resides at Ingrow West on the Keighley & Worth Valley Railway. The site of the goods yard is now covered by flats and the bridge over the Leeds & Liverpool Canal has also gone.

On the other (east) side of the canal things improve, as there is a delightful café, then access onto an embankment where an official footpath can be picked up that takes the walker all the way into Earby. Just south of Earby Junction there was an ordnance factory, in use during the First War and into the 1920s, with extensive sidings, though the site was returned to agricultural use afterwards and little remains except for a widened formation at this point.

Diverting to Barnoldswick, a supermarket has been built on the station site, but a retaining wall and surrounding houses may still be seen and these help to identify the precise position of the platform and station building. Heading out of Barnoldswick, what in 2008 was a pleasant walk along a low embankment has now vanished; similarly, access is not straightforward onto an embankment to the east of the long-gone canal bridge. With the next section built over with modern housing, all that is left to easily explore is a (private) short stretch close to the junction. Back on the main line and heading into Earby, the official path continues, though this is narrow in places as some homeowners have taken the opportunity to extend their back gardens onto the formation; it is not clear whether or not they had permission to do this and clearly these pockets of land would have to be bought back should the railway ever reopen. At Earby a goods shed and the Station Hotel survive, but a mound marking part of a platform is the only remnant of a once quite substantial station.

Access remains straightforward as the line passes through and beyond the northern outskirts of Earby, soon reaching Thornton in Craven station. Here is the best preserved of all the stations on this line, with both platforms (though the northbound platform is rather hidden away behind a hedge) and the stationmaster's house still in reasonable order. Just north of here a short branch headed west to a stone quarry on the opposite side of the A56 road. A short tunnel passes under the road, once quite accessible but now securely fenced off and flooded at its southern portal. Heading north to Elslack, the line is well used as a public path, though not clearly designated as such. As mentioned above, Elslack station was an early closure, in 1952, and the site is covered by light industry, though an adjacent row of cottages that appear in old photographs helps to identify the site.

North of Elslack there is no public access, though most of the formation is intact and the Railway Ramblers Club have previously gained permission to walk a section of around 3 miles that runs through the Tempest Estate. Approaching Skipton, a viaduct over the Aire and an adjacent lane was demolished in 1989, leaving a short, isolated section of embankment before the existing line to Hellifield is reached west of Skipton.

The Colne to Skipton line has an active group campaigning for its restoration and feasibility studies have demonstrated that restoration is possible, with the reconstruction of two major bridges and a way of crossing over or passing under the Colne bypass being the key issue. An earlier plan for the railway to be converted into a road, in fact the reason why the line was not sold off piecemeal after closure, seems now not to be on the agenda. Support for restoration has been forthcoming from local politicians of all parties but at present there is no sign of the necessary funding becoming available.

Colne to Skipton line, Thornton in Craven station, a 2022 view looking south. The northbound platform is intact but hidden behind the hedge. *Author*

Colne to Skipton line, a tunnel on a short branch to Thornton Rock Quarry, north of Thornton in Craven station. *Author*

13
Preston, Blackpool and Southport

Preston–Southport

The visitor to Preston cannot help but be impressed by Preston station, noticeably busy and bustling throughout the day, and with trains heading out to almost every point on the compass. All, that is, except south-westwards, where the direct Preston to Southport line closed in September 1964. Originally served by a separate station on Fishergate, half a mile or so to the west of the current station, the West Lancashire Railway had received its Royal Assent in 1871. But, having encountered both financial and geological problems (notably a bed of unstable sticky clay in Penwortham cutting), the line was not up and running until September 1882, though it did open a couple of weeks early to accommodate traffic for the Preston Guild, a series of community events in the city held just once every twenty years. By 1896 the now insolvent West Lancashire Railway was absorbed by the L&YR, who made some significant changes. A triangle, built on embankments, was constructed south of the river at Penwortham. Curves were built eastwards from Ribble Junction and Penwortham Junction, twenty-six chains to the south, to Middleforth Junction, from which the East Lancashire Railway's route into Preston's main station could be accessed. As a result, Fishergate station (popularly, and later officially, known as Fishergate Hill) closed in July 1900, just eighteen years after opening. This station, boasting just a single island platform, perhaps surprisingly remained in use for storage of stock and goods traffic until January 1965. The building was used for commercial purposes for a while but was eventually demolished and the site is now covered by modern housing (Colman Court). Heading south, after a short embankment and the site of a low, long-gone, twelve-arch, masonry viaduct, the crossing of the River Ribble is reached. This bridge had six piers supporting five iron spans around 50ft long. From the 1930s the bridge also carried a gas pipeline and when in 1968 the intermediate spans were removed, the piers remained in place to carry the gas pipe, a situation that remains today.

South of the Ribble lies the Penwortham Triangle, all three sides on embankments and nowadays with a static caravan site occupying the space in between. A public footpath runs parallel to the main route, from Ribble Junction to Penwortham Junction, the embanked track being largely overgrown and inaccessible at this point. South of Penwortham Junction very little remains at all, with roads and reclaimed farmland eradicating virtually the whole trackbed until Hoole station is reached, south of the minor road heading west to the south-west of Walmer Bridge. Here, slight remains of platforms can be seen, together with a very degraded level crossing gate. The formation is again lost for a while south of Hoole, but a 600-yard embankment leading to the former bridge over the River Douglas east of Hesketh Bank can still be enjoyed. This bridge consisted of an iron structure with a central pier that could swing to allow tall boats to pass. Records suggest that the bridge last opened in 1913, after which it was welded into place and additional piling was provided around the pier for added protection. It was demolished soon after the line closed in 1964. Today, only the abutments on either side remain; although the east side is clear, the western abutment can take a little finding behind summer vegetation.

Moving now to the west side of the river (a diversion of around 4 miles to the next bridge and back is required for anyone attempting a through route), a short branch just 1¼ miles long was built from Hesketh Bank, parallel to the River Douglas, south towards the riverside township of Tarleton. Opened for goods at the same time as the main route, a passenger service was started in June 1912 to complement the introduction of faster and more frequent railmotor services from Southport to Preston. Unfortunately, this proved uneconomic from the start and became one of the region's most short-lived passenger branch lines, closing less than sixteen months later, in October 1913. Provision of goods traffic, though apparently of little volume, continued until around 1925, when a track diagram records the line as being closed.

South of Tarleton, the line crossed flatter ground at the western edge of the West Lancashire Plain, passing through stations at Hundred End and Banks before reaching the outskirts of Southport at Crossens. At Banks the remains of one platform survives, alongside a public footpath, but part of the formation has been lost to a drainage ditch along this length. Moving on to Crossens, here the stationmaster's house survives, though now surrounded by modern buildings. From here into Southport, a quite different service was provided, as this station was the terminus of the eponymous 'Crossens Electrics'. This frequent and very popular service ran from Southport via St Luke's station to Meols Cop, using only the western side of the island platform, where most services reversed (some took the west side of the Crossens Triangle), before heading north via Hesketh Park and Churchtown to Crossens. In addition, for a brief period around 1900, the L&YR ran trains from Preston to Liverpool that avoided Southport, taking the east curve at Meols Cop and proceeding to Liverpool via Downholland (see Chapter 6). South of Crossens, little survives other than a few bridges, allowing views of the extended gardens of suburban houses that have taken up nearly all of the formation here.

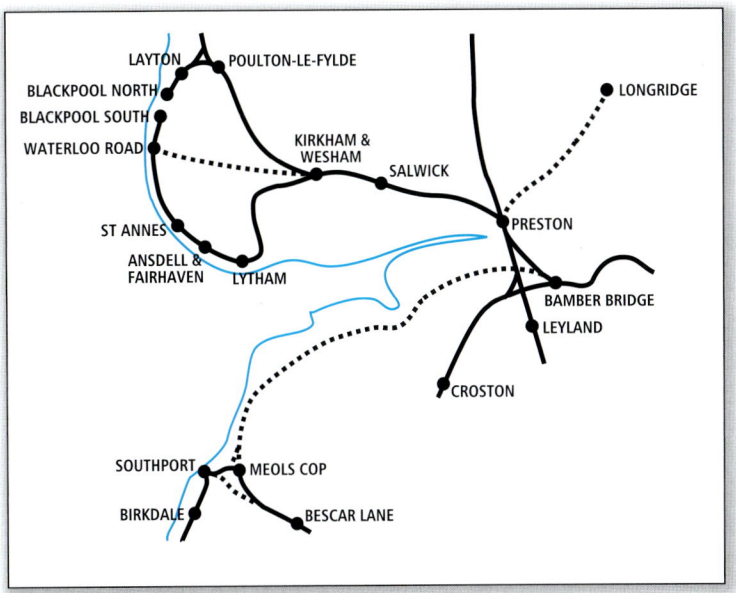

Map showing lines in the Preston area.

West Lancs Railway, Hundred End station shortly before closure in 1962. *Gordon Suggitt collection*

Above: West Lancs Railway; Stanier 4P No 42439 crossing the River Douglas in 1963 with the former 'rotating pier' in the left foreground. *Gordon Suggitt collection*

Left: Preston to Southport line, the surviving platform at Banks station. *Author*

Southport Central station, the original southern terminus of the West Lancashire Railway, had a remarkably similar history to its contemporary in Preston. Having opened in September 1882, it closed to passengers in May 1901 when traffic was diverted to the town's main station. Used as a goods station until December 1973, the building was demolished in 1982 and today a supermarket occupies the site. The best viewpoint is the footbridge at the south end of Windsor Road, where the original straight formation heading west into Central station can be viewed alongside the later slight curve needed to access the current station. To the east is the former 'straight' route out of Southport towards Burscough, with a filled in bridge under the A5267 (Ash Street) and modern housing behind. On the straight line there was a station at Blowick, closed in 1939, and a level crossing over Norwood Road just to the west, but unsurprisingly nothing of railway origin remains at these locations.

Preston–Longridge

The Longridge branch had a remarkably long (over 150 years of use) and varied history for a comparatively minor branch whose main line was less than 7 miles long. Although it closed to regular passenger traffic over ninety years ago, it benefitted at various times from four significant but very different types of freight traffic: quarry trains from Longridge, mixed freight to Whittingham Hospital, coal and other materials to Courtaulds' rayon factory and coal traffic to and from Deepdale yard.

The line opened in 1840 (thus preceding the Preston & Lancaster Junction Railway) as a horse-drawn route to carry stone from the quarries above Longridge to Preston and other Lancashire towns where ongoing building work had created a high demand. No record of the original gauge appears to exist, but it was unlikely to have been standard gauge, probably closer to 4ft. It was reported that loaded wagons heading down the gradient to Preston could reach speeds of up to 40mph, though the empties returned at a more sedate trotting pace. On 1 May 1840 a formal opening of the line to passenger services took place; these ran on Wednesdays and

Preston–Longridge line at Maudland Bridge, 2003. *Gordon Suggitt*

Saturdays only to a temporary terminus in Preston on Deepdale Street. No intermediate stops other than at Grimsargh were made and initially no proper stations were provided. At Longridge the nearby Towneley Arms provided facilities with a ticket office at the Plough Inn at Grimsargh providing the same role. Happily, the hospitality at both these pubs can still be enjoyed today.

In 1846 the local company sold out to the grandly named Fleetwood, Preston & West Riding Railway, who had received Parliamentary approval for a line from Grimsargh via Clitheroe to Elslack on the Skipton to Colne route. In 1847 work commenced at Hurst Green (a cutting was constructed south of this village that can still be seen to this day, see picture in Chapter 1) but little else was done and the project was abandoned. In 1848 the Longridge line was converted to locomotive haulage on standard gauge track. In 1870 a station building was constructed at Grimsargh and a permanent station at Longridge, attached to the Towneley Arms, was finally built in 1872. This was a single-storey building and a single platform; the layout being unusual in that at its southern end the platform faced a single track but then curved inwards to support a second track and a passing loop. Quarry traffic lasted until around 1920, though the track beyond Longridge yard to the works was not lifted until around 1943. This was thirteen years after the early closure to passengers, which was largely due to bus competition.

By 1889 a line from Grimsargh to the newly built Whittingham Hospital had been completed; this used a platform built specifically for the purpose, quite separate from the main Grimsargh station, north of the adjacent level crossing. Running until around 1957, it carried coal and other produce into the asylum but also provided a free, ad hoc, passenger service for staff and visitors. The 'main' line was last traversed in full by passengers on a Railway & Canal Historical Society railtour on 22 September 1962 to Longridge but a Branch Line Society Railtour reached Courtaulds siding on 25 October 1969, this siding to Courtaulds fabric works having operated from 1938 to 1980. The line's final use was to supply coal to Deepdale yard; these operations ceased in 1994.

Let us start our explorations at Preston station, where the branch can first be seen shortly after its junction with the Lancaster route, shortly followed by a bridge over the former course of the Lancaster Canal. Although rusty track remains, much clearing work was carried out by rail authorities in this area in 2021, though to what purpose is not entirely clear. Subsequently access here is blocked off by secure fencing (I know of people who walked through the tunnel unofficially in 2008), so the west portal of the 864 yards (in three parts) Maudlands Tunnel cannot currently be viewed. The tunnel's east portal can be seen more clearly, as can the remains of Deepdale station a little further on where one platform survives in a cutting

Above: Preston–Longridge line, Ribbleton station, 2002. *Gordon Suggitt*

Left: Longridge branch, sign at the Plough Inn, Grimsargh. *Author*

together with a much-altered station building at street level. The trackbed here is neither officially nor easily accessible, except by those agile enough to scale quite high walls, with the result that in recent years it has become quite overgrown. Next is the junction where traffic reversed to be propelled into Deepdale yard; a little further north of here access to the trackbed can finally be gained.

At this point the proposed 'Preston Tramway' should be discussed. As far back as 2010, plans were being submitted for a tramway along the branch, though heading past Deepdale Yard, rather than the original route through the tunnel, to run through roads into the University of Central Lancashire area and the city centre. Progress over the years since has been so slow, with virtually nothing happening on the ground, that many Preston people believe it will never happen, though two developments in 2021 give some reason for hope. The first is the clearing of land around the junction with the siding that led to the coal yard and the second is the acquisition by the tramway company of Ribbleton station. But before Ribbleton is reached, a pleasant suburban walk of just over a mile can be enjoyed, passing the platform of a halt that at one time unofficially served a nearby barracks. At Ribbleton itself the platform has gone but the station building has long been in a somewhat dilapidated state, often with animals such as goats tethered outside. Whether or not things will improve here following the change of ownership will presumably soon be seen.

After crossing a new footbridge over the M6 (the railway bridge having been demolished when the motorway was widened) and passing the junction with the former Courtaulds siding, a more rural section follows into Grimsargh, though not all is accessible. Currently there is no through path past the village's primary school either, though a route has been provided between the two crossings of the B6243 road in the village. Nothing of either the Longridge line station or the hospital railway platform remains, though 'Old Station Close' gives a helpful clue to the location of the former. Here the Whittingham Hospital branch used to curve away to the north-west, initially on a slight embankment. Fifteen to twenty years ago this route was a superb little expedition; remains of the hospital's concrete platform could be picked out, as could traces of a siding that continued across a grassy area to a coal store and where the outline of the sleepers used to reappear in the parched lawn after prolonged dry weather. The hospital was extraordinary too; huge buildings that formerly housed thousands of 'inmates' lying abandoned, their roofs having already been removed for their slate. A visit today, however, would find all these buildings swept away, being gradually replaced by a large housing development known as Guild Park. The best advice for a visitor today would be to head for the cricket ground; the coal siding ran on an east–west alignment just south of here, with the former station a couple of hundred yards to the east. Sadly, though, I expect that soon no remnants whatsoever of the railway will be left untouched in the old hospital grounds.

Returning to the main route, the section north to Longridge is largely private land through open fields but has been explored with permission in the past by the Railway Ramblers Club. Reaching Longridge, the station is now a visitor centre with exhibitions, local books for sale and a café providing cakes and coffee, though perhaps a more authentic end to one's day is a drink at the Towneley Arms next door where, so long ago, you could buy a ticket to Preston as well as a beer. Between Longridge station and the quarries to the east the line has long since disappeared under modern housing, but at Tootle Hill quarry a section of trackbed and a short, blocked off tunnel may still be found.

Longridge station building prior to development, 2002. *Gordon Suggitt*

Longridge station, a modern view. *Chris McFarlane*

The East Lancashire Railway South of Preston

Let us return to Preston station and note the eastern side with a section of platform curving sharply to the east before disappearing under a car park. This marks the site of the former East Lancashire Railway's platforms at Preston, giving access to an entirely separate route running south that linked with lines running east and west as well as onto the West Coast Main Line. The East Lancashire Railway also had a major goods terminus just east of Preston station at Butler Street, but this has long since been built over by a car park and shopping centre.

Opening in 1850, almost two years after the Wigan line had opened, what became known as the East Lancashire Railway's 'Preston Extension' headed south to a junction station at Todd Lane. Here, traffic could head east to Bamber Bridge and then to Blackburn or beyond, or alternatively head south to Lostock Hall Junction, where there was access to either the West Coast Main Line at Farington Junction or the line to Liverpool via Ormskirk, accessed at Moss Lane Junction. A further link was established in 1883 when the Whitehouse triangle was built, which allowed access to the West Lancashire's Railway's Southport line (described above), and particularly to allow Southport trains to use Preston's main station rather than the original one at Fishergate Hill.

As an obvious duplicate of other routes, the prospects for the 'extension' in modern times were poor. First to go, in 1968, was Todd Lane Junction, at times also known as Preston Junction, though hardly ever used as a junction with virtually all its traffic heading either in or out of Preston. In September 1972, the line south of Preston as far as Lostock Hall Gas Works, the link to Moss Lane Junction and the east curve to Bamber Bridge saw their last trains, with traffic to east Lancashire rerouted via Farington Curve Junction and Lostock Hall. Finally, in 1977 the Gas Works rail link went out of use and the rest of the system fell silent.

With the comparatively late closure and the convenience of the route as access from the south into Preston's city centre, much of the route is now an official path, albeit with some bridges removed. At Preston station, though, there is currently some confusion around where the trail should actually start. Despite public access to a car park next to the station on one side and clear evidence of a well-used path on the other, at present a metal fence blocks the right of way, close to a high bridge that leads to the impressively sited and former railway-owned Park Hotel. This hotel was sold off in 1949 by British Railways shortly after nationalisation and turned into offices but is still well worth a view in itself. Returning to the railway, after quite possibly having had to take a diversion through Avenham Park, the East Lancs viaduct over the River Ribble is reached, a haven of quiet compared with the busy viaduct just to the west. The East Lancs viaduct always carried foot passengers too, on its east side, but nowadays the railway formation is accessible too and generally that is the part of the bridge that people choose to use.

Heading south from here, the path is clear and wide and popular, though the south-west curve of the Whitehouse triangle is less distinct. Continuing south past the site of extensive sidings at the former gasworks, Todd Lane Junction station is reached. Here, where in the 1980s the outline of the island platform could easily be made out, it now lies in an official wetland, so anyone looking for remains of the station needs to equip themselves with a snorkel, flippers, and a very good wetsuit. Both curves from Todd Lane are truncated, the east curve as far as the new A6 dual carriageway, though a crossing keeper's cottage survives just north-west of Bamber Bridge Football Club, and access to the south curve ends at Brownedge Road. Walking into Bamber Bridge from here enables you to view a short-lived rail link, in operation between 1990 and 2000, that served the Bowker distribution centre, whose lorries are still a familiar site on our motorways.

East Lancs Railway, passenger deck of bridge over River Ribble, with former The Park Hotel in background, 2002. *Gordon Suggitt*

Preston Junction (Todd Lane) Station looking north, with the island platform still just about visible in 1988.
Phillip Earnshaw

A good plan here is to take the train from Bamber Bridge west for a mile or so and alight at Lostock Hall station, opened in 1984 and the opposite side of the road bridge from the original station, in use from 1849 to 1969. Adjacent to the old station is the site of Lostock Hall Shed, one of the last three still operating (along with Carnforth and Rose Grove) at the time steam traction ended in 1968. Despite being situated in an otherwise busy residential area, the site remains empty and securely locked. It is also worth visiting the site of Farington station on the West Coast Main Line, closed in 1960. There were once two platforms, one at either side along with a central island platform but all was swept away after electrification, though tracks still curve around the 'ghost' of the central island. The former route to Moss Lane Junction, largely on embankments, with a series of watery lodges to the south that are easily mistaken for a flooded cutting, can be accessed for a short distance, close to the junction in question.

Railways West of Kirkham

The direct route from Kirkham to Blackpool was a late arrival on the scene, opening in 1903, to facilitate the growing numbers of express and excursion services heading into Blackpool. This route reached both Blackpool Central and Blackpool South Stations with additional platforms being constructed on the east side of the latter location, to complement the existing ones serving the Lytham route. It closed in February 1967 when it was considered surplus to requirements, though it should be noted that Beeching's original proposal was for closure of the Blackpool North route instead. Some of it was then infilled, whilst much of the rest was to become the M55 and its link road to the south side of Blackpool. It is possible to view the engineers' siding that runs along the Marton Formation that still exists, both from trackbed level on an adjacent public footpath and alongside at a higher level. The abutment of the former up flyover of the 'new' line still survives east of Kirkham North Junction. Explorers can also view the disused northern part of the original Lytham line, sometimes known as the Wrea Green branch, which opened from Bradkirk Junction in 1846; at Whinbrick a level crossing gate was visible for many years but appeared gone on a more recent visit. At Bradkirk Junction there was also a west-facing curve; this appears to have survived until 1950, though what type of traffic used it is not clear. A station known as Lytham Junction used to stand at the junction between 1846 and 1853. This section of track was replaced by what became known as the 'Ribby Curve', heading south-west from Kirkham North Junction, in 1874.

Unused platform at Blackpool South station.
Chris McFarlane

14

Fleetwood, Lancaster and Morecambe

Poulton-le-Fylde to Fleetwood

The former line from Poulton-le-Fylde to Fleetwood, having remained in use as far as the chemical works at Burn Naze until 1999, never appeared in any of the twentieth-century books on closed or forgotten railways, so both its early and recent history is well worth recalling.

The railway arrived in Fleetwood early, as in 1841 it was believed that it would never be possible to link England and Scotland by rail, so the idea was that passengers would travel by train to the furthest possible point, to a new port at a new town – Fleetwood – named after local dignitary Sir William Fleetwood Hesketh. Services to Barrow (see Chapter 15) were also envisaged. After an overnight stay, passengers would then board a steamer bound for Ardrossan in Scotland. However, the development of better-engineered routes and more powerful locomotives meant that by 1847 a railway was built over Shap Fell and Fleetwood was no longer needed for its original purpose.

To accommodate the overnight stays for these early travellers, the North Euston Hotel (at the other end of the route from Euston) was constructed at the same time, also opening in 1841. Designed by Decimus Burton (thus named as he was a tenth son), the North Euston was the first hotel anywhere to use a curved façade, which certainly adds to the dignity and ambience of the front-facing rooms, though undoubtedly making the furnishing inside them less straightforward. Behind the hotel was a large sports or parade ground, long since built over., The hotel closed in 1859 and was bought by the War Office, who turned it into a school of musketry for officers. Later the building became residential accommodation for army officers but, by 1891, the fortunes of Fleetwood as a holiday destination had improved sufficiently for it to be reopened as a hotel.

Let us return to the railway itself. Though both Fleetwood and Blackpool were effectively new resorts, it was the former that developed first. As early as 1842, a twenty-seven-coach train had run from Preston up to Fleetwood, carrying over 2,000 Sunday school pupils and their teachers, who were apparently 'engaged in singing hymns throughout the journey'. The original route south of Fleetwood ran dead straight on a single-track stone embankment, with water splashing over it, at high tide extending for some three quarters of a mile either side. There was apparently a plan to drain and reclaim the land to the west, but this was never taken up. Traffic built up quickly and doubling of the track was soon required; this meant building an alternative inland route from Burn Naze to Fleetwood. The two single-track routes operated together briefly but by 1851 all traffic was routed via the new route and the old embankment abandoned.

The next major development took place at Poulton-le-Fylde. Here a branch to Blackpool (later Blackpool Talbot Road then Blackpool North) had opened in 1846, curving away on a sharp curve to the south-west just north of Poulton's first station. By the latter part of the nineteenth century, Blackpool had grown massively and the traffic it generated had long exceeded that taking the straight route north to Fleetwood. A solution was needed, and this became urgent after a train derailed at the junction in 1893, leading to the deaths of three people including the driver and fireman. As a result, a completely new line was built to the west, with a new Poulton station constructed on a long island platform. Now the main running line headed west to Blackpool and a branch went north to Fleetwood. There was also a west–north curve for local traffic, on which Poulton Curve Halt was built, in operation from February 1909 to December 1952.

Fleetwood itself had a new terminus, close to the ferry terminal, built in 1883. An impressive Victorian building, featuring refreshment and dining facilities divided as usual along class lines, together with an impressive array of clocks, it very much looked the part for over eighty years.

But traffic declined and Fleetwood station was closed in 1966, to be demolished two years later, with traffic cut back to the much smaller Wyre Dock station, renamed Fleetwood for the rest of its days. Next to go was the original Poulton station; after closure to passengers in 1896 it had remained open as a goods facility but by the end of 1968 this closed, too.

As seen elsewhere, many rail closures of the early 1970s seemed to be quite unnecessary and arguably the Fleetwood branch was one of them, leaving a good-sized town and popular resort for day-trippers without any service. The line closed to passengers in its entirety in June 1970, but fortunately was not lost altogether as freight traffic continued until 1999 as far as Burn Naze. The extensive rail-connected sites included chemical works on both the east and west sides of the line, together with a power station; several railtours also ran up the branch in the late 1990s.

Let us now turn to what remains to be seen and, perhaps just as importantly, what no longer does. The author remembers visiting the line around 2007, when things were quite different to now. Firstly, the junction of the Fleetwood branch; this was rusted away and out of use in 2007 but shortly after, for reasons that are now unclear, it was relayed to full specifications despite the absence of any traffic. During electrification work in 2017, however, the pointwork was removed and plain track now runs past the junction, with the former Poulton No. 3 signal box, formerly sitting in the throat of the junction, demolished at the same time. In 2007 the site of the old Poulton station was still in place, though the buildings and track had long gone; today the whole area is buried under new housing.

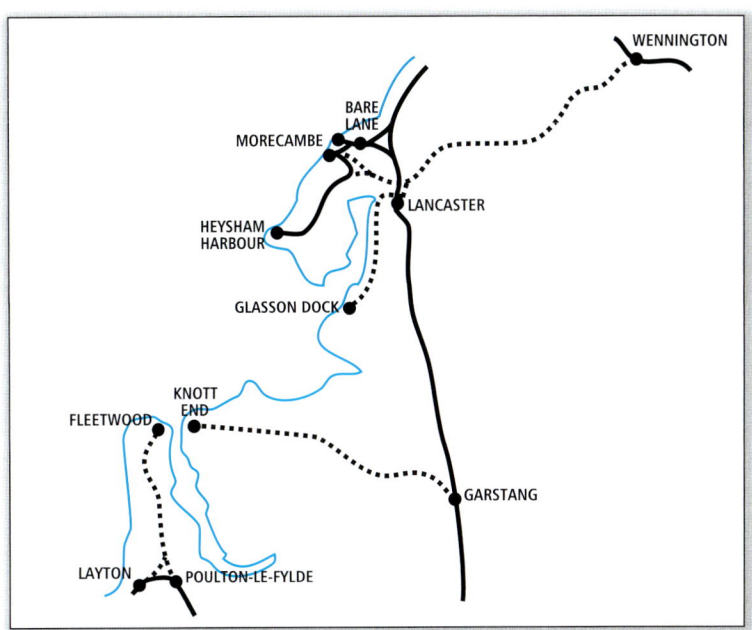

Map showing lines in the Lancaster and Morecambe area.

Turning to the track heading north out of Poulton; this had clearly been used by locals as an unofficial or desire path; despite it remaining in legal railway ownership and thus trespassing being effectively a criminal offence. Today, this section is totally overgrown with no access to anyone not equipped with a machete. Thornton station, resited north of the town's level crossing in 1925, has, however, fared rather better. Almost completely overgrown with bushes, brambles, and other sundry greenery in the early years of this century, the platforms and trackbed were cleared by volunteers from the local Poulton & Wyre Railway Society, who hope (if attempts to reopen the line to full passenger traffic fail) to run it as a preserved railway

Removing the connection to the Fleetwood line in 2017; Poulton No. 3 box, situated in the throat of the junction, had also been demolished.
Nick Melling

Fleetwood Branch, Thornton Station seen in 2006 before restoration and in 2021. *Author's collection*

Fleetwood branch, Burn Naze station, 2021. *Author*

clear. Eventually the rusty rails end and the trackbed is lost under the A585 road as it enters Fleetwood. With the docks and a retail park built across the formation, there is little to see in Fleetwood itself, other, that is, than the North Euston Hotel, still standing proudly just back from the waterfront and still very much open for business.

Garstang & Knott End Railway

By an admittedly indirect route, there was for some years a second way of getting by rail to Fleetwood. Opening as far as Pilling by 1870, the Garstang & Knot End (sic) Railway was, it is fair to say, one of the more unrealistic of railway developments; if most projected lines have the prospect of either significant goods or passenger traffic, this line had neither. Serving a flat, sparsely populated, farming area, there was little money to be made and the small town of Garstang already had a station with direct services to Preston or Lancaster. The extension to Knott End, where a (tide dependent, so never of value as a route to/from work) passenger ferry, ran and indeed still runs across the River Wyre to Fleetwood, was built as late as 1908 and hardly lasted twenty years, with the whole line closing to passengers in March 1930. For a brief period, a connecting siding south to serve salt mines at Preesall brought significant revenue but, in the 1920s, a pipeline was built across the River Wyre allowing brine to reach the chemical works at Burn Naze without the need of a very circuitous train journey around Preston. Other freight traffic, what there was of it, reached Knott End until 1950 before being cut back to Pilling and later to a coal yard at the former Garstang Town station.

Perhaps surprisingly, there is a fair bit left to see and explore. Garstang & Catterall station, where a bay platform served the branch's passenger services, has long gone but the station house and what was effectively the station's pub, the Kenlis Arms, still remain. From its junction with the West Coast Main Line, the trackbed is accessible for the best part of a mile, though a small girder bridge over the infant River Wyre is a modern replacement for the original. Through Garstang, the route is lost to housing, but on the west side of town a bridge carries the

between Thornton and Burn Naze, a couple of miles to the north. Although no buildings survive as such, the remaining walls and foundations have been presented to a high standard and are quite impressive in their own way. Further north, access to the trackbed is not possible but photographs suggest that the route past Burn Naze station, with its two long concrete platforms, is still quite

Right: Garstang & Knott End Railway, crossing keeper's house at Nateby, 2002. *Gordon Suggitt*

Below: The replica 'Pilling Pig' locomotive at Fold House Caravan Park, 2002. *Gordon Suggitt*

A6 bypass (built in the 1920s, so a very early example of this type of road) over the formation and abutments can be seen where the Lancaster Canal was formerly bridged.

Much of the middle section of the Garstang & Knott End has since returned to farmland but a number of crossing keeper's houses still exist as converted family homes, one at Nateby being perhaps the best preserved. Housing exists on the site of Pilling station but close by, at the entrance to the Fold House Caravan Park, a locomotive has been put on display. Despite having been built as late as 1955 and thus never having reached Knott End, this 0-6-0 tank engine has been given the name 'Pilling Pig'. This term had become the nickname for the line, the story being that one of the late nineteenth-century locomotives operating the line had a very loud and piercing whistle, apparently not unlike the squeal of a pig.

Approaching Knott End, the line is a public footpath for a mile, though access ends before the site of Knott End station, now a popular café. Opinions seem to vary as to whether any part of this building formed the original station, but what can be said is that a series of reconstructions has left the café looking nothing at all like a station. The goods yard, slightly to the west, is now a car park for the village. Although such a facility would not have been difficult to construct, rails were never built onto the jetty, from which the Fleetwood ferry still departs.

Glasson Dock Branch

Another 1930 closure (the LMSR apparently closed no fewer than twenty-three branch lines that year, mainly due to bus competition) was the branch from Lancaster to the small port of Glasson Dock. Glasson Dock itself was built as an alternative port for Lancaster, where silting of the River Lune meant that by the end of the eighteenth century boats of any size could no longer moor up along the old quayside. Opening in 1787, Glasson Dock was linked to Lancaster by a branch of the Lancaster Canal heading west from Galgate in 1826 and since then has been busy with both pleasure boats and commercial marine traffic, though the latter have declined in number in recent years. The railway was a good deal later to arrive on the scene, opened by the L&NWR, after many years of delay, in 1883. Passenger traffic to such a small settlement was never brisk, whilst goods traffic declined, particularly after the opening of Preston docks in 1892, but somehow hung on until 1964. The branch featured two intermediate stations, one at Conder Green and the other, a mile further north, something of a rarity in the north-west, was a private station for the first Baron Ashton at Ashton Hall. The line's closure just after the Baron's death in 1930 was thought by many locals not to be the coincidence that it undoubtedly was.

Exploring the Glasson Dock branch makes a delightful half day's walk with a bus one way, though another option is to make a circular route using the Lancaster Canal and its Glasson branch. Starting at a junction on an embankment just to the north of Lancaster station, the Glasson line initially runs north-west, curving through 90 degrees as it descends to ground level, passing the back of Lancaster Cricket Club's ground on a freely accessible embankment. From here the line is lost for a mile under an industrial estate but a rough track eventually comes parallel to, then onto, the former formation. From here, the trackbed is an official path, part of the Lancashire Coastal Way, with impressive views of the Lune estuary and low-lying land south of Heysham. Of actual railway remains there are few, the Condor Green station site now being a car park for the trail, whilst virtually nothing remains of the platform at Ashton Hall. Approaching Glasson Dock itself, you cross a fine girder bridge, and the formation remains intact right into the village, past the former station site until it is lost in a boatyard.

Lancaster to Morecambe and Wennington, the 'Little North-Western Railway'

North of Lancaster station, on an embankment with the main line climbing to cross the River Lune, two lines diverge, one to the west and one to the east. The western one leads to Glasson Dock, discussed above, but the eastern fork leads down to river level and a wholly different railway.

Lancaster had first been reached by rail from Preston in 1840, with the original Lancaster station building at Penny Street (in regular use until August 1849) a fortunate survivor, having been used as residential accommodation for nurses at the nearby hospital for many years. But by the mid-1840s there was already a campaign to build a railway along the Lune Valley and in 1849 the line from the riverside Green Ayre station in Lancaster to a temporary station at Wennington. The (still open) continuation of this route into Yorkshire was completed the following year.

Glasson Dock branch, trackbed approaching Glasson Dock forming part of the Lancashire Coastal Way. *Author's collection*

Morecambe Jetty station, 2022. *Author*

Exterior of Morecambe Promenade station, 2002. *Gordon Suggitt*

Intermediate stations were provided at Halton, Caton, Hornby, together with short-lived stations at Wray (closed 1850) and Claughton (closed 1853). The line was doubled in stages, the section between Lancaster and Hornby completing the work in 1899.

Having hit financial problems, the 'Little North-Western' Railway was taken over by the Midland Railway in 1859 and it was the Furness & Midland Joint line from Carnforth to Wennington, opened in 1862, that eventually was to provide competition for the original line. Traffic had started to decline before 1957, when Hornby station closed, and Caton was to follow in 1961.

Let us now turn to the original route from Green Ayre into Morecambe. When the line opened, slightly before the Wennington line, in 1848, Morecambe was then a small harbour village, known as Poulton. Traffic terminated at a jetty, where a small wooden hut served as the station until a new structure was constructed in 1861. Morecambe's development as a seaside holiday destination in the nineteenth century mirrored that of Fleetwood and Blackpool to the south and a gradual increase in facilities for travellers reflected this. A small station on Northumberland Road was replaced by the large and impressive Morecambe Promenade station in 1907. Meanwhile, in 1864 the L&NWR had opened their own route to Morecambe via Hest Bank, later building a second large terminus station in the town at Euston Road. Further developments came in 1904 when a deep-water port at Heysham was constructed for ferry traffic to Northern Ireland and the Isle of Man and after this time the jetty and its station fell out of use.

Aiming to cash in further on both boat travellers and, later, holidaymakers, the North-Western Railway also opened a small hotel in Morecambe. This original building, small and unpretentious, was a two-storey building of grey stone with green shuttered windows. But how peaceful a stay the guests enjoyed is a matter of conjecture; the line to the harbour passed right by and from 1902 onwards they had to put up with the noise generated by the neighbouring ship-breakers' yard of T.W. Ward. However, this little hotel was eventually to be replaced by, arguably, one of the most famous hotels in the whole of England.

As the 1920s drew to a close it was apparent that the old Midland Hotel had become inadequate for the changing times. The Depression meant that many once well-to-do people were no longer able to afford foreign holidays and this brought a new wave of custom to the English seaside, one with more sophisticated demands, and there was an urgent need for the upgrading of accommodation for visitors. The London, Midland & Scottish Railway Company was now responsible for the Midland Hotel and decided to replace the existing Victorian building with a more modern structure. In January 1932 it approved plans for a new hotel to be built on the seafront at a cost of just under £72,000. Bravely, the LMS saw Morecambe as an opportunity to make a radical new departure from traditional hotel design and selected the architect Oliver Hill to provide the company with 'a building of international quality in the modern style'. Work commenced in August 1932, the new building rising from the lawn in front of the old hotel before the latter was eventually demolished some months later.

Platforms of Morecambe Promenade station seen in 1987 with the Midland Hotel to the right. *Phillip Earnshaw*

Hill had no previous experience of constructing a hotel or anything remotely similar. Nevertheless, he readily accepted the commission from the LMS, who remarked that ... 'you have here a unique opportunity of building the first really modern hotel in the country'. Hill's design was for a three-storey, curved structure, with its convex side towards the sea, allowing good views from every room. The concave side faced the railway station and was divided by a tower containing the hotel entrance and spiral staircase. The north end was finished off on the ground floor by what was, and again is, a circular café.

Hill believed that the exterior design should be intimately linked to the interior décor and to this end he took complete control of the hotel's colour scheme, works of art, decoration and furnishings – even down to the colour of the hand towels and the shape of the door handles.

'Greyhound' bridge west of Green Ayre station, Lancaster. *Chris McFarlane*

A contemporary observer described it as 'in complete harmony with its natural surroundings ... it rises from the sea like a great white ship, gracefully curved'. Inside, the impression was one of space; from the open spiral staircase above with its cantilevered steps to the sparsely furnished entrance lounge ahead and, leading off it to the right, the sweeping curve of the dining room. But such luxuries were not to be available to the general public for long. At the outbreak of the Second World War Morecambe became an important RAF station and the Midland was requisitioned by the government for use as a military hospital. Valuable items were put into store and the interior of the building converted. On the ground floor the dining room became a large ward with some forty beds, while the circular café was adapted to serve as a physiotherapy centre. Other rooms were used for administrative purposes. Upstairs, two of the suites were turned into operating theatres and the bedrooms used for individual patients. There were also X-ray facilities, a dental surgery and a dispensary. Additional beds were provided in Nissen huts erected in the hotel grounds.

After the war, the Midland was handed back to the LMS Railway in February 1946. It was the intention of the company to reopen the hotel in the near future, but this was not possible as the building was found to be in such a bad state of repair that restoration costs were prohibitive. This prompted the company to consider selling the hotel. However, it eventually decided to renovate the building and the Midland did reopen to the public in July 1948 and continued to operate for the next three years, while becoming increasingly unprofitable. Following nationalisation of the railways, the British Transport Commission no longer saw the need for seaside hotels, though it took until July 1952 for a sale to be completed; so, nineteen years after it first opened, the Midland Hotel passed out of railway hands. The hotel prospered during the 1950s but by the early '70s it was losing both its appeal

Halton station, between Lancaster and Wennington. *Author*

and its clientele as holidaymakers deserted Morecambe and other British seaside resorts for the guaranteed sunshine of southern Europe. In 1976 the Midland changed hands again and its new owners, the Hutchinson Leisure Group, embarked on an unsympathetic refurbishment of the interior. But that same year, the building's architectural importance was recognised when it was grade II* listed. A glass sun lounge was added in 1979 running the length of the seaward side of the hotel but business did not improve as much as envisaged and by the time the Midland was bought by Family Hotels in 1989 it had become very run down. After deteriorating still further, it was eventually purchased by the Manchester-based development company Urban Splash, finally finding an owner with belief in its potential, and who proudly reopened the fully restored building on 1 June 2008. Operating at the boutique, high-level end of the hotel market, the Midland has survived the pandemic and continues to be both popular and profitable.

In 1908 the Lancaster to Morecambe (and Heysham) route was electrified, using alternating current overhead power at 6,600 volts, with power coming from the Midland Railway's own generating plant at Heysham. This system was used by local trains but there were also many steam-powered services, particularly from Bradford, with whom Morecambe had developed a close connection. After a short break in 1951 when stock was updated and power increased, the electric system operated right through to the line's closure. The high volume of local traffic was indicated by the opening of a new halt at Scale Hall as late as June 1957. But, as an obvious duplicate route between Morecambe and Lancaster and a route without a direct connection into Lancaster's main station, its days were numbered. The whole route from Morecambe, through Green Ayre to Wennington, closed to passengers in January 1966 and to all traffic the following year. One inconvenience was that from this time all Heysham traffic had to reverse at Morecambe. Further rationalisation was to take place in 1994 with the replacement of Morecambe's promenade station by a single platform about a quarter of a mile to the east, coincidentally on almost the same site as Morecambe's original station.

Let us now take a tour of what remains, starting at Morecambe and working east. First, the jetty remains fully accessible and the small station building of 1861 still survives, used as a seasonal cafe. After passing the impressive art deco frontage of the Midland Hotel we see, just across the road, the former Promenade station. Fortunately, the station building survives, from the front still looking very much the part, these days housing a café/bar and a popular arts centre. Behind this building, though, is a very different story. All traces of platforms and goods facilities have been swept away, replaced by a supermarket and a large car park. However, it is not far to the current station and just to the east of here, after the Heysham line diverges, the old route to Green Ayre can be picked up. This is accessible throughout and, taking a straight, direct, route between the two places it is a popular route for cyclists, both commuters and more leisurely riders. Some remains of the supports of Scale Hall Halt remain hidden in undergrowth. Approaching Lancaster, the line crossed the River Lune on a fine, low bridge, known locally as the Greyhound Bridge; this was converted to road use after closure and is generally busy with traffic.

Little remains at Green Ayre other than a green open space, though a small crane, originally from Hornby station, has been erected on the site. The short link up to the present Castle station is also walkable and provides a useful link between the station, the castle (until recent years a prison), and the quayside.

Heading east now, the line to Wennington passes under one of the arches of Rennie's magnificent aqueduct, carrying the Lancaster Canal high over the River Lune, then under the much less impressive structures that carry the M6 motorway and the new link road to Morecambe. At Halton, one platform and a small timber station building, still with its (non-working) clock, remain. East of Halton the line crosses the delightfully and appropriately named Crook o'Lune on two superb viaducts. A little further on, Caton station house survives as a private residence, whilst the goods shed has had a more unusual reincarnation; it now serves as a Catholic church for the village. The official path ends at Bull Beck shortly after Caton, about 6 miles from Lancaster, and the trackbed is privately owned from here right through to Wennington. Back on the trackbed, two concrete 'Beware of Trains' notices at one time remained in situ west of a level crossing at Claughton. The crossing house is now a private residence, as detailed by Quick, it acted as a short-lived station between 1851 and 1853. It is surprising how much of the formation survives between Bull Beck and Claughton, but the story is different beyond Claughton to the next station at Hornby, where much of the trackbed has vanished. Hornby station was once a delightful station with a Tudor-style building, very much in keeping with the village that it served. But it was to close in 1957 and a subsequent fire, whilst the railway was still operational, meant that, sadly, this attractive structure did not survive. The station site has today been completely redeveloped. East of Hornby, the formation is largely intact as far as Wray, which had its own station between 1849 and 1850. This station, which was reused as a crossing house has, however, not survived. A deviation is these days required into Wray to bridge the River Hyndburn, there being only remnants of the former railway bridge here and whilst private, with permission, it is possible to walk to Tatham and on to Wennington fairly unimpeded. At the latter location lies the former junction site, and also visible is the site of the former signal box west of the station where the route concludes. At Wennington the old Lancaster line runs straight into the station whilst the still open Carnforth route curves in from the north, a reminder of the original status of these two lines.

Lancaster–Wennington line; viaduct at Crook 'O' Lune with road bridge behind, 1998. *Gordon Suggitt*

15
Barrow and the South Lakes

Arnside–Hincaster

The route from Arnside to Hincaster, just under 4 miles long, was the easternmost branch of the Furness Railway; it provided an effective cut-off for traffic between Barrow, the south Lakes and the north or north-east of England, effectively forming a triangle with the third apex at Carnforth. Opened in 1876, until 1942 a passenger service nicknamed 'Kendal Tommy' linked Grange-over-Sands with Kendal via Arnside; in pre-war days, boys from Grange travelled along it to attend school at Heversham.

Although generally uneconomic and rarely busy with local traffic, the line did come into its own during the First World War, when Durham coke kept the Furness steel industry going, enabling destroyers and frigates to be built at Barrow; Lloyd George referred to the route at this time as 'the lifeline of Britain'. As late as 1960, the line was busy with several trains a day, bringing coke from south Durham to fuel the major iron and steel works at Barrow and Millom. But after the Barrow works closed, the line was little used and the section north of Sandside closed in 1963, track lifting taking place somewhat later (by 1960s standards) in 1966. The Arnside–Sandside section remained in use to serve a quarry at Sandside until 1968, though official closure of this section only took place in January 1972.

Today the line is fortunate to have an enthusiastic support group, the Hincaster Trailway, who have worked hard in recent years to convert much of the line into a usable path and in particular to create a path that allows access to all kinds of users. The group's news and activities can be followed on their website and social media pages. Starting at Arnside, it is first worth viewing the impressive Kent Viaduct. Consisting of fifty-one spans, totalling over 450m long, it was completely reconstructed between 2010 and 2011. Returning to Arnside station, the bay platform has vanished with a ranger building occupying part of the site. Continuing north-east, a most scenic path can be followed, partly on the formation and partly on a parallel flood prevention embankment, in an attractive estuary environment that, depending on the tide, is either a great expanse of sand or water. Either way, the space created allows superb views of the mountains of the Lake District on a clear day. Heading inland, the path continues north to reach Sandside, where a somewhat unattractive block of flats occupies the station site.

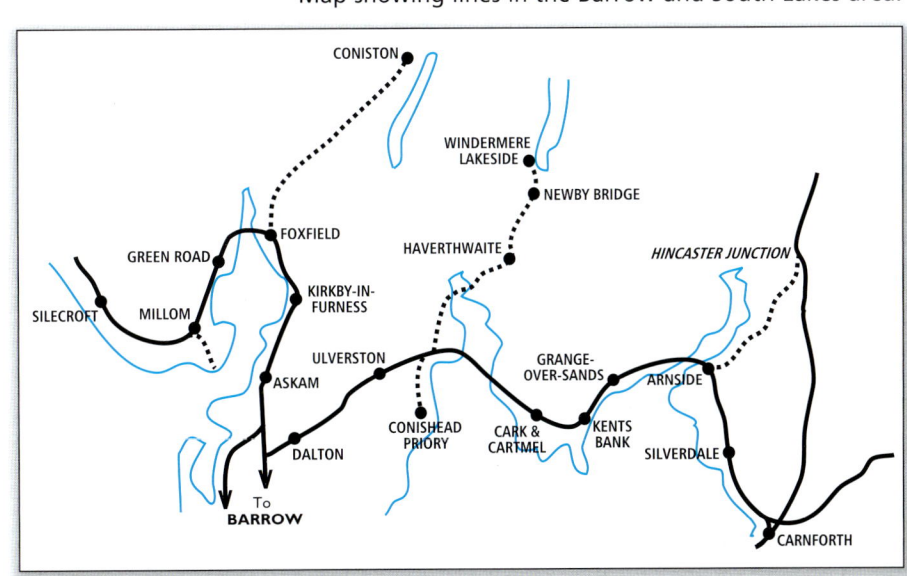

Map showing lines in the Barrow and South Lakes area.

Arnside to Hincaster line, trackbed near Arnside, looking south. *Steve Pendrill*

Arnside to Hincaster line, Heversham station, looking north. *Steve Pendrill*

Soon, the site of Beela Viaduct is reached, formerly an attractive structure with three main cast-iron spans mounted on stone arches. Not to be confused with the similarly named but rather larger structure on the Stainmore route, this viaduct, together with its northern approach, was demolished in 1973 and a diversion is required over the road bridge to the south, though the trackbed can be regained without too much difficulty before approaching Heversham. At Heversham station the overgrown platform, access path and overbridge remain, though photographs record the gradual deterioration of the site since closure. Further formation can be followed, with some overgrown stretches, though mostly on private land, right up to Hincaster Junction where the West Coast Main Line is reached. This has become a popular spot for railway photographers, particularly when a steam-hauled train is scheduled to run past along the main line.

The Lakeside Branch–Ulverston to Lakeside

The Furness Railway branch line to Lakeside, at the southern end of Lake Windermere, was somewhat unusual for a nineteenth-century venture in that it was built predominantly for the benefit of tourist traffic, though the Kendal & Windermere Railway, serving the same purpose, had opened as early as 1847. Opening in June 1869, the new line was built with a triangle at its western end, formed by Plumpton Junction (see also the Conishead Priory branch below) to the west, Leven Junction to the east and Greenodd Junction to the north. The branch also supplied coal to the Windermere steamers but additionally helped to open up trade to what had previously been a purely local gunpowder-making concern near Haverthwaite.

The early twentieth century proved to be the line's heyday, with fashionable Edwardian tourists flocking to the lake and tours combining train, steamer and charabanc travel being offered. However, the route was never as popular after the First World War and with the A590 road serving the area directly while trains virtually went to Ulverston and back, decline set in. The gunpowder works had closed in the 1930s and with tourist traffic being largely summer only, out-of-season revenue was minimal; the intermediate stations at Greenodd and Haverthwaite closed as early as 1946.

The east curve between Leven Junction and Greenodd Junction was the first to go, closing in March 1952, but access to Lakeside remained possible via the west curve from Plumpton Junction to Greenodd Junction until complete closure; much of this curve is now several feet deep in flood water. The last scheduled passenger train left Lakeside for Ulverston in September 1965, with the last known through train being a late 1967 railtour.

The post-closure history of the branch and the formation of the Lakeside & Haverthwaite Railway is complex and can only be summarised here. Initial plans to save the whole branch involved the building of a new station at Plumpton Junction as it was assumed, almost certainly correctly, that British Railways would not allow an unproven preserved railway access on main-line tracks into Ulverston. A further problem was the relative inaccessibility of Plumpton Junction, and these issues were unresolved before plans were announced to take over part of the trackbed for widening of the A590 trunk road to Barrow. This was enough to put off the original company but eventually a second group formed who were happy to concentrate on the eastern 3½ miles from Haverthwaite to Lakeside. This part of the branch opened as a predominately steam-hauled preserved line in 1973 and remains busy and popular to this day.

Returning to Plumpton Junction, if given permission for access to private areas, it is possible to walk a good deal of the route north from here. Much of the line can be followed, mostly along but in places just alongside the line, though a diversion is required around Plumpton Cottage Farm. The highlight is a superbly scenic, privately owned, stretch of a mile or so running just alongside to the estuary of the River Leven. North of a picnic area, the trackbed has been taken over by the A590 but a very narrow path exists alongside. Greenodd station and the Leven Viaduct are long gone but fortunately a footbridge provides easy access to the east side of the river. Soon an excellent stretch of trackbed is reached, over and beyond the still intact Ladysike Bridge, which also crosses the Leven. Beyond this bridge the formation is intact but private, eventually becoming a narrow minor road; the route into Haverthwaite can be followed until access is lost at an embankment above the village cricket club. Further road development has blocked access to the west portal of Haverthwaite Tunnel, but it remains open from the east side. Though largely empty these days, the tunnel was used as a stock storage facility by the preserved railway until the construction of their impressive new shed in 2016.

Lakeside branch, Ladysike Bridge Girder. *Author*

Lakeside branch, Ladysike Bridge at track level. *Author*

Lakeside branch, Haverthwaite Tunnel in 2022, now largely unused. *Author*

Lakeside branch, bridge and signals on the final approach to Lakeside station. *Author*

Close by are two gunpowder tramways; generally operated by horses as for obvious reasons they were never suited to steam haulage. The standard-gauge Blackbeck Tramway, open from the branch's opening until 1928, operated from a gunpowder mill at Bouth for about 2 miles south to Dickson's sidings, just east of Ladysike Bridge. This line can be followed south from the site of a long-gone wooden trestle bridge over a river inlet at Pool Foot. A second route, the 3ft 6in gauge Low Wood Tramway, which closed in 1935, stayed south of the river and now much of it forms a pleasant woodland footpath back into Haverthwaite. The village of Haverthwaite was once highly dependent on its gunpowder trade and a number of works buildings, including a fine clock tower, can still be viewed. The Low Wood tramway ended at Haverthwaite station yard for exchange purposes, where the gate that once guarded remains in position.

Conishead Priory Branch

Ulverston station, the start of our next route, is well worth a visit in itself, featuring in many collections of the country's finest stations. It boasts two running lines but three platforms, together with an old low, unused platform just to the east. The station itself has an Italianate-style building attached to a delightful clock tower, its impression of a church only spoiled by a chimney at the top, together with superbly delicate canopies painted in a distinctive red, white, and green colour scheme.

In the 1870s, the Furness Railway's freight services were struggling with the gradients between Ulverston and Barrow, with a climb of over 250ft from either direction to a summit at Lindal. Accordingly, Acts of Parliament were passed to allow the construction of a double-track line that would follow lower ground close to the coastline. But only the eastern two miles were ever built, together with a further few hundred further yards of embankment on which it is believed that tracks were never laid.

Conishead Priory is of twelfth-century origin, originally built as a hospital and destroyed in 1537 during the period of dissolution of the monasteries. In its place, a large country house was constructed. After changing hands many times, by 1883 it was in use as a hydropathic hotel. It was sold in 1928 for use as a convalescent home for Durham miners (special trains ran from Durham to Ulverston into the 1950s, carrying poorly or injured miners); during wartime it had a stint as a military hospital and nowadays it is a Buddhist centre, thus returning to its original spiritual roots.

Returning to the railway, a mineral line heading south from Plumpton Junction (where, as noted above, the Lakeside branch also began, but in the opposite direction) to Bardsea Ironworks had opened by 1874.

Plumpton Junction in the 1980s. The Conishead priory line still heads south behind the signal box. The abandoned and fenced off junction with the Lakeside Branch can also be made out to the right of the DMU. *Author's collection*

Conishead Priory line, Ulverston Canal Bridge's retracting mechanism. *Chris McFarlane*

Conishead Priory line, Ulverston Canal Bridge at track level. *Author*

Although the idea of a through route to Barrow was abandoned around this time, it was felt that there was sufficient traffic to the 'hydro' for a short branch line to be opened, beyond the ironworks, to a station just a short distance from the priory. Conishead Priory station was thus opened, for visitors to the priory only, and was not open to the general public. The aforementioned unused embankment, which can still be viewed, though lying mostly on private land, continued south past the priory as far as an unmetalled road to the east of Town End. Passenger services were reduced to one train a day by 1895 and struggled on until January 1917, a date when presumably leisure traffic was no longer encouraged. Tracks were not lifted until 1952. Freight traffic continued, at first to Bardsea Ironworks but later mainly serving the huge Glaxo pharmaceutical works, with oil traffic that continued running as late as 1994. Formal closure took place in 2000 when the signal box at Plumpton Junction was taken out of use and track lifting took place soon afterwards.

The Priory station building is intact but much extended since 1980, when the house was largely derelict. A building extension can be seen at one end and a conservatory at the other; it now forms luxury holiday accommodation known as South Lodge. Since 2015, a platform has been reconstructed that gives the setting much more of a 'railway' feel, if a rather inauthentic one, though an original set of buffer stops can still be seen close by.

Heading north, a crossing keeper's cottage may be viewed and the trackbed beyond is intact; an unofficial but clearly well-used footpath that avoids the need to follow the edge of the Leven estuary at high tide. At North Lonsdale Crossing there was a signal box and a small, public, station was provided, serving the settlements of Sandside, where there was a hotel, and Canal Foot, where a coastal path headed north to Plumpton Hall giving views of the Leven Viaduct. The main engineering feature of the line was the bridge over the Ulverston Canal. This structure, fixed in position since 1952 and Grade II listed since 2012, was known as a 'rolling bridge', a section of which could be retracted at an angle of 45 degrees to allow boats to pass through.

Sadly in 2014, what was then a delightful stretch of trackbed leading up from the canal crossing towards Plumpton Junction was securely fenced off and is now totally overgrown and inaccessible. It is not clear whether this land is still railway owned or has been purchased by the local farmer, but in either case there is absolutely no access here these days.

Barrow's Piel Pier Branch

Barrow is sometimes described as being situated at the end of a long cul-de-sac, though a view of a large-scale map shows that it lies, as the crow flies, not too many miles from Fleetwood, the two towns lying on opposite sides of Morecambe Bay. The idea that traffic might reach Barrow by train to Fleetwood, with onward shipping, was noted as early as 1840 by John Abel Smith, a London entrepreneur. Around this time, Smith purchased two islands just a few miles south of Barrow, Roa Island and Piel Island, with a view to providing a deep-water pier for both commercial and passenger shipping. Having reached agreement with Smith, the Furness Railway opened its branch from Roose to Roa (but always known as Piel) in 1846, despite the pier being unable to accommodate shipping until 1853. In fact, the railway never reached Piel Island, terminating at Roa Island after crossing a long causeway embankment to link the island with the mainland; the aforementioned pier was over 800ft long and could be used for slate and iron traffic as well as passenger services. At one time Piel Pier also hosted ferry services to Belfast but these were transferred to Ramsden Dock, closer to the centre of Barrow, in 1881 and the pier was demolished just ten years later. Passenger services for

Rampside; the embankment to Piel Island with the former Roa Hotel (white building, centre background) clearly visible.
Maurice Blencowe

local traffic struggled on until July 1936, when the line south of Parrock Hall Junction (where lines to Barrow's south docks and to Roosecote power station diverged) was closed to all traffic.

Today much of the line is walkable, forming a valuable part of the Cumbria Coastal Way as it provides an accessible, if not overly attractive, route past a power station and a gas terminal. At Rampside, the station building still stands, much altered, but now in residential use. The embankment onto Roa Island was converted into a road and remains perfectly accessible but nothing remains of Piel station, though the nearby (former) hotel still sits opposite its site.

Foxfield–Coniston

This line opened in stages, with a branch off the original Furness Railway at Kirkby reaching Broughton in 1848 and a fully engineered branch line opening to Coniston in June 1859. Originally built primarily to carry copper ore down from the mines above Coniston, the branch later carried tourist traffic for Coniston Water and the surrounding area. Passenger traffic was initially busy, enough to justify the addition of a third platform at Coniston in 1896. Railmotors, accompanied by a four-wheeled trailer coach, operated between 1905 and 1918 and after that time excursion trains were the main source of revenue. Closure to passenger traffic, which took place in October 1958, was controversial in that, unlike many other lines, no attempts had been made to make it more viable by reducing staffing and signalling costs. Closure to all traffic came in April 1962.

The obvious place to start exploration of this branch walk is the former junction station at Foxfield, which retains a fine water tower and large signal box. From Foxfield the line has long been pretty much inaccessible as far as Broughton in Furness, where there was once a passing loop with two staggered platforms, one from the original 1848 station and the second belonging to its 1859 successor. This station building now accommodates two private houses but can only be viewed from the back and, other than a small piece of platform facing, retains little of interest. A goods shed, still intact into the 1980s, is long gone. The first part of the route north of Broughton is a delightful public footpath, gradually gaining height, as far as a point a few hundred yards north-east of Mireside. Continuing on, the line is privately owned but the formation is still largely intact. Woodland, the next station, served a small, scattered community, also acting as the local post office. The station has been sympathetically restored with main buildings, platform facings and down-side waiting shelter all well preserved. More private land follows with superb views of the southern Lake District including the Old Man of Coniston as the gentle climb continues, though a short section of trackbed approaching Torver has been lost under a diverted section of the parallel main road.

Coniston branch, intact trackbed to the north of Broughton. *Author*

Coniston branch, Woodland station looking north in 2022. *Author*

The next station, Torver, is intact but used for holiday cottages and easily missed by the casual visitor; a goods shed slightly to the south may also still be seen. The final section into Coniston is partially walkable, with Coniston Water now visible far below on the eastern side of the line. Coniston station, superbly located on a hill above the village, was unfortunately demolished and replaced by housing, but the backdrop of hills can still be viewed, and comparisons made with old photographs. The line once continued for a short distance beyond Coniston station to serve the aforementioned mines and a fine underbridge can still be viewed on this stretch. As a tourist route to Coniston Water and the mountains beyond it would have been an outstanding preserved line, even though it should be admitted that the modern bus route via Ulverston is just as quick and probably more direct.

Millom–Hodbarrow and Haverigg

A line curving round the east side of Millom reached Hodbarrow by 1867. It served a mine that supplied coal to the huge Millom Ironworks that dominated the town until its closure in 1968; further round the coast towards Haverigg there was also a construction railway for a breakwater. This track, together with the many sidings that served the ironworks, providing access to both the harbour south of the works and the main-line railway, may be followed for some distance but the site of the works itself has now largely been reclaimed and forms a nature reserve. A more complete change of use from fifty or so years ago is hard to imagine. In October 2021 it was announced that funding had been obtained to upgrade this whole route from a rough footpath to a properly maintained footpath and cycleway, to be known, appropriately enough, as the 'iron line'.

16
Whitehaven and Workington

Sellafield–Whitehaven via Egremont

The Whitehaven coalfields were very early users of rail transport, starting with tramroads from as early as 1740 (see Chapter 2). Whilst the coastal route through to Whitehaven was completed by 1849, this provided a somewhat circuitous route to and from the coalfields that were situated to the east of the town. By 1870, a more direct route south through Beckermet to Sellafield had been opened by the Whitehaven, Cleator & Egremont Railway (WC&ER), linking with the Furness Railway at a junction just north of Sellafield station. This route had over the years quite a varied range of usage, but regular passenger services were not amongst the most successful, ceasing in January 1935, although a brief, clearly unsuccessful, revival took place between May 1946 and June 1947. Special trains were more successful, and these included excursion trains to the coast or north to Carlisle, and specials to Rugby League Challenge Cup matches at Whitehaven or Workington Town, particularly to the latter during that team's runs to the cup finals of 1952, 1955 and 1958. Workmen's trains ran into Whitehaven and, in the latter years of the line's use, south to the nuclear plant at Sellafield. However, freight was always of greater importance and as well as coal, iron ore was carried from Beckermet, which kept the northern part of the line open until 1980. There was, in the late 1960s, a plan to close the coastal line south of Whitehaven and redirect traffic through Egremont; the idea was to reduce maintenance costs on parts of the coast route that were, and still are, prone to rock falls, but nothing ever came of this.

Sellafield to Moor Row line; Beckermet station. *Author's collection*

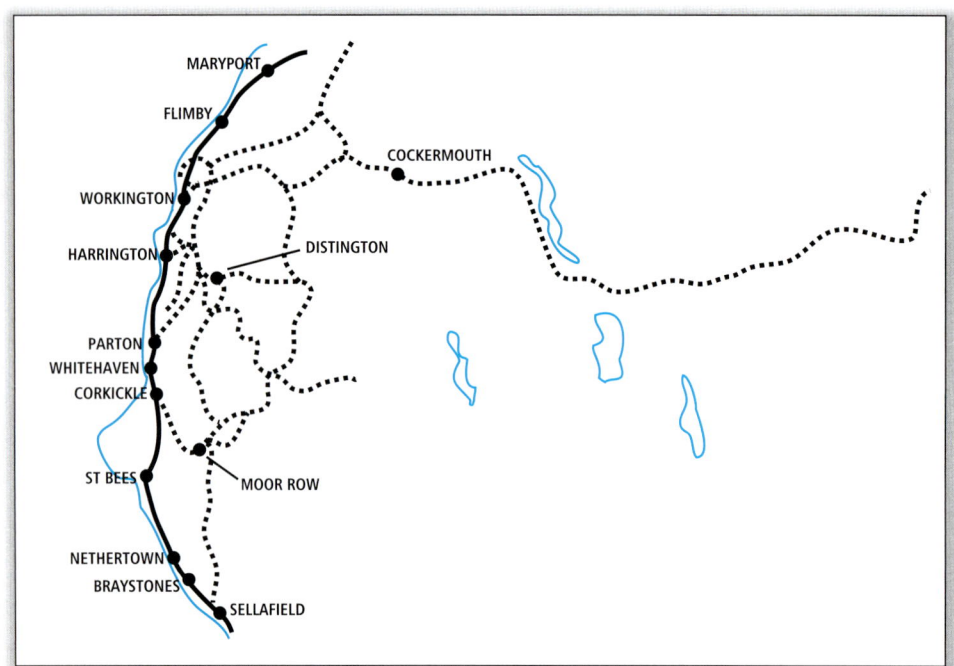

Map showing lines in the Whitehaven and Workington area.

Sellafield to Moor Row line, Woodend station. Both Beckermet and Woodend stations remain intact and in private occupation.
Author's collection

The relatively late closure of much of this line gave it a better chance of being retained as a linear route and a good deal of it has survived in that form. But let us start at Sellafield, a place very much dominated by the nuclear plant and one at which not everyone would prefer to dwell. Access to the Egremont line is via the north end of Sellafield station's car park, from where a path continues just above the coastline until the junction is reached. From here, there is a very pleasant walk along the trackbed of around a mile until forced off the line at Middlebank; a lineside hut and an intact milepost were pleasing survivors on a recent visit. North of here, though, the line is mostly inaccessible other than on a short stretch west of Thornhill, until the north side of Egremont is reached, though Beckermet station is impressive, tastefully converted into a large private dwelling. At Egremont much has vanished under a bypass, including the station and an adjacent rail-served dairy, but access resumes on the north side of town, passing the east side of a cemetery. A further section has then been lost to road development, including the area around Woodend station, though the building here again remains intact and in private use. However, from a point a mile south of Moor Row, the line is now an official path that can be followed through and around Moor Row, passing the junction for Cleator Moor and Rowrah. The cycleway ends just short of Mirehouse Junction, where a north-facing connection once connected with the coast route.

Lines East of Moor Row

The collieries and ironworks east of Whitehaven were served by what became quite a complex network of lines; the fact that a number of local companies were keen to build lines in the area shows the potential profits that could be made. The WC&ER had reached Rowrah by 1862 and Marron Junction on the Workington to Keswick line four years later, with branches serving Mowbray Colliery and Kelton Fell Quarry added in the 1870s. Once more, passenger traffic other than for workmen's trains was sparse, with all services ending in April 1931. North of Rowrah, the line closed to all traffic in 1954 but limestone traffic from a quarry at Rowrah continued to reach Whitehaven until 1978. Again, this somewhat late closure was to be crucial in the line's survival as a linear route. After lying dormant for several years, the trackbed was made available in the late 1980s for the Railway Ramblers Club to purchase. It was a somewhat drawn out process, as these things generally are, particularly as it was pretty much the first purchase of its kind, but the sale was completed in 1994 as a price of around £5,000. The line was then passed on to Sustrans, who undertook to maintain the line; an arrangement that continues to this day.

Let us now take a look at what remains, starting with the long-abandoned section south from Marron Junction. The site of the junction itself can still be identified, just south of a loop of the River Derwent north of Bridgfoot. South of here the line is fragmented with few walkable stretches,

A 2014 view of Winder station, near Rowrah. *Author*

Yeathouse signal box, west of Rowrah. *Author's collection*

though a section of a mile or so south of Ullock is now designated as a public footpath. Much of this section of the line is becoming increasingly fragmented; the best remaining feature is the station building at Lamplugh, now used as a holiday cottage. But the official path from Rowrah starts at the west end of the village and there is much to enjoy as it winds its way past Frizington and Cleator Moor before reaching Moor Row. Generally well-maintained throughout, the best features are the station houses at Frizington, Winder (where a platform also survives) and Rowrah. At Yeathouse station both platforms survive, as does a single platform at Moor Row.

Cleator Moor–Siddick Junction via Workington Central

The Cleator & Workington Junction Railway (C&WJR) was very much a latecomer to the busy and mostly quite profitable nineteenth-century west Cumbria railway scene, particularly the iron trade. With the Carlisle & Maryport and the Furness Railway having taken the easiest, coastal route through Whitehaven and Workington, what was left for the C&WJR was to take a difficult, inland route on a gradient of around 1 in 70 throughout. Opening as far as Workington (Central) in 1879 and extended to Siddick Junction the following year, the line served a mostly sparse population, so its income was almost wholly reliant on the iron trade and the coal needed to support it.

Passenger services generally started at what had become a junction station at Moor Row, then headed north through Cleator Moor (where a separate station was built from that on the WC&ER line), Distington and Harrington before reaching Workington. Cleator Moor was notable for attracting quite large numbers of Irish emigrees to staff the ironworks – one legacy being that the town's football team is known as Cleator Moor Celtic and plays in green. The C&WJR stayed independent until the 'grouping' of 1923, before marking its demise with a grand farewell dinner at Workington's Central Hotel. Like much of 'inland' west Cumbria, passenger traffic ceased early, this route being another April 1931 closure, though freight traffic continued, with a through route being available until 1963 and final closure two years later. In terms of what is left, only one station house remains, at Moresby Park, though the seven-arch Keekle viaduct, north of Cleator Moor, is an impressive if fortunate survivor. However, from Workington Central (now a car park) south to Distington, around 2½ miles of track is now a walkway, and this connects with the Lowca Light Railway (see below). South of Cleator Moor there is a further converted section, joining the paths from Rowrah and Egremont at Moor Row.

Yeathouse station platforms, 2014. *Author*

Moor Row to Workington Central line, 43004 heading through Cleator Moor in May 1963. *Author's collection*

The site of Workington Central station, now a car park, looking south. *Nick Melling*

Workington Steelworks and Docks, and the Lowca Light Railway

Workington's current station has its origins with the Whitehaven Junction Railway in 1846. The trackwork through the station has been heavily rationalised but two signal boxes still control the surrounding area. The first sits at the north end of the southbound platform (Workington Main No. 3), whilst a second sits south of the station and is the larger of the two structures (Workington Main No. 2). It is then worth proceeding from the station to view what remains of the former dock system south of the River Derwent. Until fairly recently it connected heavy industry south of the river with the port on its northern side. The demise of the steel industry finally led to its closure. The route can be traced from the yawning gap that now exists where a bridge over the River Derwent once stood; this structure was severely damaged with the floods of 2009 and has subsequently been removed. A ballasted trackbed can be followed to a sizeable yard, where reversal was possible to the various industrial sites up to and adjacent to the main line on the south side of Workington. The trackwork is visible where roads were crossed, and, in places, level crossing warning lights still stand, although long since out of commission. One interesting crossing light variant remains, which seems to relate to the various route functions for traincrews' attention rather than for the benefit of road users.

Further south, the huge void left by the demolished steelworks and associated industry is only too apparent. The next part of this route, where the line had climbed away from the steelworks site to head inland, is now blocked by a school whose grounds are now on the formation.

Lowca Light Railway, Copperas Hill near Harrington, March 1953. *Author's collection*

Lowca Light Railway, Amazon at Lowca Crossing, June 1972. *Author's collection*

Penrith to Workington line, Bassenthwaite Lake station. This station has now been fully restored into a superb café/restaurant. *Author's collection*

On the far side of the Cumbrian Coast Route the trackbed parallels the live line and is an interesting walk on a pleasant formation, although quite badly eroded by the elements. However, as it approaches Harrington, the line vanishes without trace. This route connected inland with the Lowca Light Railway and was contemporary with it until closure in May 1973.

At one time Harrington had five stations, three of which were on the Lowca Light Railway. It is possible to join the formation at the first of these, Harrington Church Road Halt, of which nothing now remains, and follow the formation on a footpath all the way to Lowca. The Light Railway passed above Harrington, affording fine views of the coastline as it passed the site of Rosehill Archer Street, where traces of the platform still remain. At Rosehill Junction another route ascended from Harrington Harbour, the major feature remaining on this branch being the abutments where the route once crossed the Cumbrian Coast Line. The climb is quite fearsome and having joined it, the Lowca Light Railway begins a 1 in 17 ascent up Copperas Hill Incline, taking the railway formation onto the cliffs. This ascent is one of the steepest adhesion gradients ever used on the British railway system. Nearing the top of this bank stood the third of Harrington's stations, Copperas Hill. The former station building still survives here, albeit bereft of its roof and crumbling badly. The formation to Micklam is easy to follow and, at least in 2013, was walkable throughout. The station at Micklam is long since gone but part of the works still remains in place on the cliffs. The rest of the route to Lowca is a heavy descent and it is difficult to imagine the industry that once stood here as it has been swept away since the 1970s.

Workington and Cockermouth to Penrith via Keswick

The first part of what became quite a lengthy cross-country route was a branch from Workington to Cockermouth operated by the London & North Western Railway. Built as a double-track route, it opened in April 1847 and carried both agricultural and coal traffic, reaching a terminus station on the west side of Cockermouth. Proposals for extending the line eastwards initially floundered, with a lack of obvious traffic and, more famously, spirited opposition from local poet William Wordsworth, delaying developments.

The situation had changed, however, by the 1860s with the development of large-scale ironworks in west Cumbria. The smelting of iron required high-quality coking coal for its operation, the nearest source being the north-east of England. Eventually built by the Cockermouth, Keswick & Penrith Railway (CK&PR) and engineered by Thomas Bouch, of Tay Bridge fame, the line constructed between these towns opened for passengers in April 1865 and as noted above, was a quite separate undertaking to the Workington and Cockermouth line. However, the advantages of through traffic were obvious, and this necessitated the construction of a new station at Cockermouth, to the south of the town, though the old station continued in use as a goods depot right up the line's closure.

The coke traffic from the north-east, which could access the line without reversing at Penrith after the construction of the Redhills curve just to the south of that town, was quickly augmented by passenger traffic, with early excursion trains running from as far away as Preston. These 'invasions' of tourists, heading into towns such as Keswick, where no facilities had been developed for them, were not initially popular but hotels and other places of refreshment were gradually provided. Built originally as single track, the sections from Redhills Junction to Blencow and Penruddock to Threlkeld were doubled by 1900, though the heavy engineering of other stretches meant that some single-track working continued. By 1913 the line carried almost half a million passengers, a remarkable figure, but first the First War and later more convenient bus and car travel led to a steady decline in passenger numbers. Coke traffic from the north-east ended in the 1920s, leading to the closure of the Redhills curve around that time; Cobb has its last year of operation as 1936, though other sources suggest an earlier date. In November 1955, diesel multiple units took over local services, significantly reducing journey times, but this provided only temporary respite. Closure came west of Keswick in April 1966, with Penrith to Keswick clinging on into the '70s, the last train running in March 1972.

It is fair that say that line has enjoyed somewhat varied fortunes since closure, with much to relate; let us start at the Penrith end first. Here a bridge over the M6 south of the station, which carries the main line and a footpath, gives a clear view of the junction with the Keswick line, though little trace remains here of the formerly adjacent formation of the Redhills Curve. Heading west, the line is mostly intact but overgrown and unsuitable for exploration even with appropriate permission. At Blencow the station and some platform remains survive behind a lorry depot, but all has gone at Penruddock with modern housing on the site. At Troutbeck the station house is the only survivor and little of the trackbed can be accessed until the impressive Mosedale Viaduct is reached. This structure is in excellent condition with a proper surface, despite not being part of an official path; its twelve arches carrying it high over the beck of that name.

From Threlkeld (where part of the former island platform still survives and can be found inside a storage depot) the Lake District National Park purchased the trackbed as far as Keswick in 1983. This section makes a superbly scenic walk, crossing bowstring bridges (some are 'inverted' bowstrings) and short tunnels en route, though the formation suffered considerable damage from Storm Desmond in late 2016 when several original structures were washed away, and only fully reopened in December 2021. Keswick station was an impressive structure, with three platforms (two as an island), a station building of slate and stone and an adjacent hotel in the same style. Today the hotel survives and has been extended with a glazed area over the former westbound platform, though the island platform has long since vanished with the area now used as a car park.

Penrith to Workington line, Derby lightweight DMU approaching Braithwaite. *Author's collection*

West of Keswick, the track can be regained, crossing Newlands Beck on a fine bridge before reaching Braithwaite; Braithwaite station has been restored and slightly extended and it is pleasing to see that both platforms are still largely intact. However, between Braithwaite and Bassenthwaite Lake stations, almost 10 miles of trackbed is buried under the modern A66 road, a diversion away from local villages but not a particularly fast one as the trackbed was only wide enough for a single-carriage road. Bassenthwaite Lake station, once largely derelict and apparently beyond repair, has been lovingly restored into a café and now makes a delightful stopover for afternoon tea and cakes. Approaching Cockermouth, a short section to the east of the River Cocker is now a public path but the station site, at one time a fire service headquarters, is now being built over with apartments. Very little of the last 8 miles into Workington is easily explored, with some track lost to road building and all five bridges that once crossed and recrossed the River Derwent having been demolished. Nothing remains of Workington Bridge station either, other than the rebuilt nearby bridge that gave it its name.

Calva Junction–Linefoot

Running almost parallel but generally around a mile to the north of the Workington to Cockermouth line, this route was built by the Cleator & Workington Junction Railway (C&WJR) to Linefoot and connected with lines north thereof, including the Solway route into Scotland. Opened in 1887, it was quite a heavily engineered line, the L&NWR's Cockermouth Railway having already laid claim to the more straightforward Derwent Valley route, so gradients of up to 1 in 50 were needed, not ideal for heavy coal or iron traffic. Passenger services were very limited indeed, although a few trains a day ran out from Workington to Seaton between 1888 and 1897, and again from 1907 to 1922. For just two months, September to November 1908, services were extended through Great Broughton to Linefoot: one of the shortest-lived such provision anywhere, though excursion traffic, at least from the former destination, continued until 1922. In contrast, the closure of this line must be on the list of the longest and most drawn-out of such measures. East of Buckhill Colliery, the railway closed in 1935 along with the Derwent branch (see Chapter 18). However, the colliery itself, closing in 1939, became the site of a military (Royal Navy Armaments) establishment, which retained a rail connection via Calva Junction right through until 1992. This meant that, on closure, the route could be acquired in one piece and converted to a footpath; it now provides 4½ miles of pleasant walking, from Camerton, east of Seaton, back down past Calva Junction into Workington.

Opposite: An apparently much-needed weedkiller train, led by a Class 20 locomotive, heads up the Buckhill branch from Calva Junction to RNAD Broughton Moor in July 1990. *Author's collection*

17 Carlisle and North Cumbria

The Mealsgate Loop

The area to the east of Aspatria, forming the northernmost part of the west Cumbria coalfield, was an early target for the local railway entrepreneurs of the mid-nineteenth century. The Maryport & Carlisle Railway (M&CR) were the first on the scene, opening a loop to the south of the main Workington to Carlisle route in 1866. Just under 8 miles long, it headed east from Aspatria, rejoining the main line at Aikbank Junction, a few miles to the west of Wigton. Climbing to a summit at Mealsgate, the line was unsuitable for heavy 'through' freight traffic and generally operated as two separate 'branches' heading in either direction out of Mealsgate, though the Aspatria end was much the busier. Passenger trains were even more of an afterthought than is usual on such lines, with just a single service provided between Mealsgate and Wigton each way on the eastern section between 1872 and August 1921, though Quick records the one intermediate station on this section, High Blaithwaite, as only opening in October 1878. The year 1930 was a bad one for the loop, with the eastern end closing completely and passenger services between Mealsgate and Aspatria (with one intermediate station at Baggrow) ceasing to run, though freight traffic to Mealsgate hung on until 1952.

For such an early closure, the formation is remarkably intact, perhaps reflecting its somewhat remote location. West of Baggrow a well-made track parallels the railway, giving clear views of the trackbed with a short section near Harriston diverted onto the formation itself. The station house at Mealsgate became a private residence and in early 2022 was undergoing major refurbishment, but unsurprisingly nothing survives at the two other station sites.

The Solway Junction Railway (Kirkbride to Annan)

Opened to goods traffic in March 1870 and to passengers in August of the same year, the Solway Junction Railway (SJR) was promoted and backed by the Caledonian Railway, which operated the line from the start and absorbed the smaller SJR company in 1895. Its aim was to provide a direct link, bypassing Carlisle, for haulage of iron ore from West Cumberland to the steelworks of Lanarkshire.

The route is most famous for its construction of the Solway Viaduct, one of the largest and boldest pieces of civil engineering to be found on a minor line anywhere in the country. Work started on the viaduct as early as March 1865

Solway Junction Railway, a bridge survives at Bromfield, but nothing remains of the station at this site. *Author*

Only these rusty pillars mark the site of the Solway Viaduct at Bowness. *Author*

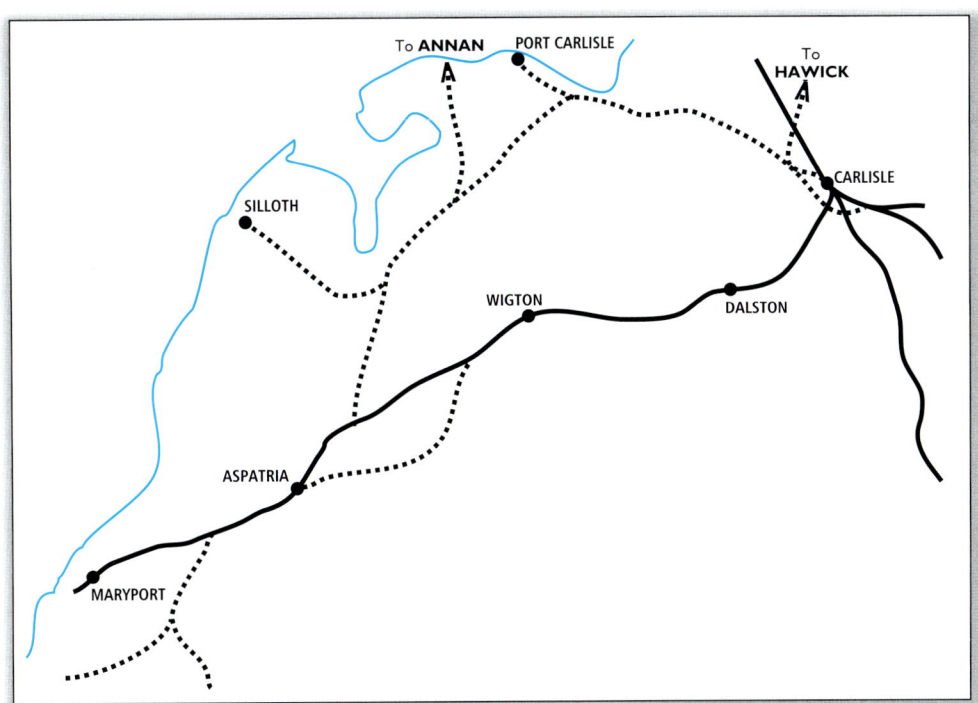

Map showing lines in the Carlisle and North Cumbria area.

and by 1868 it was largely complete but, was not passed as fit for operation until 1870. When opened, it was the longest railway viaduct in the world and was believed to have cost around £100,000 to build. At 1¼ miles long, with 181 single and twelve double piers keeping the rails 34ft above high tide, it was an extraordinary, if somewhat vulnerable structure. It was first damaged by freezing water in the winter of 1875–76 and even more so in January 1881, when ice floes backed by strong winds pounded the structure, resulting in the collapse of forty-five piers and thirty-seven girders. Somewhat surprisingly, funding was found for its reconstruction, but it wasn't until May 1884 that trains could resume their cross-border journeys across the viaduct. Final closure came in August 1921, after which it was famously used by locals from the Scottish side walking into England for alcoholic refreshment, which was otherwise denied them on the sabbath. Demolition took place in 1934–35, a dangerous undertaking in itself that sadly cost three lives. Even then the job was not finished as stones placed to support some of the piers had created small reefs that became a danger to shipping, and it wasn't until the 1950s that these were all cleared.

Passenger services seemed almost designed to avoid centres of population as much as possible. Never more than three services daily in each direction, these started at Brayton, just north of Aspatria, then briefly joined the Silloth branch before heading north through Whitrigg and Bowness before crossing the viaduct. On the Scottish side the Caledonian Railway had its own station at Annan (Annan Shawhill) and passenger services generally continued on to Kirtlebridge on the West Coast Main Line. On the English side, all services ended with closure of the viaduct in September 1921. In terms of what remains, on the English side, unsurprisingly given the date of closure there is little left to see, though just south of the viaduct around 2–3 miles of formation is largely intact. Bowness station is a private residence, and at the viaduct there remains a short piece of stone embankment with a set of rusting piers at the seaward end.

Bullgill–Brigham: The Derwent Branch

This 6-mile branch was an unusual example of cooperation between the normally highly competitive railway companies of north Cumbria. It ran between Bullgill, between Maryport and Aspatria, and Bingham on the Workington–Cockermouth route. Although owned by the M&CR, the area's main player, the L&NWR also had running rights that, together with their links with the Caledonian Railway, allowed freight traffic to reach Scotland via the Solway route. Opening in 1867, passenger services were remarkably varied: as well as more local services, there were trains between Maryport and Cockermouth, requiring reversals at both Bullgill and Brigham, together with a short-lived Carlisle to Keswick service, needing just the one reversal at Brigham.

The closure of the Solway Viaduct in 1921 ended the line's importance as a through route, and with its indirect connections to nearby towns it is perhaps surprising that passenger traffic hung on until April 1935, when the route was closed to all traffic and the track quickly lifted. Indeed, the following year there was a tragic accident during removal of a girder bridge over the River Derwent to the north of Brigham, leading to the loss of two lives. Little is left of the formation, though a short section south of Linefoot is now a public road. Dovenby station was private until 1896. Prior to that time it was used only by the Ballentine-Dykes family of Dovenby Hall and their visitors; the station building remains in use as a private house.

Linefoot, where from 1887 a further branch headed west to Workington via Seaton, was one of the shortest-lived stations anywhere, open for just two months from September to November 1908. The station at Papcastle, a village best known for the discovery in recent times of significant Roman remains including a fort, a watermill and bathhouse, also survives as a house; unusually, both its last two 'managers' were stationmistresses.

The Silloth and Port Carlisle Branches

The small coastal town of Silloth is famed for its year-round mild climate and beautiful sunsets, but its early development from a tiny village was somewhat chequered. The location had been chosen to develop a deep-water dock for north Cumbria at a point less affected by the tides of the River Solway than Port Carlisle, opened in 1823 but soon affected by silting. However, despite the North British Railway reaching Silloth via a junction with the Port Carlisle branch at Drumburgh in August 1856, the dock was not ready and much of the potential trade was lost, never to return. Silloth did develop, however, into a small, delightful, but fully planned seaside resort, with much support from the railway, and to an extent retains this role, in a rather genteel kind of way. However, the population of Silloth itself is tiny, less than 3,000, and thus generated little outbound traffic. Clearly though, attempts at running the line more economically were made, as from November 1954 the branch was the first anywhere in Britain to have its services run entirely by diesel multiple units. Unfortunately, though, it was a prime candidate for closure during the cull of seaside branches in the mid-1960s. The last trains ran through in September 1964, despite lineside protests that delayed the last train back to Carlisle by several hours. Most of the Silloth branch's formation west of Drumburgh remains intact but in private ownership and is not readily accessible, other than a short stretch heading out of Silloth itself. Station buildings survive at Kirkbride, Abbey Town and Black Dykes as private residences but sadly Silloth station, by then much altered but still taking up a prime position in the town, was demolished in 2007 with a terrace of modern housing now occupying the site.

The short Port Carlisle branch had a more unusual history. As mentioned above, the port itself opened in 1823, served by a canal from Carlisle. This was built as a broad canal with eight wide locks and no low bridges, making it possible for coastal vessels to reach the centre of Carlisle. However, by 1853, the area of the sea-lock was badly affected by silting and with several other ports available for trade nearby, the canal was closed. Somewhat surprisingly this was not the end of the story as the North British Railway purchased and drained the canal and by June 1854 had commenced passenger train services along a single-track railway laid largely on the bed of the old cut. This made the line feel like it was almost entirely in a cutting, passengers seeing little beyond the former banks of the canal.

From its opening until steam traction took over in April 1914 the Port Carlisle branch west of Drumburgh Junction was famous for its horse-drawn operation, with the carriage always known as a 'dandy' car. Although steam locomotives and later Sentinel railcars operated on the branch, there was never a population to support the service and all traffic to Port Carlisle ceased in May 1932. Much of the formation remains, but with its wide, low, and square cross-section it looks much more like the canal it once was rather than the railway it later became.

Mealsgate loop, missing bridge and trackbed west of Baggrow. *Author*

Crossing keeper's house on the Silloth branch at Causewayhead, east of Silloth. *Author*

Perhaps the most interesting surviving section is where it runs just south of the Hadrian's Wall path between Drumburgh and Burgh by Sands. Station buildings survive only at Kirkandrews and Burgh stations, but at Port Carlisle a single platform may still be found hidden away just behind the village's main road, not far from the huge, totally silted up, sea-lock through which boats once passed on their way to Carlisle.

Carlisle and the English Section of the Waverley Line

Given that the former Waverley route continues north from Carlisle for around 20 miles before heading across the border into Scotland, it is felt that this line merits inclusion in a chapter covering the north of Cumbria. Open in its entirety by 1862, its history is much more associated with north of the border: the controversial closure, depriving a whole area of Scotland of a rail service, and its subsequent partial reopening are well-known stories but the fortunes of the English end of the route have received a good deal less attention. Moved after nationalisation into the Scottish Region, ten years later in 1959 the boundary was moved south to Riddings Junction, where the Langholm branch diverged, which moved Longtown back to the London Midland Region but still left the English stations of Riddings Junction, Penton and Kershope Foot in the Scottish Region. Closure came in January 1969, despite vehement protests, but it is fair to say that few of these were rooted in the small settlements south of the border.

Port Carlisle station's surviving platform. *Author*

Let us start, though, in Carlisle itself. There is much left to see here, aside from its superb station, designed in a pseudo-medieval style by Sir William Tite and used by no fewer than seven different railway companies. Taking a roughly clockwise route around the city, a visitor can view the site of Petteril Bridge Junction and its yard, though it is no longer possible to view the former Midland shed.

'Dandy car' at Port Carlisle station. *Gordon Suggitt collection*

Derwent branch, Dovenby station house. *Author*

It is also possible to walk parallel to the main line north of Carlisle Citadel station past Caldew Junction to Dentonholme Goods. Although now a 'public' road, signage indicates that this area remains in railway property hands. After viewing the sites of Bog, Forks and Rome Street Junctions to the south of Citadel station one can continue north, eventually reaching Canal Junction, where the Silloth (and Port Carlisle) line left the Waverley route, though the precise site is now hard to discern. The Eden Viaduct, subject of proposals for conversion to a footpath/cycleway, is currently awaiting a change of ownership and some remedial work before it can again be opened for public use; it had significant repairs carried out in 2015 to stabilise and makes repairs to the piers.

Heading out of Carlisle towards Longtown, much is built over or blocked by roads and other developments, but two pleasant accessible sections remain. The first is south of the former Parkhouse Halt (serving RAF Carlisle for many years), which is now part of the Kingmoor Nature Reserve. The second stretch is north from Lyneside towards Sandysike, appearing almost untouched since the rails and ballast was removed and with a small bridge over the River Lyne still intact. Between these locations was Harker station; actually two stations, as the first closed in November 1929 but a second station opened in 1943 on an adjacent site, initially for access to a nearby ordnance factory. A fine station building and beautifully restored signal box survive at the first location. At Lyneside (another early closure in 1929) the station building also survives but the platform area has been replaced by a lawn, thus making the place look almost unrecognisable as a station.

Nothing remains at Longtown, the only place of any significance in England beyond Carlisle, but Scotch Dyke station (closed in May 1949) has fared much better, the single-storey station building surviving in private occupation together with the southbound platform and two small railway cottages that also backed onto the platform. A fine viaduct over the River Esk is another delightful survivor just to the north. At Riddings Junction the station building survives but is now enclosed within the private grounds of Riddings Farm. Just to the north the Langholm branch curved away north, crossing Liddel Water, which here marks the England–Scotland border, on another fine and sometimes unofficially accessible (from the north side) viaduct. North of Riddings the trackbed is largely intact but in private hands and not easily walkable even with the requisite permissions.

Lambley–Brampton Junction and Brampton Town (Lord Carlisle's Railway)

Although the Brampton Railway (or Lord Carlisle's Railway) probably had its origins in a short wooden wagonway at Tindale Fell Colliery in about 1776, the line heading westwards into Brampton only opened over

Waverley line; crossing of River Esk. *Phillip Earnshaw*

Waverley line; Scotch Dyke station, looking south. *Phillip Earnshaw*

twenty years later with the first wagon of coal being horse-hauled into the small town in April 1799. No Act of Parliament was obtained as the vast majority of the system was built by Lord Carlisle on his own land. By 1808 it had been relayed with cast-iron and wrought-iron rails, this being the first recorded application of the latter in a day-to-day commercial way. In 1836 a horse-worked passenger service was introduced when the track was realigned to meet up with the Newcastle & Carlisle Railway (N&CR) at Brampton Junction. This 'dandy-car' service ceased in 1890 after the line failed an inspection, and despite local campaigns was not reinstated. Eventually, in 1913 the NER took over the branch, relayed the track and introduced a steam-hauled passenger service, but traffic was clearly modest as the NER suspended passenger trains between 1917 and 1920 and the L&NER withdrew the service for good in 1923. Complete closure came shortly afterwards, and the following year the track was lifted. After this time the route started to be used by locals on foot as a way of reaching Brampton Junction, with apparently some encouragement from the railway company, and thus became one of the country's oldest railway paths.

The line to the east of Brampton Junction lies what has been called has been called at different periods the Tindale Fell Railway, the Midgeholme Railway, the Hartleyburn & Brampton Railway and simply the Brampton Railway. It also became one of the first non-Stephenson railways to convert to and adopt the standard gauge of 4ft 8½in. The year 1836 saw conversion to locomotive power, with the famous *Rocket*, newly purchased from the Liverpool & Manchester Railway, in use from the following year, though unfortunately it quickly proved unsuitable for the heavy loads that needed to be hauled. In 1947 the mines and thus the railway came under the control of the National Coal Board but six years later, after being in use for 155 years, mining ceased, and accordingly the railway closed.

The Brampton Railway, known locally as the 'Dandy Line' due to its history of horse traction, began at the former Brampton Town station and is an official path throughout. Brampton Town station lies at the north end of this route, with some remains in the yard of a local garage, so obviously access is only possible with permission here. The line then climbs gently for a mile and a quarter to Brampton Junction, becoming a pleasant, rural walk. The original, eighteenth-century alignment, last used in 1836, ran to the north-east of the later line, and some short pieces of cutting may still

The unusual 'three-tracked' incline on Lord Carlisle's Railway west of Hallbankgate. *Author's collection*

be made out here. From Brampton Junction, the 'Lord Carlisle' line headed east, though the trackbed is no longer accessible here, and after a mile ascended by a self-acting inclined plane from Kirkhouse to Planehead with gradients varying from 1 in 22 to 1 in 17½. This incline, most unusually, had three rails, each a standard gauge apart, with a division into two separate 'lines' only at a central passing place. At Kirkhouse a small shed remains, as does some cast-iron rail formerly from a siding that once served a nearby farm. A level crossing carried the line over the A689 road at Hallbankgate and slightly further east a branch headed south-east to serve a number of quarries and mines in the Howgill area. Reports indicate that some of this system remains walkable, whilst other parts have been completely obliterated. Official access can be resumed here, continuing through Bluegate to Tindale, where there were smelting works and collieries. Turning south-east towards Midgeholme, the line ran for about a mile along a high embankment, constructed in 1824, crossing the valley that divides Cumberland from Northumberland. The line then skirted the northern escarpment of Hartleyburn Common with another level crossing taking it over the A689 at Haltonleagate, shortly after which public access to the line ends. Further east, the junction with a short, north-facing branch to Roachburn Colliery is identifiable. The line terminated at Hallbankgate until an 1849 extension reached Lambley and a junction with the Alston line upon the latter line's opening in 1852.

Trackbed on Lord Carlisle's Railway at Bluegate. *Author*

18
Pennine Cumbria

In considering this area, we need to return to our definition of 'north-west'. Our lines for consideration here are those heading north and west from Kirkby Stephen and the old L&NWR route from Ingleton (and Midland Railway south to Clapham) to Low Gill via Sedbergh. The majority of both the Stainmore route east of Kirkby Stephen and the Alston branch from Haltwhistle lie outside the area and will not be discussed in detail in this volume.

Tebay–Kirkby Stephen (Stainmore Route West)

Let us first consider the background to the Stainmore route. Seen as a valuable link between the coal and coke of the north-east and the iron (and later steel) works of west Cumbria, it opened in August 1861. Passenger services through to Tebay were never numerous, though between 1905 and 1911 a Newcastle to Barrow service used this route. Although summer excursions from the north-east to Blackpool continued into the 1950s, many of the regular services were diverted north to serve Appleby, Penrith, and Carlisle instead. Local traffic ceased in 1952 but the Tebay line remained a valuable secondary link until the closure of the Stainmore line as a through route in 1962.

Starting at Tebay, where all traces of a once-substantial station were swept away by electrification works, the trackbed has been taken over by the new A685 road for around 5 miles, as far as Brownber. The road is arguably a valuable facility, linking Kirkby Stephen with the M6 motorway and bypassing local villages formerly served by a narrow road, with sharp bends, not really suited to modern-day traffic. At Gaisgill the stationmaster's house nowadays looks over the road rather than the tracks, and the wating room on the down-side platform has been tastefully converted to holiday accommodation. In addition to Gaisgill, a couple of crossing-keeper's houses can still be seen along here, but it is certainly not an ideal location for exploration on foot.

The road section ends close to Ravenstonedale station, a delightful example of a beautifully preserved, privately owned station house, situated on the up platform, though the down platform and goods shed are long gone. The trackbed east of here is privately owned, so to reach the publicly accessible section you must make use of a public footpath heading north from Newbiggin. At this point, the trackbed, heading north, becomes an access route for the Smardale Gill National Nature Reserve for almost 4 miles, though it should be noted that the route is accessible for walkers only and that cycling is strictly prohibited. En route can be seen the site of the signal box at Sandy Bank, a stone-lined cutting bereft of its metal overbridge and Smardale Lime Kilns. Smardale Gill Viaduct, spanning the valley high above Scandal Beck, is a stone, fourteen-span structure, 553ft long. The viaduct itself, 90ft high, can be best appreciated from its south-western side. It is a magnificent sight; one of three currently maintained by the locally based Northern Viaduct Trust. The viaduct was bought into public ownership and restored for public access in 1992 and has recently been resurfaced after a period of closure. However, at the time of writing the Viaduct Trust are actively trying to raise funds for more general repairs; it can only be hoped that this does not imply a long-term threat to the structure.

Passing under the Settle & Carlisle route just south of that line's own Smardale Viaduct (the highest on the S&C), the Stainmore line curves east, then south as it heads towards Kirkby Stephen. A diversion is required at Smardale station; here the stationmaster's house and platform remain but in a much-changed and modernised state, with the original structure added to on both sides by extensions. It should be noted that there was only ever one platform at Smardale, the raised area opposite the station building not being of railway origin. After Smardale, the line becomes a somewhat rough unofficial footpath past Waitby to a point where it parallels the Eden Valley branch, heading south from Penrith, at a second nature reserve known as Waitby Greenings.

Map showing lines in the Pennine Cumbria area.

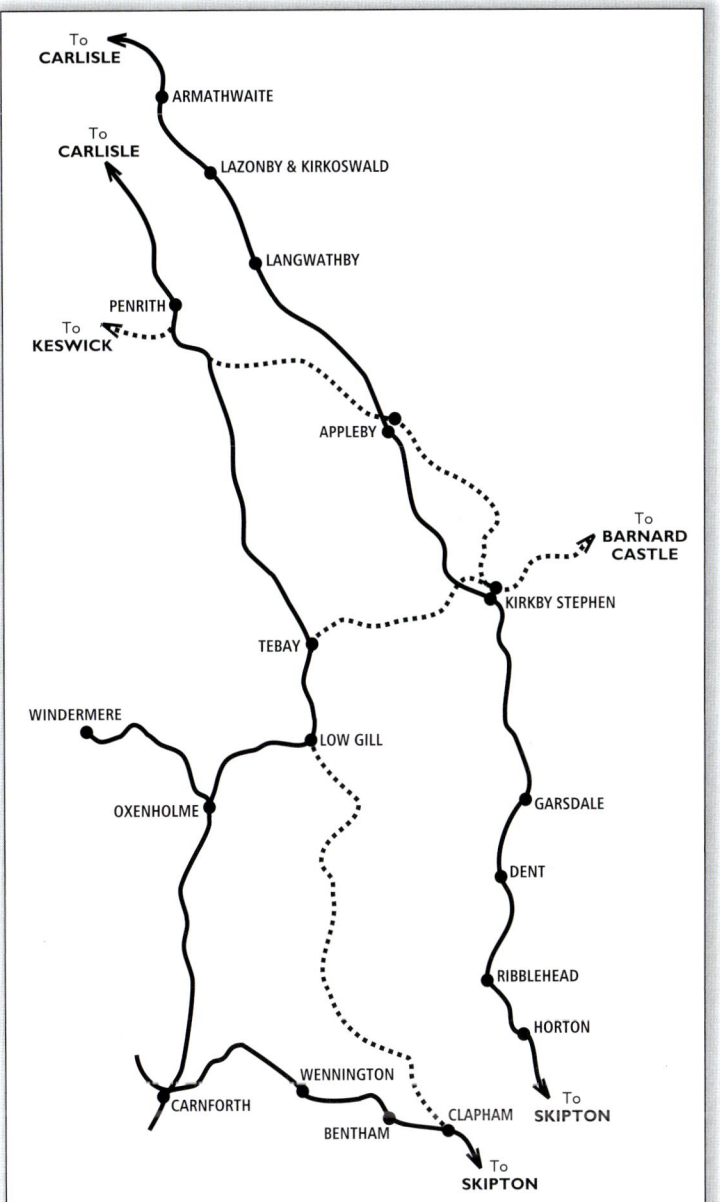

While technically the footpath ends in a cul de sac, it is not difficult to cross onto the Eden Valley line, exit onto a public footpath at Greenriggs Farm and continue south to Kirkby Stephen from there.

Kirkby Stephen–Penrith (Eden Valley Line)

The small, somewhat isolated town of Kirkby Stephen was perhaps a surprising place to find a major centre of railway activity. As well as being a junction station, it had its own engine shed (12D), housing over a dozen locomotives as late as 1956. The Eden Valley route was very much seen as a branch line when built, with 22 miles of single track. Following a valley made construction easier; unlike the Stainmore route it required little in the way of major viaducts and large bridges. Just south of Penrith, a link was made into the Keswick line, known as the Redhills Curve (see Chapter 17), giving direct access for coke trains heading into Workington. There was also a link made with the Settle & Carlisle line at Appleby; this proved valuable in later years and allowed closure of the northern section of the route after passenger traffic had ceased. In a similar way to the Tebay route, longer-distance passenger services, including Darlington–Penrith services, lasted longer than local trains, which enjoyed little in the way of patronage. Most of the village stations were early casualties, Musgrave going in 1952, Kirkby Thore and Temple Sowerby in 1953 and Cliburn in 1956, several years before final closure in 1962. However, the line remained in use, via the connection at Appleby, to serve Hartley Quarry, east of Kirkby Stephen, until 1975, when it was lifted south of Warcop.

Much remains to be seen, though the distance and the loss of Skygarth Viaduct over the River Eden south of Temple Sowerby make the line a difficult proposition as a single-day visit. Let us start at Kirkby Stephen East; here a preservation society known as the Stainmore Railway Company has its base. The station, with its distinctive small overall roof, can be visited when open, together with a 1930s buffet car providing refreshments, though much of what was at one time a larger site is now given over to industrial use. The society have relayed track for some distance to the north, and after a period of inaction were scheduled to resume running trains in April 2022.

Smardale Gill Viaduct on the Tebay–Kirkby Stephen line. *Chris McFarlane*

Smardale station, west of Kirkby Stephen. *Author*

Heading north, a wooded footpath exists, initially parallel to the Tebay line through the aforementioned Waitby Greenings Nature Reserve as far as Waitby Crossing. North of here the line remains largely intact but in private ownership, the small bridge over Scandal Beck having happily survived. South of Musgrave the viaduct over the River Eden has now gone, though do be aware than some modern maps show it as still in place. Fortunately, the parallel B6259 road provides an easy alternative crossing point. Musgrave station, the earliest on the line to close, is soon reached, in private occupation, with the station house and part of the platform still intact though the front of the building has been extended and modernised in recent times.

North of Musgrave station, a road-over-rail bridge is reached, the location of a controversial incident in 2021 when the structure was infilled with concrete by the Highways Agency. This was one of a number of such actions around the country, carried out without any local consultation and without any apparent proper professional assessment of the strength of the bridge and the traffic that passes over it. Having said that, the argument that the infilling of the bridge blocks a potential relaying of the railway is somewhat fanciful; neither the Stainmore or Warcop groups (see below) have the funding required to even consider rebuilding this section, nor, it seems, do they have any history of effectively working together towards common goals. However in June 2022 retrospective planning permission for this act was refused by the local council, with the Highways Agency being obliged to remove the infill.

After another mile or so of private land, sidings are reached that mark the southern end of operations of the Eden Valley Railway, based at Warcop. Although the station building itself, a delightful single-storey structure, is in private ownership, the railway owns a good deal of land with sidings on which it keeps its collection of locomotives and carriages. It has also restored to working order the station signal box at the south end of Warcop's single platform.

Kirkby Stephen East station. *Author*

The survival of tracks from Appleby as far as Warcop lies in its use for transport of large military vehicles to the nearby army camp and was last used for that purpose in May 1987. The line briefly became a popular venue for railtours, with the last of them running in March 1989 before the line was taken out of use. Since that time, the railway has lay slumbering. Most unusually for a route with tracks, the line was acquired by Railway Paths Ltd, though there does not seem to have been any intention to convert it into a trail. The Eden Valley Railway have since then purchased the last 2 miles of trackbed into Warcop and do run trains on this section when they can. However, they have been hampered by bridge strikes and landslips in recent years, as well as by Covid, so any potential travellers are advised to check what they are currently doing in terms of operations. Opening up to Appleby East remains a long-term objective, while heading south to link up with the Stainmore group at Kirkby Stephen is an even more long-term aspiration.

A frosty morning between Appleby and Warcop on the Eden Valley line. *Chris McFarlane*

Appleby East station, a 2022 view. *Author*

Appleby East station is both beautiful and ugly at the same time; a delightfully ornate station building still sits on its single platform with a goods shed opposite. However, the whole site is now occupied by a scrap metal firm happy to leave its scrap all over the platform and the almost buried rails. North of the station level crossing gates survive but resurfacing of the road through the crossing in 2017 took out the rails and thus removed the physical connection. There is no public access to the junction with the erstwhile short link to the Settle & Carlisle, though this piece of track can be used for turning and storage of stock and proved of value when the S&C line north of Appleby was closed due to a landslip in 2016–17.

North of Appleby, the formation disappears underneath the A66 for much of the route north, though a section north from Crackenthorpe remains and can be walked with landowners' permission. Temple Sowerby station, closed in 1953 has fared better than most; the former platform, station buildings and station house survive, as does the former weigh house. It is then possible to make your way past the abutments that once were part of Skygarth Viaduct over the River Eden. To the west, Cliburn station, closed in September 1956, now serves as a family home with its platform still clear and intact. The signal box and goods office have both been refurbished and now serve as self-catering accommodation. On an organised visit back in 2018, the owner showed us how the old railway structures had been laid out inside while retaining a lot of their original external appearance. On site could also be seen reminders of the former goods facilities at this station.

In 2017 the trackbed was severed at the level crossing to the north of Appleby East station. *Author*

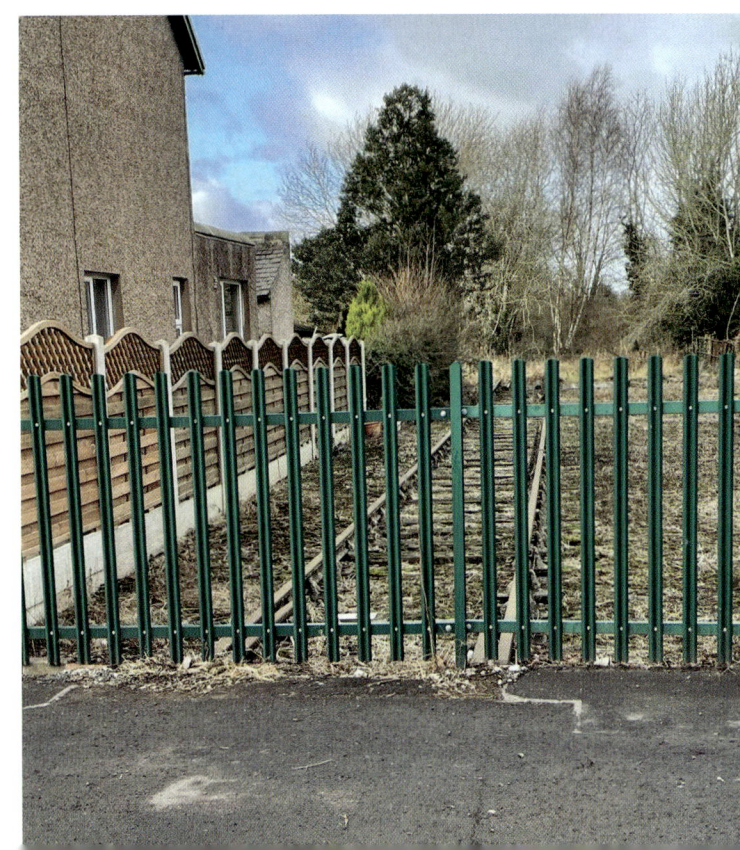

Above: Cliburn station, on the Eden Valley line between Penrith and Appleby, after closure. *Author's collection*

Left: A modern view of Cliburn station. *Author*

Clifton Moor station follows and here can be viewed the station house and main station building, another conversion to a private dwelling, A separate waiting room, once provided for local dignitary Earl Lonsdale, has been extended and serves as a separate dwelling, with the former goods yard still clear. A second building, which stood adjacent in the goods yard, whilst intact in 2015 is understood to have succumbed to high winds in the interim period. An old station lamp still survives, although a station sign, still present in the undergrowth in 2015, has now gone. The remaining formation to the junction with the West Coast Main Line south of Clifton is intact but generally inaccessible.

Clapham–Low Gill

Our last line in this section is the 'lost' south–north route through the Pennines into what was formerly known as Westmorland. The North Western Railway, often known as the 'Little North Western', built a branch from Clapham, west of Skipton, to Ingleton. This route opened in July 1849, with the Midland Railway quickly taking over the original company and assuming responsibility for operations in 1851. In the following decade, the Lancaster & Carlisle Railway also built a branch to Ingleton, south from Low Gill via Sedbergh, Ingleton being a more important and populous place in the mid-nineteenth century than it is now. Ingleton seems from this distance to be more of a strategic target than a likely supplier of profitable traffic but did also have coal mines that could have provided some business. This line opened in 1861, the same year as the impressive Ingleton Viaduct was built to connect the two lines. The northern of the two routes was soon taken over by the L&NWR, leaving an uncomfortable connection between two major companies at Ingleton. Opinions varied on how well they got on; at times there seems to have been a reasonable degree of cooperation, but both companies continued to operate their own stations at Ingleton until 1917, when the L&NWR (the northernmost) station was closed. However, some years previously, the Midland Railway had grown weary of the situation, eventually reaching the point where they built their own line to Carlisle and Scotland, the Settle & Carlisle line, which opened in 1876. From that point Clapham to Low Gill was never more than a secondary route, though in the early 1960s a case was put forward to electrify Leeds to Low Gill via Ingleton, an action that would have doubtless meant the end for the Settle & Carlisle line.

A short discussion of county boundaries is needed here before we discuss the line's demise and post-closure history. Clapham is, and always has been, in North Yorkshire, as has Ingleton. The next town up the line, Kirkby Lonsdale, was formerly in Westmorland, at one time in Lancashire and now administratively in Cumbria. Sedbergh had a similar move, from Yorkshire to Cumbria, in the 1970s but more confusingly still, remains in the Yorkshire Dales National Park area. Low Gill moved from Westmorland to Cumbria when the former ceased to exist during the same 1970s local boundaries reform. But with the majority of the line lying in modern Cumbria we are safe to include it in this volume; now let us consider its later history.

Although Sedbergh, Kirkby Lonsdale and Ingleton might be considered quite well-known towns, they are all in reality very small places, with a population of around 2,000 in each. In addition, there was never any direct route by rail to the largest nearby city, Lancaster, which was reached by buses instead. As a result, local passenger traffic was an early casualty, closing in February 1954. Occasional school traffic, mostly to Sedbergh, continued until 1963, the same year as the line was last pressed into service as a diversionary route in bad weather for the Settle & Carlisle line. The last through trains ran in 1966 and track lifting was completed by the end of the following year.

Cliburn signal box. *Author*

As a disused railway of some length, passing through superb countryside, it is a great shame that the line did not make it into an era when it might have been preserved as a linear path. In the 1960s, British Railways were happy to sell off small pieces of trackbed bit by bit to the highest bidder, but it should also be said that organisations representing walkers and cyclists were not at that time pushing hard for access to disused railways in rural locations. They saw sterile, ballasted, trackbeds, burnt back cutting sides and overly gentle gradients that they did not think would have general appeal; a classic example of how attitudes change over time.

Let us start at Clapham, a somewhat quieter junction than its south London namesake. Passing a former caravan park, the line heads north, through pleasant countryside towards Ingleton. All is private land, though at intervals views of the mostly still well-formed formation can be seen from the A65 and adjacent minor roads. Nothing remains at Ingleton station, now a car park, but this is the best starting point to allow views of the superb viaduct. Despite being apparently in good condition and situated at a point where it might provide useful access between two halves of the village, Ingleton Viaduct has always been fenced off and to my knowledge there has never been any campaign to reopen it for pedestrian use. North of Ingleton the line is somewhat fragmented but in places walkable, as far as Kirkby Lonsdale, where the station, a good 2 miles south-west of the town, survives in private ownership.

North of Kirkby Lonsdale, much of the trackbed is owned by the National Grid. Although not normally publicly accessible, the power company has in the past given permission for walks by organised groups such as the Railway Ramblers Club. Of the formation today, much is walkable between the River Rawthey and High Casterton, although all lies in private hands. Any sign of Barbon station has been erased and subsequently its site has been built over. Since closure the route between Barbon and Sedbergh has acquired a gas pipe under its surface, which also crosses the Jackdaw (or Rawthey) Viaduct. Much of the trackbed is a pleasure to walk, having a soft, grassy surface with only minor diversions required beyond Barbon, although these can be somewhat cumbersome due to the regularity of the fences/gates across the formation. The other point of note is the station house at Middleton on Lune, an early closure, in 1931, another that has been preserved and is now in private hands.

Approaching Sedbergh, prior to passing behind the public school and along the northern bank of the River Rawthey is reached the first of three fine viaducts between here and Low Gill. The aforementioned Jackdaw Viaduct is 120ft long, 53ft high and comprises a single metal span between abutments of Penrith stone. Today it is totally secure. The curved embankment to its north is intact and walkable to the A683, although the section beyond is in industrial use. Beyond the next A684 Road Sedbergh station was sited. The main station building, together with part of its platform, still exists although it is in private ownership as a holiday cottage and not visible from adjacent roads. However, the goods yard can be visited during the coal merchant's normal opening hours and contains the station's goods shed, weighbridge and hut.

The next stretch of the route that can be accessed is beyond Slacks Lane, where a glorious cutting, overbridge and accompanying milepost precedes the gradual approach to Waterside or Lune Viaduct. This grand structure consists of six arches sandwiching a central metal span crossing the River Lune some 100ft below. At 530ft long and built of Penrith stone, it is a most striking site, fitting without intruding in an area of outstanding natural beauty. The viaduct, whilst in theory walkable with permission, is highly dangerous in that the central span is extremely exposed with only narrow strips of rotting wood between the foolhardy and a likely fatality. The Dales Way makes a more sensible alternative route here, with just a small diversion required to view the viaduct. The section north of the viaduct is strictly private but with few obstacles, although one cutting can become heavily overgrown with nettles. Another milepost may be noted en route. The coup de grace of the route is the long sweeping embankment sandwiching the delightful Low Gill or Dillicar Viaduct. Spanning Dillicar Beck and built again of Penrith stone, it is a magnificent sight with its eleven arches taking the route some 90ft above the valley floor. The route ends just beyond, at Low Gill Junction, slightly east of the long-disappeared Low Gill station (closed in March 1960) on the current West Coast Main Line. The 1860 stone terrace provided by the Lancaster & Carlisle Railway for railway families still stands, and continues to provide accommodation to this day.

Opposite top: Decking of Rothay (or Jackdaw) Viaduct south of Sedbergh. *Author*

Bottom: Clapham to Low Gill line, Waterside Viaduct. *Author*

Below: Clapham to Low Gill line, Waterside Viaduct, remains of decking. *Author*

19
Exploring Tramroads

Having spent most of the regional chapters considering former standard-gauge passenger railways, I will conclude the book by discussing the exploration of former tramroads in the north-west. I will categorise the tramways that can be explored into three groups and give examples of each. First are tramways that linked with standard-gauge railways, involving an interchange of sorts, secondly tramways that served canals and finally lines that stood alone, ending at roadsides or landsale yards. In some areas, particularly the north-east of England, many tramroads led down to rivers, particularly the River Tyne, but few such examples exist in the north-west. My choice of tramways for this chapter, necessarily subjective, is based on ease of access and a reasonable geographical spread, so apologies are in order if a line familiar to you is not included.

Discovering Tramroads

First let us examine the process of discovering tramways. Unlike proper railways, there is no definitive list or comprehensive mapping; as suggested above, readers might well know of tramways in their locality that have escaped my attention. Few appear in Colonel Cobb's outstanding books of adapted maps of Britain's railways and even fewer survived to appear in Ian Allan's pre-grouping atlas. Having said that, the recent mapping of parts of Britain's railways by Joe Brown is an outstanding effort. Brown's *Liverpool and Manchester Atlas* (though it actually covers much of our area as far north as Preston and as far east as Colne) includes many tramroads, mapping their routes, giving an approximate chronology, and is a very useful starting point. Another good point of reference for the tramroad hunter is Bertram Baxter's 1960s classic *Stone Blocks and Iron Rails,* which details the history, operation, and economics of the earlier horse-drawn tramroads. Baxter also included a chapter on tracing old lines, which is fascinating and contains much that is still relevant today, such as recognising a straight(ish) track with a steady but gentle gradient as a possible tramroad, together with a gazetteer that includes many former routes while unfortunately omitting certain others.

Brooks Quarry tramroads, incline above Facit. *Author*

Maps, both old and new, are another source for research and certainly on more than one occasion I have spotted an 'old tramway' marked on a map where I did not imagine one to be. A further source of information can be walking books: for example, in the 1960s, the author George Birtill wrote a number of guidebooks to the moors, hills, river valleys and canals around Chorley. These included reference to several tramways in the area that to my knowledge have never been documented elsewhere. This returns us to the key issue; if a tramway was never documented, its dates of opening and closure never recorded, nor its use, then it will be very difficult to find, trace and explore. Often the only chronology available is by comparing old maps of different dates, though this has become much easier with the mapping now provided by the National Library of Scotland (which covers the whole of Great Britain). For example, if a tramway is marked as open on an 1880 map but is shown as lifted on an 1890 one, we can make a reasonable assumption that the line closed between those two dates. But there are short-lived lines that can miss these criteria: particularly those used for the construction of reservoirs. Another example is the short-lived line built to serve collieries at Kings Moss, west of Wigan, which does not appear at all on the 1894 map and is marked only as a track (use of the term 'disused railway', or similar, on maps did not come in until much later) in the 1909 version.

So, what are we still likely to find in place still in situ on the ground? Certainly nothing of any wooden structures – nor iron rails and nails, long since rusted away. In some places, tramways ran alongside existing roads and although this unfortunately sometimes created an ideal opportunity for widening schemes alongside busy routes, an unusually wide verge can be a telltale sign of a former line. But what you can see in many places and which form the obvious trademark of the earlier versions of these routes, are the original stone sleeper blocks, sometimes stretching for quite some distance. On closer inspection you may also be able to find two or more holes in the top of each block. Into these went the nails to secure the rails – the nails themselves having long since rusted away. But with two parallel lines of sleeper blocks you can start to imagine the scene, perhaps also the sounds, so unfamiliar to modern ears, the loud clip-clop of the horses together with the jingle-jangle of the chains connecting the wagons and the metallic roar of wheel on rail. Clearly the smell would have been somewhat different to steam or diesel, too!

Tramroads that Linked with Standard Gauge Railways

So, let us head out there. First, we will consider tramways that linked with the mainline system and here the obvious place to start is the extensive network of stone quarry tramways in the hills above Rossendale. The 3ft gauge system serving the Brooks quarries was the most extensive of these; to reach them you climb a long and quite steep incline just to the east of Clough Fold station (Chapter 8) on the Bacup branch of the East Lancashire Railway. The 'main line' of this system first reached the main quarry, Cragg, but continued on to reach Ding Quarry, at over 1,500ft above sea level. The direct route from Clough Fold to Ding was around 4 miles, but with its many branches to other quarries, the system probably totalled over 10 miles, including a point of reversal to gain extra height. These trackbeds are nearly all walkable, either on trackbed or just above shallow, flooded cuttings. But this is by no means the only railway on the moors: other tramroads reached Lee Quarry, closer to Bacup, Britannia Quarry and Bagden, west of Whitworth.

Less well known are the lines that linked with the Bolton to Blackburn line, north of Entwistle station. Here an early twentieth-century tramway reached a brickworks at Blackhill. Starting at some exchange sidings to the east side of the main line, the tramway descended and passed under the main line before taking a direct course west to these works. Pretty much the whole way is walkable, on either a grassy or stony surface, though the site of the former works itself is private. But there is more: heading north out of the brickworks another tramway soon appears (it is possible that these lines linked, but it seems unlikely from the map or from evidence on the ground) heading north on a slight embankment through delightful woodland, as good a setting for an old railway as you will find anywhere yet known to so few. Eventually a cutting appears, and the going becomes rougher and less easy to follow before the tramway ends above a very old quarry. Just a mile north of here, at Walton sidings where the once four-track section of main line reduced to double track before the approach to Sough tunnel, starts an arguably even more impressive tramway. This route heads due east, crossing the main (Roman) road at Round Barn then, dividing into several branches, heads into the extensive and still impressive sandstone quarry at Round Barn Delf. Walkable throughout, the lines that survive were clearly in use at different times to reflect the progress of quarrying. As a line that I have never seen discussed or documented, I consider it quite a find.

A further group of tramways that are well worth exploring, but do not fit quite as neatly into the above criteria, are those in the Poynton area of east Cheshire. Although, in its heyday, a busy area for coal mining, the last colliery and hence the tramway had closed by 1935. It should be said that the whole area, being quite prosperous and now a popular residential area with an easy commute to Manchester, nowadays has a very different feel to the former mining areas discussed in previous chapters. Indeed, as early as 1841, a report on the living conditions of Poynton miners found 'good earnings, well-furnished houses with vegetable plots outside and provision of savings in case of sickness', a far higher quality of life than that enjoyed by most manual workers of the time. In fact, collieries were being sunk in the Poynton area as early as the seventeenth century, with coal taken by road to either Stockport or Macclesfield and references made to eighteenth-century tramways, though these seem not to have appeared on any maps. The Macclesfield Canal,

Stone cutting on Brooks tramroads, Rossendale. *Author*

Tramway with retaining wall approaching Round Barn Delf, near Darwen. *Author*

opening in 1831, was in canal terms a relatively late arrival on the scene, but soon a line headed east from Poynton, via Prince's incline to a wharf on the canal east of Higher Poynton. The canal's monopoly on trade lasted less than fifteen years though, as by 1845 the Macclesfield & Birmingham Railway (later the L&NWR) could connect with the Poynton system at a junction just to the north of Poynton station. The tramways were originally horse-drawn with rope-operated inclines, but locomotives were introduced in 1876.

The tramways that can be explored today lie in the area roughly between Poynton and Middlewood stations; a circular walk being possible from either location. From the canal, and from Canal Pits (north of the current Barlow House Farm), we can head west, crossing over the former Marple & Macclesfield Railway, now the Middlewood Way. A right of way exists right through past Prince's Wood, where a walkable branch headed north to Park & Lawrence Pits and an adjacent brickworks. The path ends at the A523 road just north of Poynton town centre though its course further west, being almost a straight line, can be easily traced on a map. On the east side of the A523, at the appropriately named East Yard (unsurprisingly there was a West Yard on the opposite side of the road) a second main tramway, opened by 1857, headed south-west via Lady's Incline to reach a further collection of small pits near Hockley. This incline is preserved as a footpath, but a section further east is now inaccessible. This tramway was later extended to link with the new line from Marple, just north of Higher Poynton station (see Chapter 5), by 1872.

The third tramway of significance worth exploring is that of what is now Black Road, an older route running from Lord and Lady Pits at Hockley, heading north-west to a yard on the A523 close to, what is now, the Brookside Miniature Railway. All track was removed from these colliery lines by 1936 so the survival of access is fortunate indeed and is largely due to them becoming public and valued rights of way.

Tramroads Linking with Canals

Moving on to lines that linked place of industry to canals, a fine example is the tramroad that brought coal down from Outwood Colliery, south of Radcliffe, to the now disused Manchester, Bolton & Bury Canal east of Ringley. Pre-dating the East Lancashire Railway of 1846, the tramway had to be re-routed due to the large cutting that the ELR line built to the south of Ringley Road station (see Chapter 8). First, the tramway used the main road bridge at the station but later the tramway had its own bridge, a couple of hundred yards north of Ringley Road, the abutments of which can still be viewed. The highlight of exploring this tramway is the incline, quite walkable, heading down through Ringley Wood to the old canal, where a small dock once facilitated the transfer of coal onto boats.

My second example of this type is the early nineteenth-century Samuel Stock's Railway, near St Helens. This line ran north from the upper basin of the now-disused St Helens Canal past Carr Mill Dam (and under Carr Mill Viaduct) to the site of Seneley Green Colliery on the outskirts of Garswood. Samuel Stock's Railway was, at 4 miles, a lengthy tramway by north-west standards and for much of its time an exceedingly profitable one. It opened in 1838, using horses for traction other than at its inclines. There were two of these: the first being a long, rope-worked, incline (only 1 in 40 in gradient and apparently worked by locomotives after 1861) down to Carr Mill Dam; this section has been obliterated by later reservoir works. The top section, from Seneley Green to Blackleyhurst, had a gradient against the loaded wagons, requiring another incline worked by stationary engine and rope, though this engine was destroyed by a dramatic explosion on 10 April 1865. The boiler apparently blew up, sending pieces of iron into the air, destroying a chimney, then passing through the headgear of the pit and cutting the ropes of the cages, though fortunately no one was riding in them at the time. In the words of a newspaper reporter of the day, 'the works looked as if a hurricane had swept over them'. Closure of the collieries and hence the tramway came in 1880.

Our next example, rather than linking with a canal, effectively replaced one, as the Walton Summit Plateway linked two sections of the Lancaster Canal that were never joined, the cost of constructing an aqueduct over the River Ribble in Preston being forever prohibitive. Starting at a wharf north of Fishergate, close to Marsh Street, the

Outwood Colliery Tramway, incline on embankment through Ringley Woods. *Author*

tramway headed south, across an area now built over with modern buildings constructed for the University of Central Lancashire. Opening in 1803, the route then passed east of Preston station, where the remains of a tunnel under Fishergate, now widened for road access, can be seen. Always known locally as 'The Old Tram Road', the route, at a gauge of 4ft 1in, mounted on stone blocks, operated until 1868 when the line was closed, and ownership of the formation was transferred to the local council. North of the Ribble was an incline powered by a stationary engine, though all traces of this part of the route were obliterated by the landscaping of what is now Avenham Park. We then come to the tramway bridge over the river, something of a story in itself. Originally of wooden construction, after closure of the tramway the bridge remained in place until a storm in December 1936 washed away one of the timber piers. The six river piers were then reconstructed in reinforced concrete, with the aim of recreating the trestles and struts of the original bridge, but the timber decking was retained. It was not until 1964 that this decking was replaced by concrete with an asphalt surface. The bridge continued to serve as a convenient link for pedestrians wishing to cross the Ribble until 2018, when an inspection found the bridge to be structurally unsafe and it was closed and blocked off. At the time of writing (April 2022) the situation remains unchanged, and funding is still being sought for reconstruction or indeed a complete rebuild of the bridge.

South of the river the tramway becomes a delightful, tree-lined path on a small embankment; having opened as a footpath soon after 1868, this section therefore has a strong claim to be the oldest extant 'railway path' in Britain. About a mile and a half of trackbed is walkable before the route is lost, buried under a road and various residential or industrial buildings. Although I have walked this route on three or four occasions, I have never come across a stone sleeper block in situ, though in at least two places, blocks with telltale boltholes have been incorporated into the rockeries of nearby gardens. The suitably named Tramway Road, the short link running south from the end of the Walton Summit motorway link under the M65, leads to a footpath up to the tramway's southern terminus, where goods were once again exchanged onto canal boats. At Walton Summit there is little to identify the spot other than a rather grassy, nondescript area, though the former canal can then be followed, without too much difficulty, down through Whittle-le-Woods to its junction with the Leeds & Liverpool Canal south-west of Wheelton.

Tramways Not Linked to Canals or Other Railways

Let us now turn to the 'stand-alone' tramways, those that had no links with either railway or canal. These tended to be smaller operations, linking a particular mine or quarry with an industrial works, such as a reservoir, that needed the coal or stone, though sometimes it was simply a case of bringing materials down to the nearest road. Many of the very earliest tramroads took this form, some even pre-dating the canals; another feature being individual and sometimes unusual choices of gauges. The Congleton Railway, our first example, was discussed in Chapter 2.

Stocks Reservoir is situated at the north-east corner of the Forest of Bowland in Lancashire, slightly to the west of a line drawn between Settle to the north and Clitheroe to the south. Prior to the introduction of the 'right to roam' on open countryside, Bowland was rather inaccessible with very few footpaths and bridleways and as such has only become a desirable destination for ramblers and lovers of the outdoors in comparatively recent years.

Walton Summit Plateway, Old Tram Road Bridge over the River Ribble, Preston. *Author*

A circular route around Stocks has gradually been developed, with access being significantly improved in 2006 by the construction of a footbridge over the River Hodder north of the reservoir. The difference between a new map of the area, showing a quite extensive network of footpaths, and a pre-1990s map showing virtually none at all is quite stark; however, as explained below, not all the railway remains are marked on even the most large-scale maps.

In use from the start of construction in 1921 to the removal of the last materials in 1935, Stocks Reservoir was built by the Fylde Water Board. The main route commenced at a roadside yard at Tosside on the B6478 east of Slaidburn, though materials were brought by train to the nearest railhead at Long Preston, where additional sidings were provided. There were effectively three main routes: the original main line of 1921, which required a point of reversal close to Hesbert Bridge, a second main line slightly to the south, constructed in 1931 and a branch of some 4½ miles heading north-west to Jumbles Quarry. All these routes were laid to a gauge of 3ft, though some short stretches of 2ft-gauge line for construction purposes were also laid at the reservoir.

The railway's roadside terminus at Tosside (with still-extant concrete platforms) and the exchange sidings at Long Preston can still be easily seen, but the largest part of the eastern sections of both main lines now lie in a forested area; I must admit I have not attempted to work out which of the many woodland paths might be the old trackbed but anyone seeking a serious challenge is more than welcome to try. The western side of the original main line was submerged once the reservoir was filled, which leaves us to explore the western section of the second main line and the branch to Jumbles. The second main line lies south of the reservoir, passing to the north of 'Black House' and crossing the road to the east of the reservoir on the level just a couple of hundred yards to the north of a small church. A grassy path can be followed heading east, though the formation becomes less distinct until the road heading up to the car park from the B6478 road is reached at GR 736566.

The currently closed bridge over the River Ribble on Preston's Old Tram Road. *Author*

A delightful 1913 postcard of people enjoying a walk along the former Walton Summit Plateway, Preston. *Author's collection*

Stocks reservoir railway, remains of track above stream. *Author*

The real gem, however, is the Jumbles Quarry line. Other than two short sections, the line can be followed in its entirety; for the purposes of this description, we will start at the Fishing Lodge on the south-west side of the reservoir, where refreshments can be purchased on summer weekends. This is the start of a continuous path, with outstanding views of both the reservoir and the surrounding fells. It continues for the best part of 2 miles, following the contours but at the same time climbing gently as it heads north-west from the reservoir. It is clearly marked as a path on modern maps and there are no issues with rights of way. After passing a small quarry, access ends at a former level crossing near Copped Hill Clough, after which the line disappears into rough ground. The railway rambler must then take to a path and subsequently follow a minor road a short distance north to Kenibus. After passing a cottage on the left, the line comes into view again, with a missing trestle bridge and a short branch to serve another small quarry. To the north of this road the track may be regained, crossing access land. Although not marked as a path at this point the trackbed remains clearly visible as a slightly stony, slightly raised trackway as it heads north, at one point passing through a gateway. The line crossed the road on the level just south of Cross of Greet Bridge and the line briefly disappears into a modern plantation. However, by accessing a track heading west for a short distance the track can be regained near a short cutting above and to the west of the River Hodder. This last section of 1,000 yards or so of trackbed across rough ground with some sleepers and short pieces of rail in situ is a scenic delight but whilst clearly visible on the ground is again not indicated on any relevant maps. But the best is left until last; after a missing bridge over a stream, the quarry itself is reached. Here things seem to have been left pretty much as they were on the last day of quarrying: a steam crane mounted on a short piece of standard-gauge track survives, as do extensive sections of 3ft gauge track, some though now hang gingerly over the (in wintertime at least) fast-flowing stream.

My next example here fits very much into the 'undocumented' category, too: I know nothing more than the information shown on the maps of the time and what can be seen on the ground. North of Bolton, west of the A666 road leading north towards Darwen at Charter's Moss Plantation, lies a route of for just over a mile, helpfully marked as 'old tramway' on some modern maps. Running dead straight, slightly north of due west, the line can easily be walked, much of it on a slight embankment and with one small bridge over a tiny, culverted, stream. Gradually climbing onto Turton Moor, it provides stunning views on a clear day. Just the eastern end has disappeared under a short plantation. But what was it for? It would appear from map evidence that in the late nineteenth and early twentieth centuries, the route took coal from a small mine down to the delightfully named 'Turton Moor Sanitary Pipe Works'. By 1929, however, the works had gone, and all that remained on site was the 'Turton Moor Balancing Tank', which presumably didn't need coal.

Just a couple of miles further west lies another example: Belmont Reservoir, just east of the A675 north of Bolton on the Preston Road, was constructed in 1826 by the Bolton Waterworks Company to supply water to what was already a rapidly growing town. Presumably supplying stone for the construction of the reservoir, this line started at a quarry on higher ground just north of Rivington then descended gradually, whilst following the contours, passing through the north side of Belmont village. Again, walkable most of the way, a small section has been lost at Ward's Cote, but its course can be traced past its crossing of the main A675 road before reaching its goal on the west side of the reservoir.

Now let us return to Rossendale, where we started. On the south-west side of the moors lies the Scout Moor Tramway, a line with a slightly more unusual dual-purpose history. This 3ft-foot gauge line opened in 1880 in order to bring stone down from Scout Moor Quarries to a yard on the Rawtenstall–Rochdale Road, where the stone was transferred onto lorries. The line climbed gently into the Dearden Valley but needed a point of reversal to gain the height required to reach the quarry. Having worked well for twenty-five years, in 1905 the line was extended from the reversal point to the site of a reservoir being built for Bury Water Board for a further mile up the valley. Although the reservoir opened in 1909, the 'extension' continued in operation until around 1912 and, as can be seen on the ground, was never fully dismantled. The line continued in use as a stone tramway until 1939, when a large landslip carried a large section of the trackbed, including rails and sleepers, over 100ft down the hillside;

Stocks Reservoir trackbed, the Jumbles branch heading towards the reservoir. *Author*

Storeton Tramway trackbed. *Howard Harrison*

this was never made good. Although walkable right up to both quarry and reservoir, particularly after a period of dry weather, this route is not as easy to explore as most of those mentioned above. In places the formation is unclear, in other parts boggy rushes have encroached onto the trackbed and there is also the landslip to contend with. But here, if you are willing to head a little way down the hillside, you can just about see the remains, sets of wooden sleepers bound together, still with pieces of rusty rail attached, that have somehow survived over eighty winters on the moor.

Our last tramway of all takes us to the Wirral in search of the Storeton Tramway. This was a single-track, standard-gauge railway that was used to transport stone from three quarries at Storeton to Bromborough Pool. From there it was taken by barge to Birkenhead and Liverpool to be used in the construction of buildings. Before the railway was built, horse-drawn carts were used on the local roads. It may be noted that the Storeton was one of the very last horse-drawn lines to open. The idea of constructing such a railway dated back to the late 1820s, when in 1828 George Stephenson visited the quarries. He was looking for stone to use for construction of the Sankey Viaduct on the Liverpool & Manchester Railway, though the tramway was not completed in time to serve that purpose. In fact, construction of the Storeton line only began in April 1837 and was completed in August 1838 at a cost of £12,000, ironically using stone blocks bought second-hand from the L&MR. The original name was The Stourton Railway (the original spelling of the village), though it became known as the 'Storeton Quarries Tramway', finally becoming just the 'Storeton Tramway', though nowadays it is locally known as the 'wagon line'.

As noted above, the line serviced three quarries: these were, Storeton North, Storeton South and Jackie's Wood Quarry, the latter situated on the east side of Mount Road. It started at the North Quarry, then past the South Quarry, over Rest Hill Road, through Hancock's Wood and into a 60-yard tunnel under Mount Road to emerge in Jackie's Wood Quarry. It then passed across Bracken Lane, Cross Lane and Church Road (near to St Andrews Church) and onto the Quay at Bromborough Pool. From the quarries to Mount Road the wagons were hauled by horses, but after that interchange they were propelled by gravity at speeds of up to 20mph, the whole journey taking around thirty minutes. Horses provided the power for the return journey at a rather more sedate pace. By the 1890s quarrying stopped at the North Quarry, but the others remained operation into the early years of the twentieth century. The last wagon load set out from Bromborough in 1905, and the tramway was then abandoned. All three quarries were eventually infilled by spoil dug out during construction of the Mersey tunnels. During the Second World War, the Mount Road tunnel was converted into an air raid shelter by a local man, a Mr Jacques, who fitted bunks and a protective door. Later stone excavations at this site caused a collapse and it became two shorter tunnels. You can still see the cutting that approaches the west entrance to the Mount Road tunnel. Parts of the cutting to the north quarry are still visible, as are a number of stone sleeper blocks. These blocks, notable for having as many as four bolt holes, can still sometimes be spotted, built into walls and rockeries of local houses.

Acknowledgements

Thanks are due to so many people who have helped made this venture happen. Firstly, grateful thanks to those who have contributed photographs: to Hilary Blencowe on behalf of the late Maurice Blencowe, Dave Coogan, Phillip Earnshaw, John Fiander, Derek Fry, Howard Harrison, Chris McFarlane, Becca Norton, Steve Pengrill (of Steve Pengrill Photography) and Gordon Suggitt, who in addition to providing pictures of his own kindly gave access to his extensive collection of photographs that stretch right back into the 1960s.

Thanks also to all those, particularly from the Railway Ramblers Club and the Railway & Canal Historical Society, who have led and participated in walks and other events. So many of you have added extra information over the years and have been companions on many a journey to view an old line. Finally, a big thank you to to Paul Smith for all his hard work on the maps and Peter Waller and Charlotte Stear at Crécy Publishing for making this all happen. I am truly grateful.

Bibliography

The following books and atlases are recommended for further reading. It should be noted that while a number of them are either still in print or easily obtainable on the second-hand book market, others were printed in very small quantities, sometimes privately, and may now be very difficult to source.

Ashmore, O., *The Industrial Archaeology of North West England* (Manchester University Press).

Baxter, B., *Stone Blocks and Iron Rails (Tramroads)* (David & Charles).

Binns D., *The 'Little' North Western Railway* (Locomotives International).

Brown, J., *Liverpool & Manchester Railway Atlas* (Crécy Publishing).

Bushell, J., *The World's Oldest Railway* (Crown Press Keighley).

Carter, O., *An illustrated History of British Railway Hotels* (Silver Link Publishing).

Cobb, M., *The Railways of Great Britain* (Ian Allan).

Cornwell, M., *The History of the Calderstones Hospital Railway* (self-published).

Cornwell, M., *The History of the Whittingham Hospital Railway* (self-published).

Donaghy, T., *Liverpool & Manchester Railway Operations 1831–1845* (David & Charles).

Fernyhough, F., *The Liverpool & Manchester Railway 1830–1980* (Robert Hale).

Fletcher, M. & Taylor J., *Railways – The Pioneer Years* (Studio Editions).

Guy A. & Rees J., *Early Railways 1569–1830* (Shire Publications).

Harvey M., *Forget the Anorak – What Trainspotting was Really Like* (The History Press).

Holt, G., *Regional History of the Railways of Great Britain, vol 10 – The North West* (David & Charles).

Jenkins, S., *Britain's 100 Best Railway Stations* (Viking/Penguin).

Jermy, R., *The Storeton Tramway* (Avon Anglia).

Jordan A. & and Jordan E., *Away for the Day – the Railway Excursion in Britain* (Silver Link Publishing).

Jones, M., *Lost Railways of North Wales* (Countryside Books).

Jones, M., *Discovering Britain's First Railways – A Guide to Horse-drawn Tramroads and Waggonways* (The History Press).

Jones, M,. *Lancashire Railways: The History of Steam* (Countryside Books).

Lewis, S., *Boots on the Line – Walking 1000 Miles of Britain's Dismantled Railways* (True to the Line).

Lovett Jones, G., *Railway Walks – Exploring Disused Railways* (Pierrot).

Mansergh, R., *Closed Railways and Stations in West Cumbria* (self-published).

Martin, R., *North West Railway Walks* (Sigma Leisure).

Marshall, J., *Forgotten Railways; North West England* (David & Charles).

Morgan, R., *Railways: Civil Engineering* (Arrow Books).

Norton, P., *Railways and Waterways to Warrington* (RCHS publications).

Oppitz, L., *Lost Railways of Cheshire* (Countryside Books).

Pertwee, W., *The Station Now Standing* (Hodder & Stoughton).

Pixton, R., *Main Line Railways around Wigan* (Runpast Publishing).

Quick, M., *Railway Passenger Stations in Great Britain: A Chronology* (RCHS Publications).

Quinn, T., *Tales of the Old Railwaymen* (David & Charles).

Reed, B., *Crewe to Carlisle* (Ian Allan).

Roberts, B., *Railways and Mineral Tramways of Rossendale* (Oakwood Press).

Rolt, L.T.C., *Narrow Boat* (Eyre Methuen).

Russell, R., *Lost Canals & Waterways of Britain* (Sphere Books).

Smith P. & Turner K., *Railway Atlas Then and Now* (Ian Allan).

Somerville, C., *Walking Old Railways* (David & Charles).

Stead, C., *The Birth of the Steam Locomotive – a New History* (Fern House).

Suggitt, G., *Lost Railways of Cumbria* (Countryside Books).

Suggitt, G., *Lost Railways of Lancashire* (Countryside Books).

Suggitt, G., *Lost Railways of Merseyside & Greater Manchester* (Countryside Books).

Thomas, D., *The Country Railway* (David & Charles).

Thorpe, D., *The Railways of the Manchester Ship Canal* (Oxford Publishing Company).

Tolson, J., *The St Helens Railway* (Oakwood Press).

Townley C., Smith F. & Peden, J., *The Industrial Railways of the Wigan Coalfield Vols 1 & 2* (Runpast Publishing).

Townley C., Smith F., Appleton C. & Peden, J., *The Industrial Railways of Bolton, Bury and the Manchester Coalfield Vols 1 & 2* (Runpast Publishing).

Townley C, & Peden, J., *The Industrial Railways of St Helens, Widnes and Warrington Vols 1 & 2* (Industrial Railway Society).

Vinter, J., *Railway Walks: LMS* (Alan Sutton Publishing).

Vinter, J., *Vinter's Railway Gazetteer; A Guide to Britain's Old Railways that You Can Walk or Cycle* (The History Press).

Voice, D., *Hospital Tramways and Railways* (Adam Gordon).

Webb, B. & Gordon, D., *Lord Carlisle's Railways* (RCTS Publications).

Wells, J., *Railways in and around Bury* (Book Law – Railbus Publications).

Index

Abbey Town station 142
Accrington 96
    Mill Pond Viaduct 99
    Stubbins Junction (East Lancashire Railway) 96
Acton Bridge Junction 36
Acton Grange Tunnel (Moore) 6, 7
Acton Grange Viaduct 36
Adderley station 28, 29
Adlington-Boars Head Railway 60-61, 65
Aikbank Junction 140
Ainsworth Road Halt 67
Aintree-Fazackerley Railway 42
Aintree Racecourse station 42
Alderbottom Viaduct (Helmshore) 97
Alexandra Dock (Bootle) 41, 42
Altcar & Hillhouse station 49
'Altcar Bob' 49
Ann Street station 55
Annan (Shawhill) station 141
Apethorne Curve 75
Appleby 146
Appleby-Warcop Railway 7, 147-149
Appleby East station 149
Appleton (Widnes) station 55
Arpley Junction (Warrington) 34
Arnside-Hincaster Railway 123-125
Arnside station 123
Ashton-Oldham Railway 89
Ashton Canal 76
Ashton Hall station 118
Ashton in Makerfield station 53
Ashton Moss Junction 76
Ashton Oldham Road station 89, 90
Ashton under Lyne 76, 96
Aspatria 140, 141
Astley Green Colliery 79
Atherton (L&YR) station 64
Atherton Bag Lane station 64
Audenshaw station 75, 76
Audlem station 28, 29
Avenham Park 157

Bacup 155
    Bury Railway 70, 71, 155
    Rochdale Railway 93-95

station 93, 95
Bagden Quarry Tramway 94, 155
Baggrow 140
'Barlick Spud' 104
Bamber Bridge 112, 113
Barbon station 151
Barton 38
Barnoldswick Branch 13, 104, 105
Bank Hall (Liverpool) station 42
Banks Station 107, 108
Bardsea Ironworks 127, 128
Barrow 126
    Ironworks 123
Barton (Downholland) station 49
Barton Dock Containerbase 84
Bassenthwaite Lake station 136, 138
Baxenden
    Bank 98
    station 96, 98
Baxter, Bertram 155
Bay Horse (Lancaster) 7
Beckermet station 131
Beela Viaduct 125
Belmont Reservoir and Tramway 160
Bickershaw (colliery) 50, 59, 61
Bickershaw & Abram station 50
Bickershaw Junction 58, 59
Bickerstaffe 57
Bidston 24
Bidston Dock (Birkenhead) 19
Birkdale Palace station 48
Birkenhead 19, 22, 161
Birkenhead Docks 20
Birkenhead Joint Railway 18
Birkenhead North station 21
Birkenhead Woodside station 22
Birtill, George 155
Blacon station 24
Black Dyke station 142
'Black Harry' line 80-81
'Black Harry' Tunnel 80-81
Black Road (Poynton) 157
Blackbeck Tramway 127
Blackburn-Chorley Railway 65, 102, 103
Blackhill Brickworks 155
Blackleyhurst 157

Blackpool Central station	11, 113
Blackpool North station	113
Blackpool South station	113
Blackrod station	64
Blencow station	137
Blowick station	108
Bluegate	145
Boars Head-Adlington Railway	60-61, 65
Bollin Point	36, 38
Bollington station	30, 32
Bollington Viaduct	32
Bolton-Bury Railway	67
Bolton-Eccles Railway	79
Bolton & Leigh Railway	59, 62, 63, 80
Bolton Great Moor Street station	62, 79
Bootle	53
Bootle Balliol Road station	42
Bootle Midlands Goods Branch	42
Bootle New Strand station	42
Botany Bay (Chorley; former miniature railway)	7
Botany Bay Viaduct	103, 104
Bouch, Thomas	137
Bowker Distribution Centre Sidings (Bamber Bridge)	112
Bowness (Solway)	141
Bowness station	141
Boysnope Park (Irlam)	38
Boysnope Wharf (Irlam)	37
Bradford	121
Bradkirk Junction	113
Braithwaite station	138
Brampton Junction-Lambley Railway	144-145
Brampton (Junction) station	144, 145
Brampton Town branch and station	144-145
Branch Line Society	109
Brandlesholme Road Halt	71
Brayton station	141
Bredbury	75
Bredbury Junction	75
Bridgewater Canal	39, 79, 83
Bridgewater Collieries and railways	79
Brigham-Bullgill Railway	141
Brinnington	75
Brinnington Junction	73
Brinnington Tunnel	73, 74
Brinscall	12, 103
Brinscall station	104
Britannia Quarry and tramroad	155
Britannia station	93
Britannia Tunnel	93, 95
Broad Green station	43
Broadheath	36
Broadley station	94

Bromborough Pool	161
Bromfield station	140
Brooks Quarry tramroads	154-156
Brookside Miniature Railway	157
Broughton in Furness station	129
Buckhill Colliery (RNAD)	138, 139
Bullgill	141
Bullgill-Brigham Railway	141
Burgh by Sands station	143
Burnden Viaduct	68
Burn Naze	114, 115
Burn Naze station	116
Burnley Manchester Road station	96
Burscough	108
Burscough curves	8
Burton, Decimus	114
Bury-Bacup Railway (ELR)	70, 71, 155
Bury-Bolton Railway	67
Bury Bolton Street station	67, 96
Bury Gas Works Siding	69
Bury Interchange	67
Bury Knowsley Street station	67
Butterhouse Tunnel	77
Cadishead	38
Cadishead (New) station	38
Cadishead Viaduct	38, 39
Caldbeck (Cumbria)	14
Caldew Junction	144
Caldy station	18
Caledonian Railway	141
Calva Junction-Linefoot Railway	138
Camerton (Cumbria)	139
Canal Junction (Carlisle)	144
Canning Street (Birkenhead)	19, 20, 21
Carlisle	131, 141, 142, 144, 146
Carlisle (Citadel) station	144
Carr Mill Dam (and Viaduct)	157
Carrington Estate Railway	39
Caton Station	119, 122
Causewayhead (Crossing)	142
Cerestar	84
Chadderton Coal Depot	91
Chanters Colliery	59
Chequerbent	62, 63
Chequerbent station	62
Cherry Tree station	103
Cheshire Lines Committee (CLC)	22, 40, 43, 45, 46, 53, 75, 84-85
Chester	24
Chester-Whitchurch Railway	7, 13, 25
Chester & Birkenhead Railway	19

Chester (General) station	22, 88
Chester Golf Club Platform	24
Chester Liverpool Road station	22, 24
Chester Northgate station	22, 24
Childwall Station	43
Chinley	73
Chorley-Blackburn Railway	65, 102, 103
Chorlton	74
Chorlton Junction	81
Churchtown station	107
Clapham-Low Gill Railway	150-153
Clapham (North Yorkshire) station	151
Claughton station	119, 122
Cleator & Workington Junction Railway (C&WJR)	134, 138
Cleator Moor	132, 134, 135
Cleator Moor Ironworks	134
Cliburn station	147, 149, 150, 151
Clifton-Radcliffe (ELR) Railway	65, 66, 81
Clifton-Patricroft Railway	80-81
Clifton Hall Tunnel	78, 80-81
Clifton Hall sidings	81
Clifton Junction and station	65, 81
Clifton Moor station	150
Clitheroe	109, 158
Clock Face Colliery	55
Clough Fold station	72, 155
Clubmoor station	45
Cocker (River)	138
Cockeremouth station(s)	137
Cockermouth, Keswick & Penrith Railway (CK&PR)	137
Conishead Priory	127
Co-operative Wholesale Society (CWS)	83
Colne station	96, 104
Colne-Skipton Railway	12, 104
Conder Green station	118
Congleton	17
Congleton Railway	15, 16, 17, 158
Conishead Priory	127
Conishead Priory branch	127-128
Conishead Priory station	128
Coniston	129, 130
Coniston branch	129-130
Coniston station	129, 130
Coole Pilate Halt	28, 29
Copperas Hill station and incline	136, 137
Copy Pit Railway	96
Corthuld's Siding (Preston)	108, 109, 111
Coxbank Halt	28
Cragg Quarry	155
Crank station	57
Cronton Colliery branch	47, 48
Crook 'O' Lune Viaducts	122
Cross of Greet Bridge	160
Crossens station	107
Crown Street station	46
Crowthorn curve (Guide Bridge)	75, 76
Cuddington-Winsford & Over Railway	26
Culcheth (and linear park)	11, 52, 63
Culcheth station	52
Daisy Hill station	64
Dales Way	153
Dallam Shed (Warrington)	40
'Dandy Car' (Port Carlisle)	142
Dandy Car/Line (Brampton)	145
Darcy Lever cutting	68
Darcy Lever Viaduct	69
Daubhill inclined plane	62
De Trafford Junction	60
Deansgate Goods (Bolton) station	62
Dee Marsh Junction	23
Dee Marsh Junction-Mickle Trafford Railway	22, 24
Deepdale station	109-110
Deepdale Yard	108, 109, 110
Delph branch	92
Delph station	92, 93
Denshaw	92
Denton Junction	76
Denton station	76
Dentonholme Goods Yard	144
Derker station	91
Derwent branch	138, 141
Derwent (Cumbria) River	133, 136, 141
Desire Paths	11
Dicconson Lane & Aspull station	65
Diggle station	76, 77
Dillicar Viaduct	153
Ding Quarry	155
Dingle station	41, 42
'Dirty Fair' (Market Drayton)	28
Distington	134
Dobcross station	92
Douglas Bridge (West Lancashire Railway)	106, 108
Douglas Viaduct (Boars Head route)	60
Douglas Viaduct (Whelley loop line)	58, 59, 60
Dovenby station	141, 144
Downholland station	49, 107
Droylsden station	76
Drumburgh	143
Drumburgh Junction	142
Dukinfield & Ashton station	76
Dukinfield Central station	76
Dunham Massey station	36

Earby	104, 105
Earby Junction	105
Earby station	105
East Didsbury station/tram stop	73
East Lancashire Railway (ELR)	57, 65, 71, 96, 104, 111-112, 155
Eccles-Bolton Railway	79
Eccles-Wigan Railway	58, 79
Eccles Junction	50
Eccles station	79, 88
Eden Valley Railway	7, 146, 147
Eden Valley Railway (Warcop Group)	149
Eden Viaduct (Carlisle)	144
Edge Green Colliery	54, 55
Edge Hill station	46-47
Egremont	131, 132
Ellerbeck Colliery branch (Chorley)	13
Ellenbrook	59
Ellesmere Port (Docks)	22, 36
Elslack station	104, 105, 109
Entwistle station	155
Esk Viaduct	144
Ewood Bridge & Edenfield station	71, 97
Facit station	93, 94, 154
Fairbottom branch (Ashton Canal)	89
Fairfield Junction	81
Fallowfield loop line	73, 81, 82
Fallowfield station	83
Falk's Junction	27
Farington curve	103, 112
Farington station	113
Farnworth & Bold station	55
Fazackerley-Aintree Railway	42
Fazackerley Sidings	43
Ferny Knoll Colliery	57
Fidlers Ferry (Power Station)	8
Fishergate (Preston)	157
Fleetwood	114, 116, 128
Fleetwood branch	114-116
Fleetwood, Preston & West Riding Railway	109
Fleetwood station	114
Fletcher Street Junction (Bolton)	80
Forest of Bowland	158
Foulridge Canal Tunnel	104
Foulridge station	104, 105
Foxfield-Coniston Railway	129, 130
Foxfield station	129
Freehold Metrolink Stop	91
Friezland station	77
Frizington station	134
Furness Railway	123, 125, 127, 128, 129, 131
Furness & Midland Railway	119
Gaisgill	146
Galgate	118
Garstang	116
Garstang & Catterall station	116
Gartstang & Knott End Railway	116-118
Garstang Town station	116
Garston Dock	55
Gateacre station	43
Gathurst	15, 16
Gerard's Bridge Station	57
Glasson Dock	15, 118
Glasson Dock branch	118
Glasson Dock station	118
Glaxo Pharmaceutical Works	128
Glazebrook	38, 53
Glazebrook-Skelton Junction Railway	39
Godley Junction	74, 75
Godley station	75
Golborne (GCR) station	55
Gorton Junction	81
Gorton station	81, 83
Grange over Sands	123
Great Broughton	138
Great Central Railway (GCR)	50, 52, 53, 55
Great Harwood	13
Great Harwood loop	99-101
Great Harwood station	101-102
Greenbank station	27
Greenfield	77
Greenfield-Oldham Railway	92
Greenfield station	93
Greenmount station	71
Greenodd Junction	125
Greenodd station	127
Greyhound Bridge (Lancaster)	120
Grimsargh	109, 110, 111
Grindley Brook Halt	25
Grotton station	92, 93
Guide Bridge station	76, 81
Guided Busway	59
Hadlow Road station	18, 19
Hadrian's Wall	143
Hag Fold station	64
Haigh Hall Country Park	60
Halewood station	43
Hallbankgate	145
Halsall station	49
Halton (Lancashire) station	119, 121
Haltonleagate	145

Hanson Aggregates (Kelbit) Works	54, 55
Harker station(s)	144
Harrington	134, 137
Harrington Church Road Halt	137
Harrington Harbour	137
Hartford station	27
Hartley Quarry	147
Hartshead Power Station	77, 78
Haslingden station	96
Hassall Green station	30
Hattersley station	75
Haverigg	130
Haverthwaite	125, 127
Haverthwaite station	125
Havetrhwaite Tunnel	125, 126
Hawarden Bridge station	24
Haydock station	53
Haydock Park Racecourse station	54
Haydock Park Racecourse	54
Hay's Chemicals Siding (St Helens)	56, 57
Healey Dell Viaduct	93-94
Heapey	103, 104
Heapey Station	104
Heatley & Warburton station	35
Heaton Park Reservoir Railway	11
Hellifield	104, 105
Helmshore (former miniature railway)	97, 98
Helmshore station	97
Helmshore Viaducts	97
Helsby-Mouldsworth Railway	24-25
Helsby & Alvanley station	25
Herculaneum Dock and Station (Liverpool)	41
Hesketh Park station	107
Heswall station	18
Heversham station	124, 125
Hey's Crossing Halt	57
Heysham Port	119
High Blaithwaite	140
High Lane station	32
Higher Poynton station	32, 156
Highways Agency	148
Hill, Oliver	119-120
Hilton House station	65
Hincaster – Arnside Railway	123-125
Hincaster Trailway	123-124
Hincaster Junction	125
Hindley – Red Moss Railway	65
Hindley Green station	59
Hindley South station	50
Hindsford	59
Hodbarrow	130
Hodder (River)	160
Holcombe Brook branch	69, 71
Holcombe Brook station	71
Hollinwood Arm (Ashton Canal)	76
Hoole station	106
Hooley Hill line	76
Hooley Hill station	76
Hooley Hill Tunnel	76
Hooton – West Kirby Railway	18
Hooton station	18
Hope Valley line	73
Hornby station	119, 122
Horwich branch	64
Horwich Fork Junction	65
Horwich Locomotive Works	64
Howe Bridge station	59
Huddersfield Narrow Canal	77, 78
Hundred End station	107
Hunts Cross station	43
Hurst Green	12, 13, 109
Huskisson branch	45
Huskisson Docks and station (Liverpool)	43, 45
Hustler's Railway (Wigan)	15
Hyde Road Junction	81
Hyde Road station	83
Hyndburn (River)	122
Ince Waggon & Iron Works	50
Ingleton	150
Ingleton station(s)	151
Ingleton Viaduct	150, 151
Ingrow West station	105
'Iron Line'	130
Irlam	38
Irwell Vale station	71
Irwell Viaduct (Clifton)	65
Irwell Viaduct (Bury)	71
Jackdaw Viaduct	151, 152
James Street (Liverpool) station	42
Jumbles Quarry & Railway	159-160, 161
Keekle Viaduct	134
Keighley & Worth Valley Railway	105
Kelbit Works	54, 55
Kellogg's	83, 84
Kelton Fell Colliery	133
Kendal & Westmorland Railway	125
'Kendal Tommy'	123
Kent Viaduct	123
Kenyon Junction	62, 64
Kershope Foot station	143
Keswick	14, 137, 141

Keswick-Workington Railway 133
Keswick station 137
Kidsgrove-Sandbach Railway 29
King's Moss Collieries 155
Kirby Park station 18
Kirkandrew station 143
Kirkbride station 142
Kirkby in Furness station 129
Kirkby Lonsdale station 150, 151
Kirkby Stephen 146
Kirkby Stephen-Penrith Railway 147
Kirkby Stephen-Tebay Railway 146, 147
Kirkby Stephen East station 147, 148
Kirkby Thore station 147
Kirkdale station 45
Kirkham & Wesham station 113
Kirkham North Junction 113
Kirkhouse 145
Knott End branch 13, 116-119
Knott End station 119
Knotty Ash & Stanley station 43
Knowl Street Viaduct (Stalybridge) 78

Ladysike Bridge 126
Lakeside branch 125, 126
Lakeside & Haverthwaite Railway 125
Lambley-Brampton Junction Railway 144-145
Lambley 145
Lamplugh station 134
Lancashire & Yorkshire Railway (L&YR) 46, 48, 49, 50,
                                  64, 71, 79, 81, 87, 93, 102, 106
Lancashire Coastal Way 118
Lancashire Tar Distillers 38
Lancashire Union Railway (LUR) 53, 60, 102
Lancaster-Morecambe (Midland) Railway 118-119, 121
Lancaster-Wennington Railway 118-119, 121
Lancaster & Carlisle Railway 150, 153
Lancaster Canal 109, 157, 158
Lancaster (Castle) station 118, 122
Lancaster Green Ayre station 118, 121-122
Lancaster Penny Street station 118
Langholm branch 143
Langton Dock (Bootle) 42, 45
Latchford 34, 36
Latchford (New) station 35
Latchford (Old) station 34
Latchford Viaduct 13, 33, 34, 35, 37
Lawton station 30
Lee Quarry 155
Leeds & Bradford Extension Railway 104
Leeds & Liverpool Canal 45, 52, 55, 60, 96,
                                                  103, 104, 158

Lees Station (and shed) 93
Leven Viaduct (Lakeside branch) 125
Leven Viaduct (Furness Railway main line) 128
Leigh 64
Leigh branch 59
Leven Junction 125
Leven (River) 125
Levenshulme South station 82, 83
Liddel Viaduct 144
Linacre Gas Works (Bootle) 42
Linden 127
Linefoot 138
Linefoot-Calva Junction Railway 138
'Little' North Western Railway 118-119, 150
Littleborough 88
Liverpool & Manchester Railway 6, 14, 40, 43, 46,
                                    52, 53, 55, 56, 87, 145, 161
Liverpool Central station 46, 75
Liverpool Exchange station 46, 47
Liverpool Lime Street station 46
Liverpool loop line 43, 44
Liverpool Overhead Railway 41, 42, 44
Liverpool Riverside station 47
Liverpool, Southport & Preston Railway 48
London & North Eastern Railway (L&NR) 145
London & North Western Railway (L&NWR) 50, 57,
                              59, 61, 76, 79, 87, 92, 102, 118, 119,
                                                  137, 138, 141, 150
London, Midland & Scottish Railway 119
Long Preston station 159
Longridge station 108, 109, 111
Longridge branch 108-111
Longtown 144
Lord Carlisle's Railway 144-145
Lostock Hall Gas Works 112
Lostock Hall shed 99, 113
Lostock Hall station 112
Low Gill-Clapham Railway 150-153
Low Gill station & junction 150, 153
Low Hall Collieries 60
Low Wood Tramway 127
Lowca 137
Lowca Crossing 136
Lowca Light Railway 134, 136, 137
Lowton St Marys station 52
Lumb Viaduct 96
Lune (River) 118, 122
Lune Viaduct (Sedbergh) 153
Lydgate Tunnel 92, 93
Lydiate station 48
Lymm station 35
Lyneside station 144

Macclesfield-Marple Railway	30, 156
Macclesfield Canal	31, 155
Maghull	48
Malkins	30
Malpas station	25
Manchester, Bolton & Bury Canal	65, 67, 69, 157
Manchester Central station	73, 84-85
Manchester Docks	36
Manchester Exchange station	87-88
Manchester Liverpool Road station	86
Manchester Mayfield station	84, 87, 88
Manchester Oldham Road station	88, 91
Manchester Piccadilly (London Road) station	76, 84
Manchester Ship Canal	36, 39, 83
Manchester Ship Canal Railway	36, 37, 39, 84
Manchester Victoria station	76, 87, 88
Manisty Wharf (Ellesmere Port)	22, 23
Manley station	25
Market Drayton	12, 28
Market Drayton station	28, 29
Market Drayton-Nantwich Railway	28
Marple	16
Marple-Macclesfield Railway	30, 156
Marron Junction	133
Marston (salt works)	28
Martholme Colliery	101
Martholme Greenway	99, 101
Martholme Viaduct	101
Maryport	141
Maryport & Carlisle Railway (M&CR)	140, 141
Maudlands	109-110
Maypole Colliery	51
Mealsgate loop	140
Mealsgate station	140
Measurements Halt	92
Medlock Viaduct (Park Bridge)	89
Meols Cop station	48, 49, 107
Mersey, River	14-15, 55, 73
Metrolink	73, 91
Metropolitan Vickers	83
Micklam station	137
Mickle Trafford-Dee Marsh Junction Railway	22
Mickle Trafford (East) station	22, 24
Micklehurst loop	76-78
Micklehurst station	78
Middleforth Junction	106
Middleton branch and station	90-91, 92
Middleton Junction	91
Middleton Junction-Oldham Railway	90
Middleton on Lune station	151
Midgeholme	145
Midland Hotel (Manchester)	85
Midland Hotel (Morecambe)	119-121
Midland Railway	46, 73, 75, 84-85, 104, 119, 150
Middlewood curve	32
Middlewood (High Level) station	32
Middlewood (Low Level) station	32
Middlewood Way	30, 156
Miles Platting	88
Millom-Haverigg Railway	130
Millom (Ironworks)	123, 130
Mills, Hayley	93
Mills Hill station	91
Mirehouse Junction	132
Molyneux Junction	81
Monton Green station	79
Moore	36
Moor Row station	132, 133, 134
Moorfields station	46
Moravian Settlement (Fairfield)	83
Morecambe-Lancaster (Midland) Railway	118-9, 121
Morecambe Euston Road station	119
Morecambe Jetty station	118, 121
Morecambe Promenade station	119, 120, 121
Moresby Park station	134
Mosley Common Colliery	79
Moss Bank station	57
Moss Lane Junction	112, 113
Mossbrook station	48
Mouldsworth-Helsby Railway	24-25
Mouldsworth station	22
Mount Road Tunnels	161
Mosedale Viaduct	137
Mow Cop Tramway	16, 17
Mowbray Colliery	133
Museum of Science & Industry (MOSI)	86
Musgrave (bridge infilling)	148
Musgrave station	147, 148
Nantwich	28
Nantwich-Market Drayton Railway	28
Nateby	117
Neston Rock Cutting	18, 19
Neston South station	18
Newcastle & Carlisle Railway	145
Newchurch Halt (Culcheth)	11, 50, 52-53
Newchurch Tunnels (Rossendale)	71, 72
New Hey station	10
'New Line' (Bacup)	93
North British Railway	142
North Euston Hotel	114, 116
North Lancashire loop	99-101
North Lonsdale crossing	128
North Western Railway	118-119, 150

North Eastern Railway	145
Northern Viaduct Trust	146
Northwich	27
Old Mill Lane Halt	57
'Old Tram Road'	157-158, 159
Oldham	89, 91, 96
Oldham-Ashton Railway	89
Oldham-Greenfield Railway	92
Oldham-Middleton Junction Railway	90
Oldham, Ashton & Guide Bridge Railway (OA&GBR)	76, 89
Oldham Clegg Street station	89, 92
Oldham Glodwick Road station	89, 93
Oldham loop line	8
Oldham Mumps station	8, 9, 89, 93
Oldham Werneth station	9, 10
Ordsall chord	87
Ormskirk	58, 112
Ormskirk-St Helens Railway	57
Outwood Colliery and Tramroad	65, 67, 157
Outwood Trail	65
Outwood Viaduct	66, 67
Padiham	100
Padiham Greenway	101
Padiham Junction	99
Padiham loop	13, 99-102
Padiham Power station(s)	99-101
Padiham station	101
Papcastle station	142
Park Bridge Ironworks and station	89
Park Hotel (Preston)	112
Parker Waggonway (Whitehaven)	16
Parkhouse Halt	144
Parr (St Helens)	16
Parrock Hall Junction	129
Parsonage Colliery	59
Partington Junction	39
Partington Power Station	39
Partington (New) station	39
Patricroft-Clifton Railway	80-81
Patricroft Station (and shed)	80
Peak Forest Canal	16, 76
Pemberton loop line	11, 50, 61
Pendlebury Station	81
Pennington-Platt Bridge Railway	61
Pennington Flash	61
Penrith	146
Penrith-Kirkby Stephen Railway	147
Penrith-Workington (Keswick) Railway	136, 137, 147
Penruddock station	137

Penton Station	143
Penwortham Junction	106
Penwortham Triangle	106
Petterill Bridge Junction	143
Piel Island	128
Piel Pier branch (Barrow)	128-129
Pilkington's Plate Glass Works	57
Pilling	116-118
'Pilling Pig Railway'	116-119
'Pilling Pig' replica locomotive	117
Planehead	145
Plank Lane station	61
Plateways	16
Platt Bridge	60
Platt Bridge-Pennington Railway	61
Platt Bridge station	50
Plodder Lane station (and shed)	79
Plumpton Junction	127, 128
Port Carlisle	142
Port Carlisle branch	142
Port Carlisle	143
Portwood (Stockport) station	73
Post-closure History	6
Poulton & Wyre Railway Society	115
Poulton Curve Halt	114
Poulton le Fylde-Fleetwood Railway	114-115
Poulton le Fylde station(s)	114
Poynton	156, 157
Preesall (salt mines and siding)	116
Prescot	14
Preston-Longridge Railway	108-111
Preston-Southport Railway	106
Preston & Lancaster Junction Railway	108
Preston Docks	118
Preston station	106, 109, 111, 137
Preston (Fishergate) station	106, 112
'Preston Tramway'	110
Prince's Incline	156
Radcliffe	65, 67
Radcliffe Black Lane station	69
Radcliffe Bridge station	67
RAF Burtonwood (Warrington) Railway	40
Railway & Canal Historical Society	109
Railway Paths Ltd	97, 101, 149
Railway Ramblers Club	94, 105, 111, 133
Rainford Junction station	57
Rainford Village station	57
Ramsbottom station	71, 96
Ramsden Dock (Barrow)	128
Rank Hovis McDougall	83
Ravenshore Viaduct	97

Entry	Pages
Ravenstonedale station	146
Rawtenstall station	71
Rawthay (River)	151
Rawthay Viaduct	151, 152
Red Moss-Hindley Railway	65
Red Moss Junction	65
Redhills curve	137, 147
Reddish Junction	73
Reddish North	75
Ribble Bridge (Walton Summit Plateway/Old Tram Road)	157-158, 159
Ribble Junction	106
Ribble (River)	157
Ribble (ELR) Viaduct	112
Ribbleton station	110-111
'Ribby curve'	113
Richard Evans' Railway	55
Riddings Junction and station	143
Ringley Road station	65, 66
Rivington	160
Rixton Junction	38
Roa Island	128
Roachdale Colliery	145
Rochdale-Bacup Railway	93-95
Rochdale Canal	91
'Rocket'	145
Rock Ferry (Birkenhead)	20, 21
Roe Green Junction	59, 79
ROF Risley branch	53
Rolt, L.T.C.	28
Romiley	75
Rookery station	57
Roosecote Power Station (Barrow)	129
Rose Grove Junction	99
Rose Grove shed	99
Rosehill Archer Street station	137
Rossendale Quarries	155
Rossendale Valley	71
Round Barn Delf	155
Rowrah	132, 133
Rowrah station	134
Royal George Tunnel	78
Royton branch and station	90-91, 92
Royton Junction	91
Rumworth & Daubhill station	62
St Helens	16
St Helens-Ormskirk Railway	57
St Helens-St Helens Junction Railway	56
St Helens-Widnes Railway	55
St Helens (GCR) branch	53
St Helens Canal	53, 57, 157
St Helens Central station	53
St Helens Railway	55
St Werbergh's Road Metrolink stop	73, 81, 83
Saddleworth	92
Salford Trail	38
Salt Line	30
Samuel Stock's Railway	157
Sandbach-Kidsgrove Railway	29
Sanderson's Sidings	79
Sandhills (Liverpool) station	43
Sandhole Colliery	79
Sandside	123
Sandside station	123
Sandyside	144
Sankey Bridges	8
Saughall station	22, 24
Scale Hall Halt	121
Scotch Dyke station	144
Scout Moor Tramway	159-160
Seacombe branch	9
Seaforth (Docks)	41, 45
Sealand station	24
Seaton	138
Seaton Bank Tramway (Workington)	16
'Secret Nuclear Bunker' (Nantwich)	29
Sedbergh	150, 153
Seel branch (Whiston)	48
Sellafield	131
Sellafield-Whitehaven Railway	131
Senely Green Colliery	157
Settle	158
Settle & Carlisle Railway (S&CR)	146, 147, 149
Shaw & Crompton station	11
Shawclough station	93, 94
Shawforth station	94
Shell Oil Works (Partington)	39
Sherdley Hall station	49
Shotton station	24
Shotton Steelworks	23
Shropshire Union Canal	28
Siddick Junction	134
Silloth	142
Silloth branch	141, 142
Simonstone Station	101
Skelmersdale	8, 57
Skelton Junction	39
Skelton Junction-Glazebrook Railway	39
Skelton Junction-Warrington Railway	33
Skipton	105
Skipton-Colne Railway	12, 104
Skygarth Viaduct	147, 149
Smallshaw Tunnel (Ashton)	90

Index

Smardale Gill (and Viaduct)	146, 147
Smardale station	146, 148
Smith, John Abel	128
Solway Junction Railway (SJR)	138, 140-141
Solway Viaduct	140-141
Sough Tunnel	155
Southport-Preston Railway	106-107
Southport & Cheshire Lines Extension Railway (S&CLER)	48
Southport (Chapel Street) station	108
Southport Central station	108
Southport Lord Street station	48, 49
Southport St Luke's station	107
Spike Island (Widnes)	55
Spring Mill Tramway (Whitworth)	94
Stacksteads Station	72
Stainmore Railway	125, 146
Stainmore Railway Company (Kirkby Stephen)	147, 148
Staley & Millbrook station	77, 78
Stalybridge Junction	76
Stalybridge station	76
Standedge Tunnels	76, 77
Standish station	59
Stevens, Marshall	83
Stockport	76
Stockport Canal	83
Stockport Tiviot Dale station	73
Stocks Reservoir Railways	158-159, 160, 161
Storeton Tramway (Stourton Railway)	161
Stubbins Junction	71
Stubbins Junction-Accrington Railway	96
Sustrans	81, 133
Sutton Manor Colliery	55
Sutton Oak Station	57
Stoneclough Quarry (Cheshire)	17
Tame Valley Way	78
Tarleton branch	106
Tattenhall station	25
Tebay-Kirkby Stephen Railway	146, 147
Tebay station	146
Temple Sowerby station	147
Thelwall Ferry	36
Thelwall station	33, 35
Thornton station (Fleetwood branch)	115, 116
Thornton in Craven station	105
Thornton Rock Quarry Siding	105
Threlkeld station	137
'Thrutch' Tunnel	71, 72
Tindale	145
Tindale Fell Colliery	144
Tite, Sir William	143
Tiviot Dale Tunnel	73, 74
Todd Lane Junction (Preston Junction) station	112, 113
Todmorden (west curve)	96
Tootle Hill Quarry	111
Torver station	130
Tosside	159
Tottington station	69, 70, 71
Tottington Viaduct	69, 71
Trafford Park	36, 83, 84
Trans Pennine Trail	8, 34, 48
Trent & Mersey Canal	30
Turton Moor Sanitary Pipe Works (& Balancing Tank)	160
Tyldesley	50, 59
Tyne (River)	154
Ullock	134
Ulverston	13, 125, 127
Ulverston (Plumpton Junction)-Lakeside Railway	125
Ulverston Canal	127
University of Central Lancashire	110, 157
Uppermill station	77
Victoria Tunnel (Liverpool)	47
'Wagon Line'	161
Waitby Crossing	148
Walkden (Low Level) station	79
Wallerscote Light Railway	27
Walton on the Hill station	43
Walton Sidings	155
Walton Summit plateway	157-159
Warcop-Appleby Railway	7, 147-149
Warcop station	148-149
Wardleworth station	93
Warrington-Skelton Junction Railway	33
Warrington & Altrincham Railway	33
Warrington Arpley station	33
Warrington Bank Quay station	33, 88
Warrington Central station	40
Warrington Docks	36
Warrington 'Straight line'	40
Warrington (Crosfields) Transporter Bridge	40
Waterfoot Goods Warehouse	71, 72
Waterfoot station	72
Waterloo Goods station (Liverpool)	47
Waterloo Tunnel (Liverpool)	47
Waterside Viaduct (Sedbergh)	153
'Waverley' line	143-144
Wellington Road Tunnel (Stockport)	73
Wellington Street Viaduct (Bury)	69
Wennington	122
Wennington-Lancaster Railway	118-119, 121

Entry	Page(s)
Werneth Incline	91
Werneth station	10, 91
Werneth Tunnel	9, 91
Westleigh & Bedford station	52
West Derby station	45
West Kirby-Hooton Railway	18
West Lancashire Railway	48, 106, 112
West Timperley station	39
Westhead Station	58
Wheelock Forge	30
Wheelock station	30
Wheelton	158
Whelley loop line	50, 58, 59
"Whistle Down the Wind"	93
Whitchurch-Chester Railway	7, 13, 25
Whitchurch station	25
Whitehouse Triangle	112
Whitrigg	141
Whitworth station	93, 94, 155
White Bear station	61
Whitegate station	26, 27
Whitegate Way	27
Whitehaven	131
Whitehaven-Sellafield Railway	131
Whitehaven, Cleator & Egremont Railway (WC&ER)	131, 133
Whittingham Hospital and Railway	108, 109, 111
Widnes-St Helens Railway	55
Wigan-Eccles Railway	58, 79
Wigan Central Station	50, 51, 60, 61
Wigan Junction Railway (WJR)	50, 52, 60
Wigan North Western tation	59
Wigg Island (Runcorn)	36
Wilbraham Road Station	83
Willis Branch (Cronton Colliery)	47
Wincham (salt works)	28
Winder Station	133, 134
Windermere (and Lake)	121, 125
Winnington Chemical Works (Northwich)	27, 28
Winsford & Over-Cuddington Railway	26
Winwick Hospital Railway	40
Wirral Way	18
Withnell	103
Withnell station	103-104
Woodend station	132
Woodland station	129
Woodley	75
Woolfold station	71
Woolfold Viaduct	69, 71
Workington	131
Workington-Penrith (Keswick) Railway	133, 136, 137
Workington Bridge station	138
Workington Central station	134, 135
Workington Docks	136
Workington Steelworks	136
Worsley station	79, 80
Wray station	119, 122
'Wrea Green branch'	113
Wyre Dock (latterly Fleetwood) Station	115
Wyre (Knott End-Fleetwood) Ferry	116
Yeathouse station	133, 134
Yorkshire Street Viaduct (Rochdale)	93

Northern Rail Steam
Allan Heyes

One of our most well received railway titles in recent years was *Northern Rail Rover*, a selection of photos taken in the final years of steam on Britain's railways by photographer, Allan Heyes. In this new collection of photographs by Heyes, *Northern Rail Steam* continues this story and takes the reader on a journey, recorded in over 200 previously unpublished images which starts in North Wales and then moves on through Chester to Merseyside. There follows a roughly circular itinerary starting around the Wigan area and south east Lancashire before heading to the north east and Cumbria before returning to Lancashire.

While the majority of photos cover steam on the BR network, some explore the colliery and other industrial lines which fed traffic onto the main lines. Sequences of pictures at certain locations will recreate the lineside experience of many enthusiasts at this time and will bring them to life for those too young to remember those days. *Northern Rail Steam* also focuses on the infrastructure and the environment of the steam railway so much of which has been swept away in the decades following the end of steam on Britain's railways.

A key feature of the photographs of Allan Heyes is they honestly and accurately portray the reality of those last years of steam. There is no attempt to glamorise the subject, the dirty and unkempt nature of engine sheds and their locos is here for all to see. This personal account of the decline of steam is an essential companion for all railway enthusiasts.

Hardback, ISBN: 9781800352520
224 pages, **£22.50**

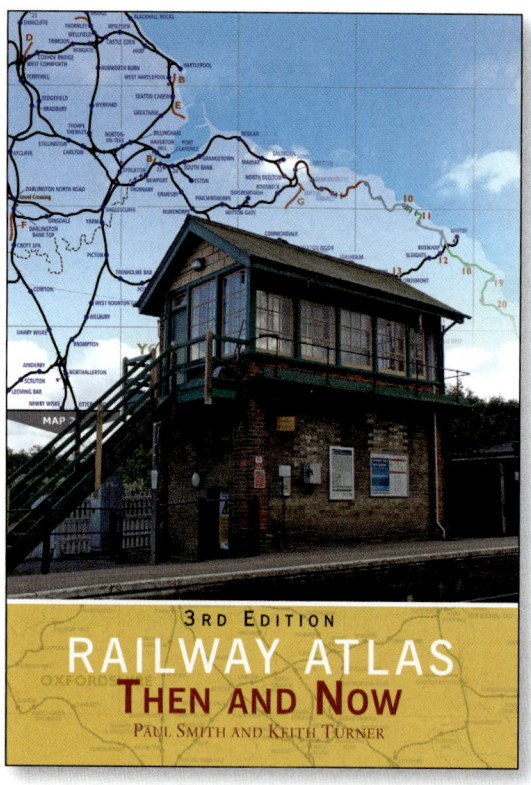

Railway Atlas Then and Now
3rd Edition
Paul Smith and Keith Turner

Railway Atlas Then and Now 3rd Edition is a new, revised and fully updated edition of one of the most popular and successful railway atlases of recent years.

As before, the 1923 maps are set opposite the same area maps of the 2020 rail network, showing clearly the full extent of closures and reopenings made in the intervening years, as well as the new uses closed lines and stations have been put to. Other information includes the location of steam sheds, railway museums and a wide range of modern commercial narrow gauge and miniature railways.

The new edition of this unique publication can be used either for pleasurable browsing or as an aide for more detailed research into how the railway network has changed over a period of close to 100 years.

Hardback, ISBN: 9780860936985

128 pages, **£20.00**